Elusive Consumption

Elusive Consumption

Karin M. Ekström & Helene Brembeck

Oxford • New York

First published in 2004 by
Berg
Editorial offices:
1st Floor, Angel Court, 81 St Clements Street, Oxford, OX4 1AW, UK
175 Fifth Avenue, New York, NY 10010, USA

Berg is the imprint of Oxford International Publishers Ltd.

Library of Congress Cataloguing-in-Publication Data
A catalogue record for this book is available from the Library of Congress.

British Library Cataloguing-in-Publication Data
A catalogue record for this book is available from the British Library.

ISBN 1 85973 763 3 (Cloth)
1 85973 768 4 (Paper)

Typeset by Avocet Typeset, Chilton, Aylesbury, Bucks
Printed in the United Kingdom by Biddles Ltd, Guildford and Kings Lynn

www.bergpublishers.com

Contents

Notes on Contributors

Russell W. Belk is N. Eldon Tanner Professor at the David Eccles School of Business at the University of Utah. He is past president of the Association for Consumer Research and the International Society of Marketing and Development, and is a fellow in the American Psychological Association and the Association for Consumer Research. He has received two Fulbright Fellowships and holds honorary positions at universities in Australia, Asia and North America. He has published over 300 articles and papers, dealing especially with culture and the meanings of possessions and materialism.

Helene Brembeck is associate professor at the Department of Ethnology, Göteborg University and research leader at CFK. She has been in the lead of several research projects concerning children, childhood, parenthood and consumption and is now one of the leaders of the 'Commercial Cultures' project at CFK. She is also coordinator of NordBarn, a research network for the studies of Nordic conceptions of childhood. She has published several books and articles, most recently *Det konsumerande barnet* ('The Consuming Child'), a study of the representation of children as consumers in Swedish newspaper advertisement during the twentieth century.

Colin Campbell is professor of sociology at the University of York, England. He is the author of *The Romantic Ethic and the Spirit of Modern Consumerism* (Blackwell, 1987) and co-editor of *The Shopping Experience* (with Pasi Falk, 1997). He is also co-editor of the series Studies in Consumption and Markets. He has published extensively on the sociology of consumption as well as on the sociology of religion and sociological theory. He is currently finishing a major work on cultural change in the West.

Miriam Catterall is a senior lecturer in management at the Queen's University of Belfast (Northern Ireland) where she is responsible for marketing and research methods programmes. She has considerable business experience in the market research industry and in management consulting. Her research interests lie in consumer research, feminist issues in marketing and in qualitative market research, particularly in focus group theory, methodology and practice.

Notes on Contributors

Franck Cochoy is professor of sociology at the University of Toulouse II, France. He authored *Une histoire du marketing, discipliner l'économie de marché* (Paris: La Découverte, 1999) and *Une sociologie du packaging ou l'âne de Buridan face au marché* (Paris: Presses Universitaires de France, 2002). He has also published many papers and chapters on the sociology of market issues. He is working on the technical and human mediations which connect/shape supply and demand in the market economy (marketing, packaging, standardization, quality, traceability, etc.).

Karin M. Ekström is associate professor at the School of Economics and Commercial Law at Göteborg University, Sweden. She is one of the leaders of the 'Commercial Cultures' project at CFK. A current research project is 'The meaning of consumption and consumers relations to artefacts'. Other research areas are collecting, family research, consumer socialization and the historical development of consumer research. She has been a teacher/guest researcher at the University of Wisconsin, USA, University of Odense, Denmark and Thammasat University, Thailand. She is the initiator and director of the Center for Consumer Science, CFK.

Richard Elliott is a fellow of St. Anne's College, Oxford and professor of marketing and consumer research in Warwick Business School at the University of Warwick. He is a visiting professor at ESSEC, Paris and Thammasat University, Bangkok. He is associate editor of the *British Journal of Management* and European editor of the *Journal of Product and Brand Management*. His research focuses on consumer culture and identity, the symbolic meaning of brands and the dynamics of brand ecology.

Margaret K. Hogg is senior lecturer (associate professor) in consumer behaviour at Manchester School of Management, UMIST, England. She read politics and modern history at Edinburgh University, followed by postgraduate studies in history at the Vrije Universiteit, Amsterdam and an MA in business analysis at Lancaster University. She had six years of industry experience with K Shoes, Kendal before completing her PhD in Consumer Behaviour and Retailing at Manchester Business School. She was the joint winner of the 1999/2000 UMIST Prize for Teaching Excellence. Her research interests centre on the interrelationships between identity, self and consumption within consumer behaviour and marketing history. Her work has appeared in several refereed journals.

Robert V. Kozinets is an assistant professor of marketing at Northwestern University's Kellogg School of Management. A marketer and anthropologist by training, he has consulted with over 500 companies. His research encompasses high technology consumption, communities (online and off), entertainment, brand management, consumer activism and themed retail. He has written and published articles on retro brands, Wal-Mart, online coffee connoisseurs, ESPN Zone, Star Trek and the Burning Man Festival for journals such as the *Journal of Consumer Research*, the *Journal of Marketing*, the *Journal of Marketing Research* and the *Journal of Retailing*.

Pauline Maclaran is professor of marketing at De Montfort University, Leicester. Her research has two main strands: gender issues in marketing and consumer behaviour; and the experiential dimensions of contemporary consumption, particularly in relation to utopia and the festival marketplace. Much of this work draws on the tools and techniques of literary theory to gain insights into the symbolic aspects of consumer behaviour.

Daniel Miller is professor of material culture in the Department of Anthropology at University College London. He is author and editor of nineteen books mainly concerned with material culture and consumption. Recent works include *The Dialectics of Shopping* (Chicago, 2001), the edited volumes *Car Cultures* (Berg, 2001) and *Home Possessions* (Berg, 2001), and with D. Slater, *The Internet An Ethnographic Approach* (Berg, 2000). *The Sari* (written with Mukulika Banerjee) was published by Berg in 2003

Lisa Peñaloza is associate professor of marketing at the University of Colorado, Boulder. Her research is concerned with how consumers express culture in their consumer behaviour, and in turn, how marketers negotiate various cultures of consumers. Market subcultures examined in her work relate to ethnicity/race, nationality, gender/sexuality, and most recently industry and region in the commodification of western culture at a stock show and rodeo. Her work has been published in the *Journal of Consumer Research, Journal of Marketing, Public Policy and Marketing International Journal of Research in Marketing*, and *Consumption, Markets and Culture*.

Jonathan Schroeder is director of the marketing programme at the Royal Institute of Technology (KTH) in Stockholm, Sweden. He is also a research affiliate with the European Center for Art and Management, Stockholm, and a visiting professor of marketing semiotics at Bocconi University, Milan. His research focuses on the production and consumption of images, and is particularly concerned with interconnections between art, consumption and representation. He has published widely in marketing, psychology, law and design journals. His book *Visual Consumption* (Routledge, 2002) introduces a theoretical perspective on visual issues in consumer research.

John F. Sherry, Jr. joined the Kellogg Marketing Faculty in 1984. He is an anthropologist (PhD Univ. Illinois, 1983) who studies both the sociocultural and symbolic dimensions of consumption and the cultural ecology of marketing. He has researched, taught and lectured around the globe. Sherry is a past president of the Association for Consumer Research, and a former associate editor of the *Journal of Consumer Research*. He sits on the editorial boards of four other journals, and is an ad hoc reviewer for a dozen journals in the fields of social science and management. Sherry's work appears in a score of journals, in numerous book chapters, in professional manuals and proceedings. He has edited *Contemporary Marketing and Consumer Behavior: An Anthropological Sourcebook*, as well as *Servicescapes: The Concept of Place in Contemporary Markets*; he is co-editor of *Advances in Consumer Research, Vol. 19*.

Craig J. Thompson is the Churchill Professor of Marketing at the University of Wisconsin-Madison. In broadbrush terms, his research focuses on the ideological circuit formed by individuals' creative acts of self-definition through consumption and, reciprocally, the market monitoring activities and technologies by which marketers adapt their ideological appeals to a heterogeneous and dynamic marketplace. His research has been published in a number of leading journals including *Journal of Consumer Research*, *Journal of Marketing Research* and *Consumption, Markets, and Culture*. He is co-author of *The Phenomenology of Everyday Life*. He is an associate editor for the *Journal of Consumer Research*.

Richard Wilk is chair of the Department of Anthropology at Indiana University. He has done research in the rainforest of Belize (with Mayan people), in West African markets and in the wilds of suburban California. He has published on topics as diverse as beauty pageants, household decision-making, economic anthropology and the effects of television on culture. Most of his recent work concerns the global environmental impact of mass consumer culture, gender and consumer culture, and the history of the global food system. His most recent publication is *The Anthropology of Media*, co-edited with Kelly Askew, and he edits a book series on Globalization and the Environment for Altamira Press.

Introduction

Karin M. Ekström & Helene Brembeck

Nowadays, research on consumption is carried out within a broad field of disciplines ranging from the humanities and social sciences to technology. Researchers with different theoretical and methodological traditions such as anthropology, sociology and marketing do, however, seldom meet even though they often use each other's methods and theories. The ethnographical methods introduced by anthropologists now appear in the toolbox of any consumer researcher. Also, the anthropologist Marcel Mauss's work on gift-giving is frequently referred to by researchers from many different disciplines. Anthropologists have traditionally been interested in how relations are maintained in foreign cultures by the exchange of goods, symbolic or material, and in the importance of rituals involving consumption. Today, when researchers study their own neighbouring streets and corner stores, the fruitfulness of importing traditional anthropological theories and concepts in a modern, western context is highlighted.

Sociological forefathers such as Weber and Veblen are also often to be found in lists of references. They were both interested in goods as signs of social status. Expensive lavish objects communicated power and the ability to show off in front of others. Later, with Barthes and the semiotic revolution, merchandise increasingly turned into a language able to formulate subtler meanings. The primary focus was the way identity was expressed within different social groups. Research on lifestyles and youth culture are good examples with many followers.

Consumer behaviour was introduced within marketing as a research area during the 1950s, and has since become increasingly interdisciplinary. A paradigm shift towards increased acceptance of interpretative research and ethnographic methods happened in the mid 1980s. The Consumer Behavior Odyssey when, during one summer, two dozens of consumer researchers travelled from Los Angeles to Boston in order to study consumption and interview consumers along the way, was a highly contributive factor.

Not only disciplines studying consumption, but also the actual act of consumption itself, have become more and more porous. Consumption (and consumerism) is gradually trickling into all areas of human life. It is closely related to all aspects of being an individual, and is – for good or bad – the foundation of human existence. This leaking and absorbing character of modern consumption makes it impossible to pin it down to certain phenomena or lock it within specific disciplines, theories and methods. Not even the concept of consumption is self-evident, as we will show in this volume, for it also has a number of meanings, referring to several inconsistent metaphors. There is nothing stable or obvious at all about consumption.

This book is the result of a gathering of a large number of internationally renowned consumer researchers at a conference in June 2002 at the newly established Center for Consumer Science (CFK) at the School of Economics and Commercial Law at Göteborg University. The aim was to problematize the elusive concept of consumption inviting researchers from a vast area of disciplines from both sides of the Atlantic to reflect on new perspectives, theories and methods within consumer research. The contributors represented the disciplines of anthropology, marketing and sociology, which are not often combined within one conference. These disciplines complement and compete at the expanding fields of consumption studies. This brew came out in the most interesting way suggesting multidisciplinarity and plurality of theories, methods and topics as well as an opening of borders and reciprocal exchange between researchers and disciplines. The layout of this book is an attempt to keep this pot boiling, constantly mixing disciplines and perspectives.

In the first part of the book, 'Grasping the topic', Richard Wilk, Colin Campbell and John Sherry reflect on the basic meanings of consumption and consumer research. *Richard Wilk* opens by analysing the very term of consumption using recent research in cognitive linguistics. By exploring the structure of the concept of consumption, disembedding central metaphors like 'fire' and 'eating' that link its meanings together, Wilk guides us to a better grasp of this elusive topic. He also shows us how to avoid some of the pitfalls that often occur in the social sciences when we use folk-categories as if they were empirical and universal.

Colin Campbell grabs the baton in arguing that the fundamental assumption of modern consumerism is an emphasis on feeling and emotion using a practice and ideology that is markedly individualistic. It is by exposing ourselves to a wide variety of products and services and by monitoring our reaction to them that we 'discover' who we 'really are'. This makes for an individualist epistemology, in which the 'self' is the only authority in matters of truth and an emotional ontology where the fact that I do desire intensely helps to reassure me that I do indeed exist. Moreover, the idea is that feeling – if intensely experienced – can directly change the world. This represents a truly magical world-view, shown in, for example, the interest in New Age. Campbell concludes that we not only live in a consumer society or in a consumer culture but in a consumer civilization.

John Sherry reflects on the subdiscipline of postmodern consumer research in marketing departments by surveying its principal contours and probable programmatic progress. He explores the ways the subdiscipline has fulfilled some of its promise, and examines some of its shortfalls. In particular, he dwells on the possibilities of rapprochement between the postmodern tradition of consumer research in marketing and the investigation of consumption arising in contiguous disciplines in the social sciences and humanities. Sherry is hoping for a new era where orthodoxy is suffused with otherness and complementary holism witnessing the birth of a discipline that researchers from various disciplines could recognize simply as 'consumer research'. He envisions in the future both the rise of a vastly reconfigured multidisciplinary 'spanning' association of scholars interested in consumption broadly constructed, as well as the proliferation of specialist associations devoted to the micro-granularities of consumption rooted in local perspectives.

In the second part of the book, 'Odysseys in Time and Space', Russell Belk and Lisa Peñaloza discuss consumer culture and multiculturalism as elaborate multidimensional concepts of essential importance in consumer research. Consumer culture illustrates the central position of consumption in society. *Russell Belk* views consumer culture as a personal and cultural orientation toward consumption, and emphasizes that it is not a production phenomena. Consumer culture is also distinguished from concomitant changes including industrialization, economic development, globalization, urbanization, capitalism, wage labour and colonialism. Belk views consumer culture as an ongoing ever-changing phenomenon, neither inherently good nor evil. He argues for a definition that acknowledges the ancient roots of consumer culture as well as the possibility that contemporary consumer culture can exist in the less affluent world. Consumer culture is a way of looking at, and seeking to derive, value in the world that has far reaching consequences. Multiple dimensions for evaluating the effects of consumer culture need to be recognized. The impacts of consumer culture are individual, social, cultural, economic, political, moral and much more. A brief assessment of two prominent examples of consumer cultures: collecting and Christmas is also provided.

Even though much scholarly research has focused on the centrality of consumers, less attention has been directed to the centrality of markets. In the literature, the market has often been discussed as an essential dimension of culture, often in terms of where cultural conflicts occur. *Lisa Peñaloza's* chapter is about crossing borders and studying the intersection of markets and cultures, also involving the complex interfaces between multiculturalism, capitalism and democracy. She explores the limits of market enfranchisement by taking into account specific dynamics of market inclusion, and comparing them to more traditional forms of political representation and agency for Latinos in the USA. There is a need to understand cultural differences in marketplaces better.

Peñaloza prefers to look at ethnic minority communities as communities that consume rather than as subcultures. The former have their primary agency in community identity rather than consumption, even though consumption is important as well. Peñaloza argues that markets are needed for developing communities, but markets also require political oversight.

The third part of the book, 'Performing identities', focuses on a topic that has attained massive attention during recent decades, and is often considered emblematic of postmodern consumption, namely the issue of identity, previously introduced in the first section of the book. Daniel Miller, Richard Elliott, Pauline Maclaran, Margaret Hogg, Miriam Catterall and Robert Kozinets advocate a breakaway from purely linguistic understandings of the consuming subject, and instead include more of body and materiality. In Chapter 6 *Daniel Miller* enters an ethnographic expedition in order to investigate the role of 'the little black dress'. Just having finished fieldwork in India about saris in rainbows of colours and effusions of print, he can't help wondering why the western female party dress has been leached into standard black. After having interrogated a row of suspects – capitalism, history and modernism – he turns to the ethnography of consumption. Using findings from fieldwork conducted in and around a London street, Miller finds the culprit to be the possibility and experience of freedom and the particular form of modernist anxiety this evokes. He advocates that black is not a neutral absence, but an assertive presence. We pretend that choosing shades of grey is more subtle and sophisticated, since we don't dare to bear the burden of freedom. This lesson from the field teaches us that understanding consumption requires more than studying commerce or modernism. Miller argues that it requires experiences of the population and the kind of generalizations that social science can make about these experiences and what underlies them.

Richard Elliott discusses consumption as a symbolic vocabulary and resource for identity construction and maintenance through communities of practice. Locating identity within communities of practice integrates the self with the social and the material and identifies the emergence of a repertoire of resources for the negotiation of meaning. We can problematize the study of the consumer by widening the focus of research to include embodied performances, communities of practice and ritual; by recognizing the historical limitations on the social construction of the self; and by acknowledging the negotiated and contested nature of meaning. Elliott also argues that we ought to take a further step towards dealing with the complexities of human life by inviting informants to be co-researchers. He maintains that by adopting a wide range of quasi-ethnographic methods, such as giving informants dictaphones to report their feelings and reactions, we can little by little increase our ability to cope with the complex social practices of consumer culture.

The next chapter by *Pauline Maclaran, Margaret Hogg, Miriam Catterall,* and *Robert Kozinets* deals with the intersection between technology and computer-mediated communications (CMC) in computer-related online communities. A methodology of 'netnography' in combination with discourse analysis is proposed in order to enable researchers to explore the nuances of gender effects online better. The authors draw on findings from an online consumption-related community – a digital camera discussion forum – to illustrate how the consumption of CMC may exhibit important gendered and gendering effects. Their study implies a two-way mutually shaping relationship between gender and technology. There is a symbolic gendering of technology with material effects. Most computer games are, for example, oriented to male subject positions and cultural competencies. Conversely, gender is considered as performed rather than preformed and in the fragmentary and diverse online communities there is considerable room for individual manoeuvring across an extensive continuum of gender positions. However, the authors conclude that a lot of interesting research lies ahead to achieve better understanding of the many, varied performances of gender and consumption.

In Part IV of the book, 'Visualizing visuality', Craig Thompson, Franck Cochoy and Jonathan Schroeder reflect upon newer perspectives and approaches for understanding consumption in relation to images. They emphasize that images do not exist in a vacuum, but that cultural contexts should also be considered. *Craig Thompson* discusses the ideological framing of advertisements and refers to the increased usage of self-reflexive advertising campaigns that lampoon image-oriented marketing pitches. A polysemic analysis of natural health advertisements is grounded in the collective meanings expressed by ardent consumers of holistic health alternatives. He argues that advertising ideologies appeal to the interests of specific audiences by offering mythic resolutions to salient cultural contradictions and tensions. His argument is a reader-response adaptation of Roland Barthes's sociosemiotic classic *Mythologies*. An integration between critical and reader-response perspectives on advertising can provide theoretical insights into a number of important issues that conventional critical analysis ignores, such as the rhetorical structures that imbue advertisements' ideological representations with symbolically enticing and resonant qualities. It can also enrich reader-response analysis by better theorizing the meanings through which advertisements leverage the collective viewpoints of different consumer groups for ideological effect.

Franck Cochoy invites us to look at what the consumers look at, not the actual products, but the packaged products; his programme being to subordinate the study of consumers and producers to the sociology of packaging. He warns us against spending too much time studying the symbolic side of products and directs our attention to all of the dimensions that are built into packaging that criticism fails to see, such as content, eco-labelling, health, legal and even polit-ical information and the bar code, speaking not to the consumer but to the scanner. While the symbolic dimension moves us away from the materiality of the product, these other dimensions point directly at the product's material components. Packages argue for different action patterns, speaking to us on, for example, emotional, logic, political or routine terms. It is thus not only the producer but also, for example, the health authorities or the European Union who are given voice. So Cochoy asks where our preferences come from. From within ourselves or from the packaging surface? Is it we or the package who make the choice? Inspired by the works of Bruno Latour, rejecting the alternative between active and passive voices, the answer is obvious, i.e., we neither choose products nor are we chosen by them. Packaging makes us choose. Packaging is both the condition and the solution of choice.

In the last chapter, *Jonathan Schroeder* focuses on the idea that the image, now as in the past, provides a key to understanding how we make sense of our world. The focus is on images and their interpretation as foundational elements of elusive consumption. He argues for research on the production and consumption of images drawing from art history, photography and visual studies to develop an interdisciplinary, visual approach to understanding consumer behaviour. A theo-retical approach to visual consumption is proposed. By visual, he means not just visually oriented consumer behaviour such as watching videos, tourism or window-shopping, but also a methodological framework to investigate the inter-connections of consumption, vision and culture, including how visual images are handled by consumer research.

The conclusion of this book is that consumption is elusive in that it is not possible to identify with one single definition or some clearly demarcated prac-tices. The elusiveness of consumption is both challenging and inspiring. Studies of consumption need to reflect the mysterious, obscure, subtle and sometimes indefinable moments in our lives when we consume, sometimes as a joyful expe-rience and at other times out of necessity. Consumption is often described in terms of symbols of progress even though it also involves not only fulfilment of fantasies and desires, but fear and exploitation of resources. We have come a long way from the 'economic man' model of consumer behaviour, emphasizing rationality and utility by viewing consumption in a consumer culture context. However, the complexity of consumption still needs further exploration. According to postmodernism, consumer research is not simply a manifestation of reactance, but a progress in the understanding of consumption as ever intriguing and elusive phenomena. It should not be understood as merely an alternative involving a suboptimal choice, but as an indispensable perspective for understanding consumer society.

One of the lessons of this book is that the elusiveness of consumption makes it impossible to take a unidimensional research approach for studying consumption and consumer culture. A multiplicity of perspectives, theories and methods from a variety of disciplines·is needed as well as encompassing a variety of phenomena. We need to include not only consumers, but the laws and politics of the market, producers and marketers, the imagery of advertising, the packages making us choose, the challenges of the Internet, global-local marketplace dynamics, consumer welfare, as well as interrelations. Ethnography should also continue to have a privileged position in the future for understanding consumption, consumers and producers, and for attaining the closeness to the subjects and phenomena studied. The understandings and practices of the consumers is a necessity, needless to say, but new versions of ethnographic methods need to be included as well as ethnography combined with other perspectives, theories and methods. This would also contribute to a continuous process of building theories and methods for understanding consumption in its many varied performances.

A challenge for the future might be to include more of moral, ethical and political concerns in consumer research. Renewed attention must be devoted to global-local marketplace dynamics, to the political implications of consumption, to the unequal distribution of the world's diminishing resources and to the practices of resistance, accommodation and co-creation consumers adopt in marketplaces around the world. We need to understand the impacts of consumption from an individual, social, cultural, ecological, economic, political and moral perspective. It is important to recognize that the consumer is also a citizen whose actions and non-actions and negotiations have implications not only for her/himself, but for the community and for society as a whole.

This kaleidoscopic research agenda makes the elusive character of consumption more visible and attainable. This book and the preceding conference shows the need for common meeting grounds, be they conferences, seminars, books, magazines or the Internet, to stimulate creativity among researchers representing different disciplines and perspectives. This is the way to keep the pot boiling. We think it is time to invert the expression that too many cooks spoil the broth and introduce instead a plurality of cooks, each one contributing with ideas on ingredients, recipes, ways of preparing and stirring the broth in order to make it as spicy and invigorating as possible. We hope the reader will find the brew innovative, illuminating, imaginative, inspiring, intriguing, invigorating and irresistible.

Part I
Grasping the Topic

1

Morals and Metaphors:
The Meaning of Consumption

Richard Wilk

Introduction

I was inspired by the provocative title 'elusive consumption' to delve into the vague, undefined and intangible nature of the concept of consumption that most social scientists use in their work. Consumption turns out to be one of those common-sense concepts that usually 'goes without saying', meaning that we rarely argue about whether something really belongs in the category. In practice, the harder you try to define the term, the fuzzier its meanings and boundaries become, which suggests that there is indeed something important hidden behind our casual agreement about its meaning.

In the process of trying to find the elusive meaning of consumption, I have encountered some familiar problems and issues. Scholars working on problems and issues of consumption have long noted the close linkage between consumption and morality. Almost every aspect of consumption is laden with moral value and meaning, so that attitudes and values towards consumption are shaped by moral and often religious values that have very little to do with acts of consumption themselves (the modern scholarship on this topic begins with Douglas 1966; see also, Horowitz 1988). My approach to defining consumption explains why moral issues are an inevitable aspect of consumption; they are built into the meaning of the term at a fundamental level.

Some have tried to define consumption as an activity specific to particular groups of people, sectors of society or sections of the economy. Others take a more abstract approach and see consumption as a process diffused throughout the world, defined as reducing or destroying matter, energy or order in a way that reduces their value to humans (Stern 1997). Both approaches pay little attention to the way people use the term in everyday speech, and assume that the scientific usage can be entirely divorced from the folk-meaning, a prospect we find both unlikely and unfruitful. To understand the meanings of consumption, we follow a suggestion by Belk, Ger and Askegaard in an important paper called 'Metaphors of Consumer

Desire' (1996), and use the tools of cognitive linguistics. This takes me far from my usual field of expertise in economic and historical anthropology, and I am not by any means a trained linguist or cognitive scientist. I have only been able to venture into the new field of cognitive linguistics with the help and guidance of George Lakoff, who is one of the intellectual founders of the discipline.

I have to add one further qualification, which is that my analysis is based entirely on American English. I suspect that many of the idioms and expressions have equivalents in other European languages, but how relevant this analysis is to other languages is an open question.

What is Cognitive Linguistics?

Cognitive linguistics is a relatively new discipline that cuts across the conventional fields of linguistics, cognitive science, mathematics and philosophy. Its tenets are stated in a series of works by George Lakoff and collaborators (Lakoff & Johnson 1980; Lakoff 1987; Lakoff & Johnson 1999); this is in turn based on work by cognitive psychologists like Rosch, anthropological linguists like Berlin and Kay, and ultimately the philosophy of Wittgenstein. I will provide a very compressed and partial tutorial in the discipline, since it forms the basis for my analysis of the category of consumption as a cognitive domain.

The classic theories of language and grammar tell us that the world is composed of discrete entities and concepts like 'chairs' and 'balls', all of which share a certain set of qualities. The category is determined by the minimum common list of shared qualities, for example four legs and a back. Cognitive linguistics says instead that concepts and categories are typically complex, often fuzzy, and without clear boundaries or common shared qualities. Instead they are structured in particular ways:

- They have a prototypical object or action at the centre – an idealized typical chair with four legs and a back, for example.

- Other members of the set can be more or less central, more or less chair-like, so membership may be graded rather than categorical.

- They often have a radial structure – the prototype is at the centre, and other members can each be related to the prototype in different ways. All members of the set are bound together by their relationship to the prototype, not their relationship to each other. Some instances of the category may be related to the central prototype through metaphor.

According to cognitive linguists, the categories of speech and thought are interconnected in many different ways. The most obvious, and most studied relationships are hierarchies and other typologies, so that, for instance, a stool is a kind of chair, or the seat is one of the parts of a chair. However, Lakoff finds these cases to be relatively trivial. The most important key to understanding the relationships between concepts is founded in the fundamental way the human brain works, which is often through metaphorical linkages between categories. Typically, we map *abstract* concepts and categories onto more concrete and physically experienced categories through metaphor. The concept is made tangible through a metaphorical linkage to a class of object with which we have direct physical experiences.

To use one of his examples, modern Americans have come to comprehend the abstract concept of time through a metaphorical link to resources, especially money (Lakoff & Johnson 1980: 7; Lakoff 1987: 209–10). Resources in general, and money in particular, are used not only in everyday speech, but also in the way we reason, as a common metaphorical source for time: we spend it, save it, waste it and so on. This is more than a linguistic curiosity; the qualities of money actually affect the way we behave towards time, which is treated as if it were divisible, valuable, measurable and interchangeable, as if each minute, like each penny, has exactly the same size and value. Metaphor therefore does a lot more than structure categories of speech.

Lakoff says that basic level concepts are often grounded in direct bodily experiences like pain or hunger that all human beings share. In addition, hundreds of 'primary metaphors' that we use both in reasoning and as the basis for action are also grounded in common everyday experiences, sometimes so common that they give rise to metaphors that arise spontaneously in many cultures around the world. Examples include: *Desire is Hunger, Anger is Heat,* and *Achieving a Purpose is Getting a Desired Object* (Lakoff 1987: 380–415). There are also conceptual metaphors that are specific to particular cultures.

Conceptual metaphors are based upon non-metaphorical concepts of various kinds:

- *Kinaesthetic Image Schemas* – based on basic body perceptions of directions, basic sensory-motor schemas like containers, part-whole relationships, liquids and surfaces. The sequence of Source → Path → Goal is one of the most common image-schemas.

- *Frames,* including *scenarios* – conceptual structures that may take the form of a conventionalized story or sequence, such as 'rain' which includes a whole stereotypical scenario of clouds, humidity, rainfall and lingering mud.

Many complex concepts can be understood in terms of two or more metaphors. Lakoff shows that for Americans, anger is metaphorical fire: it burns, boils, steams and explodes. But anger is also a wild animal (out of control), and a kind of insanity (crazy). Fire is the most important, primary metaphor, but the others must be included to understand the way Americans visualize, and act out, their anger.

Furthermore, in his book *Moral Politics*, Lakoff shows that within a single culture, there can be conflicting and contending metaphorical systems. In his example, American conservatives see government as a metaphorical 'strict father', while liberals are more likely to cast the political system as a 'nurturant parent'. The contending metaphorical systems also inform and structure quite distinct models of moral behaviour, gender roles, attitudes towards capital punishment, etc. So these metaphors have real power; they help people visualize, simplify and judge complex situations, and find actions that seem consonant with their more fundamental beliefs about parenthood and authority. The implication is that, faced with new problems and issues, people tend to use old and established metaphors. Changes in behaviour need to be based on new metaphorical linkages, which is why so much public and private argument and debate is so rich in visual schemas and prototypical scenarios.

Economic Metaphors

When I was trained as an archaeologist, consumption was not a category of analysis; it did not exist. Instead, archaeologists started with objects instead of people, and developed a model of 'the life cycle of the artefact'. The notion was that 'raw' materials existed in nature, until taken up by humans and modified into artefacts, which were then used until worn out, and then discarded (cf. Schiffer 1976), so the basic cycle looks like this:

PRODUCTION → USE → DISCARD

This 'life cycle' metaphor is based on the fundamental human experience of ontology, the growth and development of an organism from origin to demise.

BIRTH → LIFE → DEATH

The metaphorical construction here is that *Objects are People*, and therefore they have lives. The speech of museologists, archaeologists and collectors of objects and antiques are full of these kinds of life-cycle metaphors that personify objects. In the long spans of time that archaeologists study, types of objects are 'born', and they eventually 'die out'. One subtle effect of this metaphor is that people become invisible, because the objects substitute for them. The basic model of the economy that appears in most economics textbooks accomplishes the same end with a similar metaphorical construction. Economists divide the economy into a productive sector, a market and the household sector, again with a flow between them.

PRODUCTION → EXCHANGE → CONSUMPTION

The life-cycle metaphor then tells us that consumption is like senility, loss of energy, decline in value, ultimately death and disappearance. For economists, all the action and excitement has always been in the first two stages; consumption is just the part of the economy where things end up after all the interesting activities take place in factories and markets. The clearest implication from this metaphorical construction is that *Consumption is Death.* As with an individual life, the flow of an object's life is inexorable and irreversible, so there is no possibility, for example, that demand could precede supply. The economist sees production as the vital force that drives the engine of the economy forward.

The life-cycle metaphor leaves all the activity, value and economic growth on the production side, while consumption is a passive process of decay and even waste. Just as with a life, any growth must be followed, and eventually balanced by decline, production has to be balanced with consumption, or the entire system is out of balance. The 'magic of the market', so beloved of neoclassical economists creates just this balance, at least in the imagination.

Another common economists' metaphor that de-emphasizes consumption is that *money is water.* This is a particularly good example of what Lakoff and Johnson call 'entity and substance metaphors'. These generally involve viewing events, activities, emotions and ideas – none of which are concrete objects – as entities and substances (1980: 25). Economists use a whole series of hydraulic metaphors, which portray the substance of economic transaction, money, utility or value as liquid. Economic transactions are *flows* that can *slow to a trickle under pressure*, before *pouring* forth into the marketplace. Economists speak of *rising tides, liquid assets,* economic *pumps,* spending like *water,* dangerous *leakage,* bringing things to a *boil,* and even pouring money down the *toilet.* The economy is therefore often visualized as a system of plumbing, but the wells, pumps and piping are the interesting part, and consumption is just water going down the drain. Adam Smith said that 'Consumption is the sole purpose of production', (1985: 338), but the hydraulic metaphor leads economists to think that consumption needs no analysis. Whatever is pumped forth naturally drains away.

Economic hydraulics is a specialist metaphor, used by a small professional class and politicians as part of their persuasive rhetoric (see McCloskey 1985). I am more concerned here with the folk models of consumption that inform everyday life and behaviour, because they, perhaps more than economic rhetoric, are the basis of consumption metaphors in the other social sciences.

In everyday American English, 'consumption' is what Lakoff calls a radial category, with a prototype at the centre, and the other members of the category belong by virtue of their relationship to the prototype, rather than through their coherent relationship to each other. So, for example, putting a painting on the wall, lying on the beach in the sun, and flushing the toilet, are all acceptable examples of consumption, but it is otherwise impossible to see how they are alike (and many scholars have strained to try to write a definition of consumption that does find their common characteristics). They are related to each other only because of their metaphorical connections to the prototype at the centre.

Consumption is also a graded category. Some things strike us as better examples of consumption than others. Borgmann says, 'plants consume carbon, animals consume plants ...' (2000: 418), but the transformation of carbon in the process of photosynthesis seems to be less like consumption than cows eating grass. Or think about burning a pile of leaves, versus putting the same leaves on a compost pile. Burning leaves seems more consumption-like than composting, just as going shopping, moving up and down the aisles hunting for the right shirt, is more consumption-like than sitting in a car listening to the radio. Some things seem more like consumption than others because of their proximity and resemblance to the prototype.

Consumption is Fire

What makes many of these disparate activities into consumption is their metaphorical relationship to the prototypical act of *eating*. Eating and consuming are also connected to each other through their common metaphorical relationship to fire, and the act of burning. Burning is historically the first English usage of the verb consume, attributed to the Wyclif Bible in 1382, in a biblical passage where a sacrifice 'with fier shal be consumyd.' (Lev. 6:23). Other early usages include 'unto ashes they will a man consume' (OED places this in 1430, Lydgate 1555: 19). Some other actions of fire – destruction, wasting away and vanishing – were also applied to consumption. Fire is still a powerful metaphor for consumption that destroys completely, leaving behind nothing useful.

- People have *money to burn*.
- Fortunes go up in a *puff of smoke*.
- Overindulgence in drugs causes total *burnout*.

Fire of course has a dual nature – both destructive and useful. It warms, comforts, and purifies; it lies at the centre of the hearth, and sanctifies the sacrifice. It is not surprising that consumption, as metaphorical fire, also has both destructive and utilitarian connotations (see Nordman). It can run out of control and become wanton gluttony, excessive luxury leading to corruption and ruin, while at the same time it is the daily 'fuel' that keeps the human 'engine' going, the centre of social life and domestic commensality.

It is no surprise that two of the Old Testament God's most important acts involved miraculous fire. He appeared to Moses as a bush that burned, but was not consumed, and during the siege of Jerusalem, he kept the temple lamp burning for seven nights with oil sufficient for only one. Later, Christians saw the fire of the lord as holy in itself; being consumed by god's fire was an act of giving up one's volition, submitting and becoming fuel in a larger fire.

As a natural (an even supernatural) force, fire metaphors do not portray humans in the central role in consumption. Fire consumes what you feed it; it dies if it is not fed, and if you let it loose it can consume everything in its path, but it has a will of its own and we are often helpless before it. The *Consumption is Fire* metaphor tells us that people consume what they are given; the rich consume more than the poor because they have more fuel. During the twentieth century, though, Americans came to believe that consumption was a matter of individual volition and will, and that consumption was not so much a natural force like fire, as something under conscious control that expresses the inner identity and essence of an individual. *Eating* as a metaphor puts the human at the centre, with the impersonal forces of the economy and nature providing the fuel and carting away the waste.

Consuming is Eating

Eating is a complex prototype, rooted in a common human bodily experience. Rather than a single act, it is normally broken down into stages (though cultures may do this in different ways) as part of a prototypical scenario.

HUNGER → FINDING & PREPARING → CHEWING & SWALLOWING
→ DIGESTING → EXCRETING

In this scenario a substance flows through a person, and this flow links the acts together into a single conceptual process, with a beginning, middle and end. It is important to remember that this series of stages is not natural categories; many of the elements are culturally specific and arbitrary.

With eating as a prototype, the more an act is like eating, the more it seems like real consumption. This is why listening to music seems less like consumption than burning gasoline while we drive in our car. The metaphor of eating tells us that when we consume something, it should be gone when we finish, transformed into waste. After we consume music, it does not disappear, and many people can listen to the same music at the same time – while the eating metaphor tells us that two people cannot consume the same bite of food, and you cannot both possess and consume the same thing ('you can't have your cake and eat it too'). Much of the vocabulary of consumption draws directly on the eating metaphor.

- She sucked the marrow from every experience.
- I have acquired a taste for furs.
- My customers lapped up the new ties.
- Shopping ate up all of our savings.
- I am always hungry for new experience.
- My attic is full to bursting.
- Consumers have gobbled the new cars up.
- That new dress is a feast for the eyes.

Because of the power of the *Consuming is Eating* metaphor, we associate the physical sensations of eating with those we experience in other kinds of consumption, particularly those associated with shopping. If you cannot get enough food, you are constantly hungry and you feel a nagging need. We visualize consumption as similarly driven by a desire just like hunger, which we can only satisfy by consuming, hopefully not so much that it makes us sick (see Belk, Ger and Askegaard 1996). *Desire is Hunger*, so that *Satisfying Desire is Eating* and consuming is a special case of *Satisfying Desire*. The result is that *Consuming is Eating*.

Similarly, the bodily experience of being satiated, full of food, relaxed and lazy, is extended to other acts of consumption, so that enough shopping or collecting should satisfy needs for a while, make people comfortable and satisfied, and no longer in need of more shopping, buying and consumption. In *The Affluent Society*, Galbraith said that once each American family got a small house, a car, and basic appliances, their needs would be satisfied once and for all. People would no longer want goods, and would instead seek satisfaction through more leisure, cultivating hobbies and self-improvement, and spending more social time with friends and family (1958). He did not recognize that even after the most sumptuous meal, people still get hungry. But the sense that consumption satisfies a need, and should satiate the appetite, appears in many consumption metaphors, often admonishing people for the sin of gluttony if they are not satisfied after a bout of consumption.

- Enough is enough!
- Your closet is already stuffed, how could you want more?
- One more coat is all I need.
- I always splurge on shoes in the spring.

- He has bitten off more than he can chew this time.
- Your clothing budget is already bloated.

Orderly consumption is like eating a meal. We have a need, we find the things to meet the need, buy them, use them and eventually, when they lose their value, they are ejected (thrown away) as waste. When we have a need we are anxious and uncomfortable; we enjoy the hunt and the purchase, are satisfied and almost unconscious of the actual process of use (digestion), and then would rather not talk about the elimination of wastes. The prototypical sequence of modern consumption is based on a metaphor for getting food and eating it. The sequence of desire → shopping → buying → using → discarding, is a clear analogue of the sequence of looking for food and eating, leading to a series of equivalences.

- *Desire is hunger.*
- *Shopping is hunting.*
- *Buying is catching.*
- *Using is eating and digesting.*
- *Discarding is shitting.*

Many expressions for the various activities involved in consumption are derived from the stages of the *Consuming is Eating* metaphor.

- I have been *beating the bushes* for a good shirt.
- I *bagged* three sweaters at the sale.
- Those rings are so beautiful I could *eat them up.*
- Throw those *crappy* old shorts away.
- I love bargain *hunting.*
- What a *waste* of a nice pair of pants.

By implication, shopping, like hunting, is exciting and challenging, even a bit dangerous. Wanting something is sheer misery and torture. Making a good buy is satisfying. Using the object is usually much more prosaic – sometimes a treat, other times a simple necessity, or a big disappointment. And disposing of waste is dangerous, private, and often left to specialist areas, equipment or personnel.

Pathology

The disorders and moral pitfalls of consumption have metaphorical equivalents in the pathologies of eating. Some of us become gluttons, suffering from an uncontrollable urge to eat more, though we know it is not good for us. The metaphorical equivalence of gluttony and wealth is made clear in the classic illustrations of the greedy and overindulgent rich. Even more egregious are those who have plenty of food, but who hoard it and hide it and deny it to themselves, and their families and friends; they are the classic biblical figures of the thin and miserly rich person. Both live off the fat of the land, gobble up resources, suck blood, while the cream they skim from others' labor feeds their bloated coffers. The moral failures of greed, avarice and miserliness are the same as those of gluttony and self-starvation, and we tend to treat all with the same degrees of approbation.

There is a moral ambiguity to all consumption, just as there is to eating. We eat because of need, but food also has power over us. It can seduce us and even addict us, to the point where we are powerless to stop eating. In biblical times of scarcity, eating well was a mortal sin. But in the overwhelming wealth of middle-class developed America today, being fat no longer means that other people are being deprived. Some estimate that 30 per cent of Americans are clinically obese, and 70 per cent are overweight. Gluttony is an understandable weakness, just giving in to normal appetites, the temptations of sinful foods.

The *Consuming is Eating* metaphor tells us that *Wealth is Fat*. Americans extend the same ambivalence they have towards food and gluttony to money, wealth and the rich. Rather than being evil, the rich are more likely to be seen as victims of the temptations offered by goods and glitz, as if they were at a giant Las Vegas smorgasbord.

At the other extreme, poverty is the equivalent of starvation, to the point that 'poor and hungry' is a cliché. Starving people are hungry all the time, obsessed with food and, given a full meal, they may stuff themselves to the point of being sick. Since poverty, lack of consumption, is the equivalent of starvation, we expect the poor to be living with a sense of deprivation. They should be obsessed with wealth and goods they can't have, and given some money they are likely to lose control and splurge with no thought for the consequences. This explains the extremely close supervision placed on those in poverty who are given food-stamps as a form of assistance, but who are bound by all sorts of rules about what kinds of things they can purchase with them (despite abundant evidence that poverty and hunger are far from the same thing). Similarly, our *Consuming is Eating* metaphor leads us to a simple explanation for poverty – poor hunting skills (see Chin 2001).

The *Poverty is Starvation* metaphor structures a host of moral attitudes towards consumption, especially those towards ethnic minorities and the countries that have been deemed 'underdeveloped', or 'impoverished'. Because the poor are supposed to be hungry, when they go ahead and buy a television or a bicycle, they are accused of misspending on things they don't need. The panic in environmental circles over what is going to happen to the environment as wealth increases in China and India is a good example. We expect them to act like starving people, which means they will binge and gorge themselves on rich goods as soon as they have the money, instead of investing it in their farms and businesses, or sending their children to school.

The same metaphor poses a fundamental problem for the proponents of voluntary simplicity or simple living. People who starve themselves amidst abundance, once called misers, are now labeled anorexics, considered mentally ill, and are sent off for treatment. Anyone who would voluntarily choose poverty is someone who will allow their children to go hungry when good food is put before them; insane if not criminal. As long as *Consuming is Eating*, it is hard to imagine any mass movement towards metaphorical anorexia.

Why Worry

It is not hard to see why many critics of the global economy draw on the *fire* and *eating* metaphors in their arguments about consumption. To say that resources are being eaten up, that consumerism is a raging fire or a ravenous beast, gives visual and visceral force to messages about the state of the planet and its resources. But these metaphors also obscure and confuse many key issues about consumer culture. While some aspects of consumption really are like eating and burning, there are many ways that they are completely unlike.

I have already touched on an obvious example. With food, you really cannot have your cake and eat it too – when you consume, you destroy the original form and devalue it. Many consumer goods are like this; marketers have worked assiduously over the last century to make as many things as possible disposable, but there are still many durable goods that never wear out, can be repaired, improved, customized and even passed down through generations. Think about gold jewellery, golf clubs, fine bamboo fly rods, oak furniture, comic book collections, books and china. We can share a song, a walk in the countryside, or an evening watching a DVD movie for the tenth time; in each case sharing increases, instead of diminishing our pleasure, and nothing has been destroyed, excreted or burned.

The eating and burning metaphors tell us that the inevitable result of consumption is ashes and waste, of little or no value, malodorous and filthy. In fact there are some kinds of consumption that actually raise and increase the value of things; Grant McCracken's argument about the way patina gives value to antiques makes just this point (1988). You buy a house on the market, and consume it very much the way you consume a car or a television set, but a house is usually more valuable after ten years than it was when you bought it. The CD you listen to once and take back to the store is physically indistinguishable from one that is brand new – your listening did no physical damage and there was no waste or residue. Nor does listening to more and more music constitute gluttony, since your brain does not fill up and get fat.

The metaphor that *Waste is Shit* may also present a series of problems, not least of which is the general attitude in most western societies that the end products of consumption should be removed from sight by invisible means, and disposed of by specialists. Thus, the entire sector of the economy that deals with objects after someone has discarded or rejected them is symbolically separated from the parts of the economy that deal with 'virgin' materials. The activities of 'waste management' take place largely out of public sight, except when there is some danger of 'overflow' or 'leakage'. It makes great metaphorical sense that the United States Government is pursuing a long-term policy of dumping its most dangerous radioactive waste into deep holes in the ground, even if most scientific panels have questioned both the urgency and the logic of the process.

Of all the parts of the *Consumption is Eating* scenario, the *Desire is Hunger* metaphor is especially misleading. Every account I have ever read of Cortés's conquest of Mexico says that he was driven by an insatiable hunger (or thirst) for gold. But what does this really explain? Greed is *not* like hunger in many ways. The metaphor makes it seem like greed is a *natural* impulse gone astray, though there is in fact no biological or genetic basis for it. Greed is much more complex and historically situated than the metaphor would allow; Cortés's greed for gold was driven by an intense desire for the status and privilege of nobility, and the confirmation of pure blood, and it has to be understood in the historical context of the recently completed reconquest of Spain from the Moors. These are far, far different from the kinds of motives that drive modern moguls like Bill Gates. Lumping together all the different motives for accumulating goods and resources as a natural force of greed is an easy, but non-explanatory, solution to the problem of understanding the multiplicity and variability of human desires. It also suggests that all forms of accumulation are products of greed, which hardly accounts for the multiple motives that drive both public and private collecting (Belk 1995).

A whole series of other moral and practical arguments about proper consumption flow from the *eating* metaphor. Moderation is a good thing. Don't eat too quickly. Strong spices can give you indigestion. Chew thoroughly before you swallow. Don't eat food served by strangers. Give yourself time for digestion after a meal, etc. These all have equivalents in precepts about not spending all your money in one place, enjoying the things you have instead of buying new things, buying solid long-lasting items instead of flashy ones, and on and on. But urging moderation and conformity to community standards is not necessarily the best form of consumption, either for the individual, or society as a whole. Consumption is not always a moral balance between too little and too much. Environmental scientists and ecologists have pointed out many cases where recycling is actually harmful to the environment, where consuming more of certain products could be beneficial, or conserving is wasteful (Lilienfeld and Rathje 1998).

Metaphors have a peculiar power to silence common perceptions that contradict the basic metaphorical structure. Consider, for example, the idea that consumption is a form of leisure that gives pleasure, just like a good meal. This is why increasing consumption is a form of progress; everyone will be well fed and therefore happy! The idea that abundant consumption brings pleasure is deeply rooted in many puritan critiques of consumer culture, since too much pleasure is corrupting and causes moral decay. But is consumption really leisurely and satisfying? Many people actually find everyday consumption activities to be a chore and an obligation, something required but hardly enjoyable. In fact, a good deal of consumption is work, not leisure. The reality in the last twenty years in much of the developed world is that the purchase of a major consumer durable requires careful research and comparison shopping amidst a bewildering variety of options and models, followed by unpleasant interactions with salespeople, and hours of assembly, reading manuals, and often months of frustration in learning to make the item work properly. Academics have had to resort to constructions like 'productive consumption' and 'consumptive production', to account for this, but the problem only exists at all because of the power of the *Consumption is Eating* metaphor. In the real world, there are no simple boundaries between consumption and production or work and leisure.

Finally, the *Consumption is Eating* metaphor creates a peculiar dilemma for the question of human agency in consumption. Eating is a natural, biological activity, driven by hunger that drives us whether we like it or not. But eating is also an act of volition; we can cultivate tastes to the status of an art, and eating is an intensely pleasurable activity for many people. In eating we must all face the boundary between nature and culture, and recognize that we have both basic needs and aesthetic pleasures in the same activity. Our own agency is called into question by the natural compulsion of need, which leads us to constantly search for the dividing line between necessity and luxury, the needs-driven, and the wants-driven. From very early civilizations, eating has posed weighty philosophical questions about the ability of individuals to know and control their passions (Davidson 1997).

We carry the same problems and contradictions of agency, need and desire forward to all other forms of consumption through metaphor. We may say, for example, that we need at least one clean shirt for our trip, but taking ten is a wasteful luxury. But this kind of need is always relative, and is socially and culturally constructed, rather than being driven by the biological force of hunger. Nevertheless, the eating metaphor lends its physical weight to statements of need; when we speak of 'children in need' we imply that their very survival is at stake. The problems of defining consumption 'needs' for housing, clothing, entertainment and the like are always at issue in the practice of development assistance, in assessing poverty, in deciding who is poor. The ugly truth is that all such needs are arbitrary because they are not biological needs of the same order as the hunger for food, and we know that even in the realm of food there are many degrees of starvation and hunger. Wanting implies agency, but needing is visceral and physical. This dichotomy divides nature and agency in a way that conceals a complex politics of value that works along several dimensions and continua. There really is no clear dividing line.

Is there Hope?

One can never abandon metaphor. The idea of perfect scientific objectivity about consumption is a futile illusion because metaphor is an essential part of our cognitive process (Lakoff & Johnson 1999). There are good reasons why our thought about consumption is embodied, grounded in physical and practical experience. The *Desire is Hunger* metaphor is not about to go away, nor is its extension the *Consumption is Eating* metaphor. The question is whether we can find other metaphors that make more sense of the realities – and possibilities – of consumption. New metaphors open new possibilities for thought, and provide openings for new actions and ways to educate people.

Activists in the environmental and anti-world-trade movements have already been creative in asserting new meanings for consumption. *Adbusters* magazine (a publication of the Media Foundation), for example, chronicled a number of campaigns in California during the late 1990s that defaced advertising bill-boards, some likening the flood of modern consumer goods to an alien invasion. Other images appearing in the magazine show people drowning in a sea of prod-ucts, or being forced to consume by corporate authorities and advertising icons like Joe Camel. Designer Tibor Kalman, somewhat more hopefully said, 'Consumption is a treatable disease' (Adbusters 1999). Here he draws, perhaps purposely, on the Victorian usage of the word consumption to describe the disease of tuberculosis. Unfortunately, none of these metaphors has the wide-spread, if not universal, grounding of *Desire is Hunger*. Effective activist messages will probably have to draw on metaphors that are extensions of the established system, instead of trying to build new metaphors entirely.

Where does all of this leave the anxious social scientist? Do we abandon the subject of consumption entirely? If nothing else, consumption is so firmly estab-lished in the modern world as a folk-concept, we need to study it as just that – an object with a history and a cultural context. On the other hand, any enterprise that sets out to find an objective category of consumption as a simple category of objects or activities that is 'out there' as a bounded and measurable group, is doomed from the start.

Acknowledgements

I was very fortunate to have the help of George Lakoff on this paper, beginning with congenial conversations on the topic of consumption, and extending to a close proofreading of the final draft. He is of course not responsible for any way that I have mangled or misused his ideas, but he certainly provided most of the intellectual fuel that drove this paper from origin to destination!

References

Adbusters, July/August 1999, No. 26. Back Cover.
Belk, Russell (1995) *Collecting in a Consumer Society*, London: Routledge.
—, Güliz Ger and Søren Askegaard (1996) 'Metaphors of Consumer Desire'. *Advances in Consumer Research* 23: 368–73.
Borgmann (2000) 'The Moral Complexion of Consumption', *Journal of Consumer Research* 26(2): 418–22.
Chin, Elizabeth (2001) *Purchasing Power*, Minneapolis: University of Minnesota Press.
Davidson, James (1997) Courtesans and Fishcakes: *The Consuming Passions of Classical Athens*, London: HarperCollins.
Douglas, Mary (1966) *Purity and Danger*, London: Routledge and Kegan Paul.
Galbraith, John (1958) *The Affluent Society*, Boston: Houghton Mifflin.
Horowitz, Daniel (1988). *The Morality of Spending*, Baltimore: Johns Hopkins University Press.
Lakoff, George (1987) *Women, Fire, and Dangerous Things*, Chicago: University of Chicago Press.
— (1996) *Moral Politics*, Chicago: University of Chicago Press.
— and Mark Johnson (1980) *Metaphors We Live By*, Chicago: University of Chicago Press.
— (1999) *Philosophy in the Flesh: The Embodied Mind and Its Challenge to Western Thought*, New York: Basic Books.
Lilienfeld, Robert and William Rathje (1998) *Use Less Stuff : Environmental Solutions For Who We Really Are*, New York: Ballantine.
Lydgate, John (1555) *The auncient historie and onely trewe and syncere cronicle of the warres betwixte the Grecians and the Troyans*, London: In Fletestrete at the signe of the Princes armes, by Thomas Marshe.
McCloskey, Donald (1985) *The Rhetoric of Economics*, Madison: University of Wisconsin Press.
McCracken, Grant (1988) *Culture and Consumption*, Bloomington: Indiana University Press.
Nordman, Bruce (no date) 'Celebrating Consumption', Lawrence Berkeley

Laboratory, 90–4000, Berkeley, CA. Online at http://eetd.lbl.gov/ea/build-ings/bnordman/c/cons3.html

Schiffer, Michael (1976) *Behavioral Archaeology*, New York: Academic Press.

Smith, Adam (1985) *An Inquiry into the Nature and Causes of the Wealth of Nations*, edited by Richard Teichgraeber III, New York: Modern Library.

Stern, Paul (1997) 'Toward a Working Definition of Consumption for Environmental Research and Policy' in P. Stern, T. Dietz, V. Ruttan, R. Socolow, and J. Sweeney (eds), *Environmentally Significant Consumption*, Washington, DC: National Academy Press.

2

I Shop therefore I Know that I Am: The Metaphysical Basis of Modern Consumerism

Colin Campbell

Introduction

I would hazard a guess and suggest that metaphysics is not a term that most people would normally associate with the activity of consumption. Indeed it seems more likely that these two would be regarded as polar opposites; the one concerned – as the dictionary puts it – with 'first principles, especially in relation to being and knowing', the other with the routine, the practical and the mundane. How then is it that I am suggesting that there might be a connection between the two? Well I arrived at the intimation of a link largely as a consequence of my attempts to seek an answer to the question of why consuming has come to occupy such a central place in our lives. Why, in other words, are the activities generally associated with the term 'consumption', such as the searching out, purchasing and using goods and services that meet our needs or satisfy our wants, regarded as so extraordinarily important? Because it seems self-evident to me that, in general and with some significant exceptions, that is precisely how they are regarded by the majority of people in contemporary society, as especially important if not actually central to their lives. It also seems largely self-evident that this has not been the case in previous eras

Now this is not the same question as 'why do we consume?' For there are several widely accepted answers to that question, ranging from the satisfaction of needs, the emulation of others, the pursuit of pleasure, the defence or assertion of status, etc. However, in seeking to understand why consumption has such importance in people's lives one is implying that it might be fulfilling a function above and beyond that of satisfying the specific motives or intentions that prompt its individual component acts. In other words, it might possess a dimension that relates it to the most profound and ultimate questions that human beings can pose, questions concerning the nature of reality and the very purpose of existence – with issues of 'being and knowing' in fact. That, at least, will be the thesis upon which – in true metaphysical fashion – I wish to speculate in this chapter.

The Nature of Modern Consumerism

In order for my argument to make sense it is important that I make it quite clear, at the very beginning, just what I consider to be the two crucial defining features of modern consumerism, that is those that distinguish it most clearly from earlier, more traditional forms. The one is the central place occupied by emotion and desire, in conjunction to some degree with imagination. This is an argument that I have developed elsewhere and hence shall not repeat at length here (see Campbell 1987).

So let me just emphasize my belief that it is the processes of wanting and desiring that lie at the very heart of the phenomenon of modern consumerism. This is not to say that issues of need are absent, or indeed that other features, such as distinctive institutional and organizational structures, are not important. It is simply to assert that the central dynamo that drives such a society is that of consumer demand, and that this is in turn dependent upon the ability of consumers to experience continually the desire for goods and services. In this respect it is our affectual states, most especially our ability 'to want', 'to desire' and 'to long for', and especially our ability to experience such emotions repeatedly, that actually underpins the economies of modern developed societies.[1]

The second, and closely associated, critical defining characteristic of modern consumerism I take to be its unrestrained or unrestricted individualism. Obviously not all consumption is individualistic in nature; for there continues to be a significant element of collective consumption even in the most modern and capitalist of societies, that is goods and services which are consumed by the community (such as defence or law and order) or owned by the community and then allocated to individuals rather than purchased on the open market (local government housing, for example). Yet it is quite clear that a distinctive hallmark of modern consumption is the extent to which goods and services are purchased by individuals for their own use. Again this is in marked contrast to the earlier pattern, in which these were either purchased by, or on behalf of, social groups, most especially the extended kin or household, or the village or local community, or alternatively allocated to individuals by governing bodies. Even more characteristic of modern consumerism is the associated ideology of individualism. That is the extraordinary value attached to this mode of consumption in conjunction with the emphasis placed on the right of individuals to decide for themselves which goods and services they consume.[2]

Now these two features strongly support each other, combining to define the nature of modern consumerism. And the crucial link between the two is the simple fact that modern consumerism is by its very nature predominately concerned with the gratification of wants rather than the meeting of needs. The significance of this development being that, while needs can be, and indeed generally are, objectively established, wants can only be identified subjectively. That is to say, others can always tell you what it is that you need. Indeed you may not be qualified to assess those needs for yourself and hence have to seek the assistance of experts in order to identify them, as in the case of one's medical 'needs'. But no one but you is in a position to decide what it is that you want. When it comes to wanting only the 'wanter' can claim to be an 'expert' (Campbell 1998). Naturally therefore it follows that such a mode of consumption is inherently individualistic, with the authority for decision-making located firmly within the self.[3] To summarize modern consumerism is more to do with feeling and emotion (in the form of desire) than it is with reason and calculation, while it is fiercely individualistic, rather than communal, in nature. And these two features provide the most obvious connection with the larger culture as well as providing the basis for the claim that modern consumerism rests on metaphysical assumptions.

Ontology and the Search for Meaning: Identity as Defined by Desire

In my initial remarks I observed that there seemed little obvious connection between the subject of consumption and metaphysical matters. There is however one topic where it is relatively easy to see a connection between the two, and that concerns the issue of identity. This is an issue central to many discussions of modern consumerism, where an emphasis is frequently placed on the significance of consuming in relation to the affirmation, confirmation or even the creation of identity. At the same time it is fairly obvious that the question 'who am I? is one of the most fundamental and basic that human beings can pose.

It is at this point that I become acutely conscious of the fact that the spectre of postmodern thought is hovering at my shoulder, and much as I would like to ignore its presence this is hardly possible. So I shall briefly acknowledge it and hope that by doing so it will be persuaded to fade into the shadows. For my position on the 'postmodern phenomenon' or the 'postmodern movement' is that this should be the object of sociological investigation. I regard it as a mistake to view this body of philosophical speculation as an intellectual or academic 'resource', useful as an aid to an understanding of the social and cultural world. To adopt this attitude is to my mind equivalent to assuming that astrology can serve as a useful guide to an understanding of the universe. What we need, as Mike Featherstone has said, is a sociology of postmodernism, not a postmodern sociology (1991: x). Unfortunately few social scientists seem to have followed this eminently sensible suggestion, with the result that many postmodern speculations concerning the contemporary world are frequently repeated as if they were indeed established truths. And one of the more widely reported of these concerns personal identity and the activity of consumption. Here the widespread presumption is that the contemporary or 'postmodern' self is exceptionally open and flexible. That is to say, it is assumed that individuals – by making use of the wide-ranging and ever-changing products on offer in a modern consumer society – are regularly engaged in the process of recreating themselves: first adopting and then casting off identities and lifestyles in just as easy and casual a manner as they do their clothes. This is made possible because, as Ewen and Ewen have put it, 'Today there are no ... rules, only choices.' And hence 'Everyone can be anyone.' (Ewan & Ewan 1982: 249–51). At the same time it is commonly suggested that individuals have little choice but to behave in this manner since what Lyotard has called 'grand narratives' are no longer credible, with the direct consequence that there is no longer any firm cultural anchorage for the individual's sense of identity. Thus one commonly encounters the view that the activities of consumers should be understood as both a response to a postulated 'crisis of identity' and an activity that in effect only serves to intensify that very crisis.[4]

I fully accept that it is probably true to say that an individual's sense of identity is no longer clearly determined, as once it was, by their membership of specific class or status groupings (Bocock & Thompson 1992: 149). I also accept that consumption is central to the process through which individuals confirm, if not create, their identities. But what I would dispute is the suggestion that individuals in contemporary society have no unitary or fixed concept of the self (Hollinger 1994: 113–14). While I would wish to maintain that consumption, far from exacerbating the 'crisis of identity' is indeed the very activity through which individuals commonly resolve just this issue.

The 'personal ads' sections of newspapers and magazines make fascinating reading and it could be that you, like me, are drawn to them because of what they reveal about our fellow human beings. This section of a newspaper or magazine is the place where individuals advertise for 'partners' either with just short-term friendship and fun in mind, or alternatively with a view to establishing a long-term, if not necessarily permanent, relationship. And, in order to attract the right kind of person, individuals set out to describe themselves (as well very often as the person they are looking for) in the advertisement. Now they usually only have a few lines in which to do this, so obviously they need to think carefully about what to say. What most people want to do is to give as clear and accurate impression of the sort of person they consider themselves to be – even if in the process there is a tendency to convey something of an over-flattering image. So what, typically, do people say when given only a restricted space in which to describe themselves? Well they say things like this: 'Bohemian cat-lover, 46 going on 27, totally broke and always working, likes red wine, working out, Pratchet, Tolkein & Red Dwarf.' Or 'Outdoor Girl, 50s, loves long country walks, jive dancing & Tate Modern. Seeks partner to share interests and maybe more.' One final example, 'Slim, professional, lively, reflective 40 year-old, enjoys Moby, Mozart, the Arts, and watching sports, seeks compatible male.'

Now what I find especially interesting about these ads is that the individuals concerned appear to be defining themselves – that is specifying what they see as their essential identity – almost exclusively in terms of their *tastes*. That is to say in terms of their distinctive profile of wants and desires. For, if we set aside the inclusion of what we might call the 'fixed basic facts' about a person, that is their gender and age together with some indication of appearance, occupation or class, then what is provided in these ads relates almost entirely to an individual's tastes. The things most commonly specified being, as my examples suggest, their tastes in music, literature, the arts, food and drink, together with leisure-time pursuits. Now why should that be? Why should people concentrate upon defining themselves in terms of their tastes? Well I would suggest that it is because these are what we feel define us more clearly than anything else, and that when it comes to the crucial issue of our 'real' identity then we effectively consider ourselves to be defined by our desires, or profiled by our preferences.

Let me be quite clear that I am not suggesting that it is our 'interests' or 'hobbies' that define us. Those people who define themselves in these ads in terms of their liking for red wine or country walks are unlikely to be looking for a partner to join them in organized wine-tastings, or in meetings of The Ramblers Association. After all, if these are indeed your hobbies then you can meet people with similar interests simply by joining the relevant societies concerned. No, what these people are identifying are less their serious interests or hobbies, than their 'tastes' (similar in effect to their sexual 'tastes', details of which do indeed appear in the more specialized and salacious variety of personal ad.). Nor am I suggesting that what we might call 'tribal identity' has ceased to be significant. Clearly these identities still matter, especially after what Americans call 9/11. In that sense the answer to the question 'Who Am I?' will still include such basic definers as gender, race, nationality, ethnicity and religion. But what I would like to suggest is that these identifiers do no more than 'frame' the parameters of who we consider ourselves to be. They do not specify the fine lines of our identity – merely its general outline. While the person we really consider ourselves to be, the 'real me' if you like, is to be found in our special mix or combination of tastes. This is where we are most likely to feel that our uniqueness as individuals – our individuality – actually resides.

Now of course if this argument is valid it means that the proliferation of choice characteristic of a modern consumer society is essential if we are ever to discover 'who we are'. For a wide range of variation in products is crucial for us to 'test ourselves', as we continually seek to answer the question, do I like this or that? Do I like this fabric, or this colour? Does this music, or those images, turn me on? Do I enjoy this experience, or does it turn me off? Viewed in this way the activity of consuming can be considered as the vital and necessary path to self-discovery, while the marketplace itself becomes indispensable to the process of discovering who we really are.

It should be clear that I am not suggesting that identity derives from the product or service consumed, or that, as the saying goes, 'people are what they purchase' (Ritzer, Goodman & Wiedenscroft 2002: 413). Of course, what we buy says something about who we are. It could not be otherwise. But what I am suggesting is that the real location of our identity is to be found in our reaction to products, and not in the products themselves. Hence I am not arguing that as consumers we 'buy' identity through our consumption of particular goods and services. Rather I am suggesting that we 'discover' it by exposing ourselves to a wide variety of products and services, and hence it is by monitoring our reaction to them, noting what it is that we like and dislike, that we come to 'discover' who we 'really are'.

It is important to realize that this manner of conceiving of self-identity is very new. Indeed considered against the backdrop of historical time it has only just happened. It is very unlikely that our grandparents, if not our parents, would ever have conceived of themselves in this way. For them, identity was far more likely to be primarily a matter of their status and position in various institutions and associations, with family, occupation, religious adherence, race, ethnicity and nationality all counting for more than something as insignificant as taste. Consequently their self-definitions would have tended to emphasize such statuses as farmer, fisherman, father, Presbyterian, Catholic, Englishman or Swede, etc., and not their taste in wine, literature, music or leisure-time activities.

If the suggestion that identity is discovered rather than purchased sounds a little too abstract or far-fetched let me quote April Benson on the subject of shopping. She writes,

> Shopping ... is a way we search for ourselves and our place in the world. Though conducted in the most public of spaces, shopping is essentially an intimate and personal experience. To shop is to taste, touch, sift, consider, and talk our way through myriad possibilities as we try to determine what it is we need or desire. To shop consciously is to search not only externally, as in a store, but internally, through memory and desire. Shopping is an interactive process through which we dialogue not only with people, places, and things, but also with parts of ourselves. This dynamic yet reflective process reveals and gives form to pieces of self that might otherwise remain dormant...the act of shopping is one of self-expression, one that allows us to discover who we are ... (2000: 505)

'I Shop therefore I Am'

These quotes come from a book entitled *I Shop Therefore I Am*, which might seem an apt slogan in the context of the argument I have just advanced. However, strictly speaking, 'I shop in order that I might discover who I am' would be a more accurate summary of the claim I have just made. By contrast, 'I shop, therefore I am', modelled as it obviously is on Descartes's famous 'I think, there-fore I am', implies something a little different. It suggests not so much that the activity of shopping is a means through which people discover who they are than that it provides them with the basic certainty of their existence. Now April Benson's book is about compulsive shopping so it is possible that the title is meant to indicate – if humorously – a situation in which this activity has come to totally dominate the lives of those subject to this addiction. Viewed in this light it simply refers to people for whom there is no other activity of any significance in life except that of shopping. I do believe however that this slogan is applicable to all consumers in modern society, whether compulsive shoppers or not, and in relation to exactly the same ontological issue that was of concern to Descartes. However before developing this argument I need to say something about the nature of the epistemology that underlies modern consumerism.

A Consumerist Epistemology

There are two popular sayings that are important pointers to the nature of the epistemology that is implicit in the metaphysical assumptions that I am suggesting underlie modern consumerism. The one is *'de gustibus non est disputandum'*, or in English, 'there is no disputing about tastes'. This saying originally referred to the fact that it was simply a waste of time trying to convince someone, by means of rational argument, to like or dislike certain foods or drink. However, it also resonates very clearly with the point I have just made about the self-defining significance of personal taste. That is to say, our tastes are unques-tionably 'ours' in the sense that they cannot be legitimately challenged by others. The second well-known, if not well-worn, saying, is that 'the customer is always right'. This originally gained currency because it was the motto that store managers or proprietors were wont to instil in their staff in order that their partic-ular retail outlet or chain might acquire, or keep, a reputation for good service. It was, of course, never intended to be taken literally, that is in the sense of being a statement of epistemological principle. However, I would suggest that this is indeed precisely what it has become; that is, in the form 'the consumer is always right.' Indeed I would suggest that the assumptions embodied in these two sayings – that there is no disputing tastes, and that the customer is always right – have become the basis for a widespread and largely taken-for-granted individualist epistemology, one in which the 'self' is the only authority in matters of truth.

We can see ample evidence to support this claim in the growing tendency to reject both the authority of tradition and that of experts in favour of the authority individuals claim for their own wants, desires and preferences. This is apparent in an area like health, for example, where there has been a rapid growth of complementary and alternative medicine at the expense of more conventional medical practice (see Fuller 1989). For it is clear that this development is a direct consequence of the assumption that the consumer is better placed than any so-called 'experts' to judge what treatment is in his or her best interests. Another area where exactly the same change is apparent is religion. Here too the authority of the churches, in the form of the clergy, is rejected in favour of the individual's claim to select his or her own version of 'eternal truth'; a process that has led to the development of what is often referred to as the 'spiritual supermarket'.[6]

In effect what has happened is that the authority of the old-style 'expert', that is someone who told you what you 'needed' and who gained their authority primarily from their institutional role, has been rejected, while their place has been taken by 'gurus' or 'enlightened ones', that is people whose role is to help you discover what it is that you really 'want', or 'desire'. Of course this is precisely what we would expect to happen in a society in which the gratification of wants has come to displace the satisfaction of needs. For as noted, when it comes to the identification of wants, 'the customer or consumer is of course necessarily always right'; always right, that is, in their judgement of what is ulti-mately true. In precisely the same way that it is generally assumed that no one else is in a position to tell you what you want so too is it assumed that no one else is in a position to tell you what is true. Hence we arrive at the popular notion of 'your truth, my truth' and the rampant relativizing of all claims to veracity that accompanies such a slogan. At the same time the process through which indi-viduals discover what is true for them is always and everywhere the same, and it is modelled on the manner in which they 'know' what they want. For a consumerist epistemology now prevails in which 'truth' is established in the same manner as the existence of wants; that is, through a scrutiny of one's internal emotional states.

The Search for Ontological Security

I would now like to return to the issue of ontology and the Descartes-style quote mentioned earlier, the famous 'I shop therefore I am'. So far I have suggested that modern consumerism embodies, or is predicated upon, a specific theory of personal identity together with a distinctive individualistic epistemology. But it is clear that it also contains a distinct ontology, or theory of reality, one that follows logically from the distinctive features of modern consumerism noted earlier. In fact, in the contemporary world epistemology is little more than an adjunct of ontology anyway, as I shall imply. That is to say, the former is commonly treated as simply an indicator of the latter; there being a greater desire to experience the real than to know the true.

I suggested earlier that consumption, and more especially perhaps shopping, could be seen as a process through which individuals resolve the 'problem' of personal identity. That is they 'discover who they are' by monitoring their responses to various products and services and therefore establish their distinctive tastes or desires. But, as the postmodernists are fond of emphasizing, individuals in contemporary society may change their tastes and preferences as, either following fashion or seeking higher status, they undergo the process of 'recreating' themselves. Now this may seem to argue against the suggestion that consumption enables people to discover who they really are, since if they had indeed found the answer to this question why would they subsequently abandon that particular identity in favour of another? Indeed, why would they continue to engage as enthusiastically as before in the search for new products and services if they have already resolved the issue of personal identity? I believe that the answers to these questions can be found in an understanding of the ontological function that modern consumerism currently fulfils.

The first critical point to appreciate is that if individuals do indeed change their pattern of tastes or preferences this does not represent any change in the *manner* in which identity is recognized or conceived, for this is still primarily a matter of the self being defined by desire, of having our profile traced through preference. In this respect, the much-emphasized variability and changeability in the perceived content of identity is not as significant as the continuity manifest in the processes involved in its 'discovery'. In fact the changes in content become quite understandable once one shifts the focus from the nature and content of individual identity to the deeper underlying human need for reassurance concerning the reality of the self. For consumption, which in the sense I have emphasized here can be viewed as an activity that involves the exploration of the self, can also be seen as constituting a response to ontological insecurity or existential angst. That is to say, it can comfort us by providing us with the certain knowledge that we are real authentic beings –that we do indeed exist. In this respect, the slogan 'I shop therefore I am' should indeed be understood in a truly literal sense.

Obviously in order to accept the truth of this assertion it is necessary to appreciate the extent to which we live in a culture that embraces an 'emotional ontology' and consequently accords consumption a remarkable significance. By emotional ontology I mean that the true judge of whether something is real or not is taken to be its power to arouse an emotional response in us. The more powerful the response experienced, the more 'real' the object or event that produced it is judged to be. At the same time, the more intense our response, the more 'real' – or the more truly ourselves – we feel ourselves to be at that moment. Very simply put, we live in a culture in which reality is equated with intensity of experience, and is hence accorded both to the source of intense stimuli and to that aspect of our being that responds to them. If then we apply this doctrine to the question of identity and the 'self' we can conclude that it is through the intensity of feeling that individuals gain the reassurance they need to overcome their existential angst and hence gain the reassuring conviction that they are indeed 'alive'. Thus although exposure to a wide range of goods and services helps to tell us who we are (by enabling us to formulate our tastes), this self-same exposure fulfils the even more vital function of enabling us to be reassured that our self is indeed 'authentic' or 'real'. Hence while what I desire (and also dislike) helps to tell me who I am, the fact that I do desire intensely helps to reassure me that I do indeed exist. To quote again from April Benson, 'I believe that reframing shopping as a process of search, a vital activity that reaches far beyond traditional associations with buying or having, can aid in [the] quest for identity and meaning.' (2002: 498). She continues, 'Conscious shopping, shopping as a process of search, is not about buying, it's about *being*' (2002: 502 emphasis added)

Of course one does not have to go shopping, or indeed engage in any other consumption activity, to undertake the quest for identity and meaning; let alone in order to gain reassurance concerning the reality of one's own existence. Any experience that provides an opportunity for a strong emotional response can serve this purpose; a fact that perhaps helps to explain the popularity of extreme sports and adventure holidays in our culture as well as the continuing popularity of horror and science fantasy films, as well too of course as romantic love, with its promise of passion, intimacy and desire. Yet it is worth observing that shopping is an ideal context in which to pursue this quest for meaning. Ideal because there is a purity of self-expression attached to the activity that is not commonly experienced in these other activities (as long as one is not thinking of routine provisioning or gift purchasing but activity directed to meeting the wants of the self). This purity derives from the absence of any need to consider either the feelings or demands of others on the one hand, and the sheer volume and variety of stimuli on offer on the other.

However, to return to the issue of changes in taste and preference and hence in identity, the key point here is that gaining reassurance concerning the 'reality' or if you like the 'authenticity' of one's existence through exposure to experiences that produce an emotional response in oneself is not a one-off requirement. Rather it is a psychological need that requires repeated satisfaction. However, it is impossible for the same stimuli – that is to say, the same products and services – to produce the same intensity of response in us when we are exposed to them a second or third time as they did on the first occasion. On the contrary it is more than probable that we will become bored as habituation sets in. Consequently, we need regular exposure to fresh stimuli if boredom is to be avoided and the continuing need for ontological reassurance satisfied. In this respect, boredom is seen as threatening because it undermines our sense of identity – we risk losing our sense of who we are once boredom sets in – hence our grip on reality falters. As a result there is a continuing need for fresh stimuli, ones that will produce a strong reaction in us. Hence the importance of fashion – as a mechanism for the regular and controlled introduction of 'new' products – as well as the fact that consumers may indeed be tempted to make significant changes to their 'identity' on a regular basis.

These changes should not be seen, however, as indicating that earlier attempts to establish the 'real' or 'true' nature of the self had failed. On the contrary, since the desires and preferences that defined that identity were experienced intensely at the time this 'proves' that it was 'real', just as the intensity attached to the new desires similarly demonstrates the authenticity of the novel 'replacement' self. The fact that such different selves can both be viewed as equally 'real' is recon-ciled – if indeed any reconciliation is seen to be necessary – by perceiving the true identity of the individual as being 'developmental' in nature. That is to say, as individuals we are conceived of as beings who are in an endless process of 'becoming', such that each new 'identity' emerges butterfly-like – from a deeper and hence more authentic level of the self – out of the discarded chrysalis of its predecessor.

A Consumerist Ontology

It should be clear by now that what I am claiming is that an emanationist or idealist ontology, or theory of reality, provides the foundation for modern consumerism. Of course an emanationist assumption has always underpinned the traditional economic paradigm for the analysis of consumption, being embodied in the central concept of the 'latent want'. That is to say, this paradigm neces-sarily presupposes that real consumer activity in the world, the selecting, purchasing and using of products, is to be understood as a process that results from the manifesting or 'making real' of something that previously was merely latent. Now I have criticized this concept in the past, pointing out not merely that the only evidence for the existence of latent wants is the actual behaviour they are supposed to explain, but also that wants should be considered as emergent constructs, the products of psychological 'work' on the part of consumers (Campbell 1987: 43–4). I still believe that these criticisms are valid. However this is not to deny that modern consumption rests on fundamentally emanationist assumptions. For, as I have already emphasized, its dynamic is built upon the ability of individuals to perform a particular psychological 'trick', that of producing desire where none previously existed. For consumers to accomplish this however – that is to perform the 'trick' of wanting what they had never wanted before – they have to engage in a highly creative process. In effect they have to 'conjure up' a specific positive feeling for an object or experience out of thin air. It is then the ensuing 'want', which has been conjured in this way, that becomes the cause (assuming they possess the necessary resources) of the subsequent and very real gratifying experience. It is thus not entirely fanciful to suggest that consumers do indeed create their own reality. That is to say they are themselves responsible for creating the necessary conditions for their consumption experiences. I believe that it is this fundamentally idealist and emanationist ontology that has in effect become the underlying paradigm for the modern consumerist view of the world; one in which all of reality, and not just the items we consume, is regarded as capable of being 'conjured up' in a similar fashion.

This claim might seem unduly fanciful, but I think it appears less so if we stop and consider just how the many objects that surround us in our own homes have actually come to be there. For most, if not all, of the products that we have purchased, and which now fill our homes – such as the furniture, the books, the CDs, the pictures and works of art, etc. – are only really there because at some stage we 'wanted' them. In that particular sense their presence in our world is the direct outcome or result of our emotional state, specifically of our desire. If we had not felt desire for them they would not be part of our everyday reality. Of course one could argue that these goods would still exist, even if we had not desired them, since they would probably have remained on the shelf in the shop where we first saw them. However it can also be argued that it is still primarily desire, one which in this case is shared with very many other people, that has brought these goods into existence in the first place, manufactured, as the producers might say, simply in order to 'meet demand'. Hence one could argue that it is not simply our purely personal world of possessions that should be regarded as 'conjured up' through a process of wanting but that the whole modern consumer economy is built upon a similar 'magical' process.

It was while I was speculating along these lines – that is on the possible pervasive nature of such an idealist and emotionalist ontology in our society – that I was prompted to think of the modern phenomenon of the 'wannabe'. Usually a young person, a 'wannabe' is an individual who is characterized by an intense desire (or 'want') to be famous and successful, most commonly as a pop star. What I find so interesting is the extent to which these young people appear to believe that their wanting – if intense enough – will be sufficient to secure the outcome they desire. Typically this belief is fiercely adhered to despite both the astronomical odds against their being successful and the fact – obvious to others if not to most wannabes themselves – that they lack the requisite talent. In this respect they are the supreme example of the now widespread belief that anyone can have, or do, anything, if only they *want* it enough. Now I used to imagine that when people uttered this sentiment they were endorsing the belief that success would come to those whose desire was such that they were prepared to put in the long, hard hours of work or practice required to achieve success. But now – and in line with the argument that I have just outlined – I am increasingly inclined to believe that contemporary wannabes actually interpret this phrase in a far more literal sense. That is to say, they actually believe that the wanting itself will bring them success, provided of course that it is intense enough. In other words, these young people exemplify just that idealist and emotionalist ontology that I have claimed underlies consumption, the idea that feeling – if intensely experienced – can directly change the external world.

Now of course the belief that you can change the world through mental or emotional effort alone conventionally goes by the name of 'magic'; something that most of us might associate either with the world of music-hall entertainment and children's parties, or a much earlier, more primitive and superstitious stage in human evolution. However, to think in this way would be to reveal just how out of touch one is with the contemporary world. It is not just in the world of children's books and the cinema that magic currently features so prominently, dominated as these are by the persona of Harry Potter and fantasy epics such as *The Lord of The Rings*. Magic also features prominently in both the New Age and neo-pagan movements that are currently enjoying such success in modern Western societies.[7] And how is magic defined by the spokespersons for these movements? Well it is defined as the ability to alter oneself and one's environment through attitudes, thoughts and emotions alone.[8] While if we take the trouble to examine the precise nature of that New Age philosophy which has found so many adherents in recent years we find that it contains an idealist ontology. In other words, New Agers believe that reality is really ideational and spiritual in form, not material. So here we find exactly that ontology which I have speculated might underlie modern consumerism, and in a very explicit form. In fact we can discern in the New Age world-view all those elements of a consumerist metaphysic that I have indicated above.

The New Age World-view and a Consumerist Metaphysic

This, of course, raises a very interesting question concerning cultural change and the nature of contemporary society. Could it be that the very extent and pervasiveness of the activity of consuming has helped to change our view of reality? That the marked degree to which the world that we experience is one that has increasingly been moulded by us to meet our desires means that we now accept – if only implicitly – a theory which regards reality as the product of our wishes?

With the result that the New Age world-view can be regarded as coming into existence as a consequence of a process of extrapolation from the assumptions that underlie modern consumerism? Or could it be that, on the other hand, we should understand modern consumerism as gaining its explicit cultural legitimation from a cultural development – the New Age movement – that had its origins elsewhere (see Heelas 1993). These are fascinating questions concerning the dynamics of cultural change. However this is not the place to explore the precise nature of the relationship between a New Age-style world-view and modern consumerism. Hence I shall restrict myself to noting the close parallels between the two.

Before doing so however it might be wise of me briefly to anticipate the objection that the New Age movement is so insignificant – and indeed in the twenty-first century so passé, so 70s and 80s, – that it cannot really be credited with a significant role in contemporary society. Now it is quite clear that nothing is further from the truth. For in fact New Age beliefs and attitudes are now so widespread and pervasive in our society and its culture as to effectively dominate all areas of life (just look carefully at the shelves in your local bookshop next time you are there if you don't believe me) (York 1995; Heelas 1996).

There are three principal parallels that we can discern between the metaphysic underlying modern consumption and a New Age world-view. The first – and most obvious – is what Roy Wallis has called epistemological individualism (1984: 100). This is the assumption that authority lies with the self, and that there is no true authority outside the self. As the New Age spokesman Sir George Trevelyan expresses it, 'Only accept what rings true to your own inner self (quoted by Heelas 1996: 21).' This, as we have seen, is also the central tenet of the modern consumer ideology, the assumption that personal experience and personal experience alone – largely in the form of wants and desires –constitutes the highest authority. Second, as we have also seen there is a shared ontological idealism or emanationism. This is the belief that reality consists of mind and spirit rather than matter. While the third, as suggested, is the fact that they share a basically 'magical' philosophy in which the 'external' or 'material world' is generally considered to be directly subject to the power of human thoughts and desires.

The second of these similarities, the shared belief in an idealistic metaphysic, provides me with an opportunity to cite the last of those well-known and popular phrases that have commonly been applied to consumption. In this case the term I have in mind is 'retail therapy'; a phrase that, in my experience, is almost always employed in a humorous context, or at least spoken of in a light-hearted or flippant manner. However, once again I would like to suggest that we should treat it with all seriousness, regarding it not as a metaphor or as a joke but as an accurate and meaningful descriptor. For when the belief in an idealistic ontology is applied to individuals it leads to the idea that the 'authentic self' is located deep within the human psyche and can only be discovered through what are essentially processes that 'express' or 'release' this underlying reality. Naturally this belief casts all restraint or constraint of any kind, whether imposed on the individual from without, or more significantly by individuals themselves through excessive self-control or inhibition, as the cause of all that is false, inauthentic or harmful. Now the term 'retail therapy' is commonly used to mean little more than that the activity of shopping, understood as a form of self-indulgence, may have the effect of making us feel better. However I would like to suggest that the term, if taken seriously, actually means that we should regard this activity as directly comparable with something like participation in an encounter group; that is, as an important means of overcoming inhibitions or 'psychic blocks' and directly expressing powerful feelings. Obviously I don't mean by this that people regularly hit out at irritating shop assistants, or for that matter routinely hug the kind and helpful ones. What I mean is that in selecting and purchasing products that we want (not ones we 'need') we are directly acting out our feelings – and hence throwing off unhelpful restraints – in just the same basic fashion as in the self-consciously constructed therapeutic contexts. Certainly shopping does indeed commonly (although obviously not always) resemble therapy as New Agers understand that term (see Button & Bloom 1992: 131–46; Heelas 1996, ch. 3). That is to say it is essentially a process in which healing and 'self-transformation' is achieved by encouraging direct emotional expression, and hence can indeed be seen as one means of 'liberating' the 'real self'. Indeed at least one New Age author explicitly identifies shopping as a means to this end (Ray 1990: 135–7).

Conclusion

The aim of this chapter was to explore some of the fundamental assumptions that could be considered to lie behind the phenomenon of modern consumption; to seek out those ideas concerning the nature of knowing and being that are implied in the beliefs and attitudes typically associated with such apparently mundane consumption practices as shopping. The conclusion I have reached is that there are indeed significant metaphysical assumptions underpinning modern consumerism, assumptions that, intriguingly, do not appear to be limited to the sphere of consumption itself but are also present in many other areas of contemporary life. What this could be seen to indicate is that the activity of consuming – with its implied emanationism and faith in the power of 'magic' – has become a kind of template or model for the way in which citizens of contemporary Western societies have come to view all their activities. Since, as we have seen, more and more areas of contemporary society have become assimilated to a 'consumer model' it is perhaps hardly surprising that the underlying metaphysic of consumerism has in the process become a kind of default philosophy for all of modern life. Viewed in this light the fact that consuming has acquired a central significance in our lives could indicate something very different from the common suggestion that we are all victims of a selfish materialism and acquisitiveness. Quite the contrary in fact, it could be seen as implying an acceptance of a fundamentally idealistic metaphysic. If so, then this would mean that consuming should no longer be viewed as a desperate and necessarily futile response to the experience of meaninglessness, but rather as the very solution to that experience. The suggestion being that consumption itself can provide the meaning and identity that modern humans crave, and that it is largely through this activity that individuals discover who they are, as well as succeed in combating their sense of ontological insecurity. Hence it is exactly in this aspect of their lives that most people find the firm foundations upon which their grasp of the real and the true are based, while also providing them with their life's goal. Consequently it is on the basis of this diagnosis that I would suggest that it is justifiable to claim not simply that we live in a consumer society, or are socialized into a consumer culture, but that ours is in a very fundamental sense, a consumer civilization.

Notes

1. In relation to this point I do find it interesting that economists increasingly appear to recognize that our economy is ultimately dependent on the psychological capacities and mental states of individuals. That is to say they generally recognize the important role played by what they call 'consumer confidence'. Yet this simple concept does not really encompass the full extent to which our economy is dependent on the psychic skills and mental dispositions of individuals. For it is our ability continually to manufacture wants that really provides its underpinning.
2. See, for one example among many, Kumar's observation that one of the key features of modernity is individualization, by which he means that 'the structures of modern society take as their unit the individual rather than, as with agrarian or peasant society, the group or community' Kumar (1988: 10).
3. These two characteristics can also be seen to largely account for most of the other characteristic features of modern consumerism, such as the importance of fashion for example, and the extensive proliferation of choice of products offered for sale.
4. See for example Don Slater's observation that 'Consumerism simultaneously exploits mass identity crisis...and in the process intensifies it' (1997: 85).
5. These ads have been taken from 'Soulmates' *The Observer Review*, 9 June 2002, p.19.

6. 'The Spiritual Supermarket: Religious Pluralism in the 21st Century' was the title of a conference organised by INFORM and CESNUR held in London in April 2001.
7. For accounts of the rise of the New Age and neo-pagan movements see Michael York, *The Emerging Network: A Sociology of the New Age and Neo-Pagan Movements*, New York: Rowman & Littlefield, 1995; and Paul Heelas, *The New Age Movement: The Celebration of the Self and the Sacralization of Modernity*, London: Blackwell, 1996.
8. See William Bloom's discussion in Button and Bloom 1992: 89.

References

Bocock, R. & Thompson, K. A. (1992) *Social and cultural forms of modernity*, Cambridge: Polity.
Button, J. & Bloom, W, (1992), (eds.) *The Seeker's Handbook: A New Age Resource Book*, London: Aquarian/Thorsons
Campbell, C. (1987) *The Romantic Ethic and the Spirit of Modern Consumerism*, Oxford: Blackwell.
— (1998) 'Consumption and the Rhetorics of Need and Want' *Journal of Design History* 11(3): 235–46.
Featherstone, M. (1991), *Consumer Culture and Postmodernism,* London: Sage.
Fuller, R. C. (1989), *Alternative Medicine and American Religious Life*, New York: Oxford University Press.
Heelas, P. (1993) 'The New Age in Cultural Context: the Premodern, the Modern and the Postmodern', *Religion* 23 (2): 103–16.
Heelas, P. (1996*). The New Age Movement: The Celebration of the Self and the Sacralization of Modernity*, London: Blackwell
Hollinger, R. (1994), *Postmodernism and the Social Sciences*, Thousand Oaks, CA: Sage.
Kumar, K. (1988), *The Rise of the Modern West: aspects of the social and political development of the West*, Oxford: Blackwell.
Lane Benson , A. (ed.) (2000), *I Shop Therefore I Am: Compulsive Buying and the Search for Self,* Northvale, New Jersey: Jason Aronson Inc.
Ray, S. (1990), *How to be Chic, Fabulous and Live Forever*, Berkeley, CA: Celestial Arts.
Ritzer, G. Goodman D. & Wiedenscroft, W. (2002) 'Theories of Consumption', in Ritzer, G. & Smart, B. (eds), *The Handbook of Social Theory*, London: Sage.
Slater, D. (1997) *Consumer Culture and Modernity*, Cambridge: Polity.
'Soulmates', *The Observer Review,* 9 June 2000.

Wallis, R. (1984), *The Elementary Forms of the New Religious Life*, London: Routledge.

York, M. (1995), *The Emerging Network: A Sociology of the New Age and Neo-Pagan Movements*, New York: Rowman & Littlefield.

3

Culture, Consumption, and Marketing: Retrospect and Prospect

John F. Sherry, Jr.

Backstory

Not quite fifteen years ago, as I policed my kitchen, cleaning up after dinner, refereeing a loud squabble between two of my sons and calming an incessantly barking dog that couldn't decide whether the scuffle interrupting her own foraging was an invitation to play or flee, the domestic din was joined by the jangling of the telephone. For some foolish reason, perhaps the welcome relief promised by what surely must be the placid monotone of a telemarketer's script, or the expectation that the bell would send all combatants to a neutral corner, I picked up the phone and put into motion the events that have led to this chapter.

On the other end of the line was Hal Kassarjian, who had tracked me to my home to outline his vision of a comprehensive handbook of consumer behaviour, which would serve as a training guide for doctoral students in the area. Three seconds into the conversation, I knew Hal wanted something from me, since his salutation had not included the words 'Jesus Christ, what the hell is all that racket going on over there?', but rather had begun with gentle ritual inquires into my current state of being, before blending seamlessly into the protracted sales pitch. By the time he had reached me, Hal had convinced many of the luminaries of our field to contribute a chapter to his project, but he lacked what he called a 'final' chapter, one that would capture the 'other stuff' that had been going on in the discipline over the last few years. As Russ Belk was apparently unavailable for the project, I had become the go-to 'other guy' for this 'other stuff'.

Already an experienced 'other', I negotiated a loose set of ground rules with Hal. I would provide an idiosyncratic account of the area, told from the point of view of a participant-observer who was also an informant, essentially confounding emic and etic distinctions. The chapter would be part sociology of the discipline, part literature review and part projection of the area's trajectory. Hal was convinced of the potential of this 'other stuff', and was eager to get its canon into the hands of doctoral students. Ever the practical anarchist, or *agent provocateur*[1], he acceded to my wishes, and promised to edit with a light hand. I remember the words he spoke after sealing the deal, just prior to ringing off: 'Jesus Christ, what the hell is all that racket going on over there?'

Thus, in the cacophony of my kitchen, were the first few notes of Joshua's horn replayed. This 'other stuff' was being offered a seat at the institutional table, and I was being given the honour of representing the work of so many guerrillas engaged in the paradigm wars; of getting the Trojan Horse inside the walls. How best to proceed? As a native Chicagoan, I heard the words of Mayor Richard J. Daley echoing in my mind's ear. He had occasion to remark, accurately as it turned out, that, 'The police aren't here to create disorder. The police are here to preserve disorder.' A sound analogy, I thought. If I could preserve the disorder being mobilized by researchers marginalized by the minions of modernism, and amplify the polyvocal chatter as characteristic of my academic department as my kitchen, then a good time might be had by all.

As a marketer, I knew I couldn't hang the tale on Hal's category label 'other stuff'. By then, the heyday of 'otherness' (and kindred concepts such as 'marginalization', 'hegemony' and 'subalternity') in contiguous social science disciplines had started to wane, even as it was making its way to consumer research, and both its stridently critical (albeit warranted) ethos and implicitly dismissable connotation were the wrong positioning statements for a marketing audience. The label 'alternative' was appropriately countercultural, but also struck me as somewhat stigmatizing, implying, as I thought, a suboptimal choice. 'Interpretive' was a label increasingly being ascribed to this 'other' research, less often in the sense of the 'interpretive turn' said to have been taken by disciplines growing more interested in richly nuanced readings of behaviours treated as hermeneutic texts, than in the sense of projective fantasy exercised in the absence of rigorous data analysis. Again, a pejorative ascription, but, with a certain flippant caché: every inquirer interprets, but some do it more reflexively, with greater integrity. I needed a label that would capture the inchoate, amorphous, rebellious, ludic irruption promising to rock our disciplinary world.

The *mot juste* I selected was a contentious one, flanked by weasel words but unpacked, I thought, scrupulously. A patchwork quilt of inquiry, a confederacy of autonomous regimes reading consumption against the disciplinary grain, a heterotopia of heterodoxies, Hal's 'other stuff' became 'postmodern' consumer research, a label of convenience purporting to embody the weirdness of the moment in which the foundational became fungible, the essential evanescent. This 'new consumer behaviour research', as Russ Belk (1995) came to construe it, seemed to arise as our disciplinary membrane mutated from selectively permeable to porous. As boundaries were blurred and transgressed (eventually to be redrawn and reinforced, inevitably and lamentably, by neo-orthodoxy), the promise of apotheosis stirred in the literature. Our thought leaders were challenged with the prospect of being otherwised. Difference seemed about to have its day.

The postmodern alternatives I described in that early effort (Sherry 1991) were unfolding in an era of rapidly accelerating and highly politicized pluralism. Ontology, epistemology, axiology and praxis were each touched by the successive waves of researchers eager to understand consumption in more holistic, comprehensive fashion. Refugees from and freeholders in other disciplines explored consumption from vastly different perspectives than the economic and psychological ones that had dominated our field. Danny Miller (1995) would eventually advocate that consumption should replace kinship as the lodestar of the anthropological enterprise. Russ Belk would continue to argue that consumer research as a field had actually yet to emerge. Shelby Hunt (1999) would eventually indict nonpositivist research for the decline and fall of Western Civilization. I also made a few projections about the fate of our field in the wake of the pluralist perturbations the postmodern moment provoked. In the balance of this chapter, I revisit and revise the projections and offer a few more in their place. In so doing, I hope not only to preserve, or at least prolong, the disorder of our area, but also to misdirect at least as many subsequent inquiries as I did with the original effort.

Reprise

In my chronicle of the emergence of this 'other stuff', I described the changes underway in consumer research in terms of Victor Turner's (1974) model of the social drama, wherein positivist and postmodern paradigm-bearers contested in a four-act exhibition of disciplinary theatre. At the time of the writing, both Acts One (public breach) and Two (escalating crisis) had been completed, and the curtain had just risen on Act Three (redressive action). Having identified the fault line, the field had begun searching for ways to contain the rift. The past fifteen years has been a period of rapidly escalating social change in the discipline, directed, I think, primarily toward bringing down the curtain on Act Three.

Several signal events have occurred during this protracted Act. Of primary importance has been the complete reconfiguring of the editorial structure of the field's flagship journal, the *Journal of Consumer Research*. In the service of decentralized decision-making and paradigm-appropriate review, *JCR* has evolved to provide its editor guidance first from advisory editors, and thence from associate editors, and from an increasingly diverse Editorial Review Board. Over time, more segments of the journal's franchise have gained greater share of voice, resulting in a more diversified publication. Recent structural changes to the journal have permitted intramural and extramural thought leaders to challenge the field with provocative essays, and encouraged researchers at large to reinquire into fundamental tenets of the discipline, thus harnessing some of the energy of scholarly ferment to catalyse social scientific advance. Further, awards for Best Article published during a three-year period in *JCR* have been made across the research 'camps', which have both validated emerging regimes and provided exemplars for emulation, thus contributing to the efflorescence of the 'other stuff'. (In fact, by my informal count, at least 50 per cent of the awards have gone to 'other stuff'.) Finally, the launching of a monograph series under the aegis of the *Journal of Consumer Research* portends significant increase in the 'reach' of postmodern inquiry, whose practitioners often chafe at the page restrictions imposed upon them by the conventional journal article.

Act Three has also been driven by events occurring at the level of the professional society. The Association of Consumer Research (the most active contributor of *JCR's* twelve member association sponsors) has held conferences of irregularly accelerating diversity and balance, striving mightily to meet the needs of its increasingly heterogeneous membership. Its presidential leadership continues to oscillate nominally across the research camps, further helping to assure breadth of coverage and diversity of intellectual initiative in the society's undertakings. ACR has partnered with Sage Publications over the years to nurture book-length treatments of consumption issues, recognizing the value of monographic accounts in a field dominated by journal readers.

While it is difficult to pinpoint the dawn of a new intellectual era – are we truly in the Seventh Moment of the history of qualitative research (Lincoln and Denzin 2000) and not still the Sixth? Or yet the Eighth? – the theatrical trope demands the staging of a fourth and final act. Act Four (reintegration or irreparable schism) is where, I believe, our field currently finds itself. Imagine consumer research, paused, like a deer in the footlights, poised to begin the next leg of its journey, with several paths looming ahead. Fifteen years ago, I saw Turner's dénouement as an either-or proposition, too close to call. Among the forces of reintegration at work have been a transmogrified *JCR*, a more variegated ACR, and the gradual articulation of a philosophy of inclusiveness by our institutional leaders. No new professional society has yet arisen to co-opt the energies of postmodern consumer researchers, (with the possible exception of the Society of Consumer Psychology), and little institutional outreach to other disciplines has occurred. Ironically, and tragically, one legacy of the 9/11 terrorist attack against the United States may prove to be a heightened realization of the role of consumption as a central agent of cultural stability and change at work in the world today. Hopefully this realization will lead directly to more enlightened ways of understanding and tempering the forces of consumption, a normative challenge the entire discipline may renounce to our collective peril.

The centripetal forces I saw moving our field toward schism have continued unabated. 'Alternative' journals have arisen to accommodate parochial interests.

Here is just a partial list: the *Journal of Consumer Psychology, CMC: Culture, Markets and Consumption*, the *Journal of Marketing Theory*, the *Journal of Consumer Culture, Qualitative Inquiry, Qualitative Marketing Research, Consumer Dimensions*.

We have seen a rise in the number and frequency of specialist conferences within the field and around the globe. In an era of reduced academic travel budgets, this embarrassment of riches will lead to fragmentation, as specialists are forced to make more efficient choices. As these conferences thrive, the flagship interdisciplinary conference may experience attrition, especially among older, more seasoned researchers who find less of relevance in their former haunts.

Outside our discipline (whose motherland has steadfastly remained the departments of marketing), contiguous fields have embraced consumption with ever greater fervour. Psychology, sociology, anthropology, cultural studies, political science, communications, architecture, literature, film, psychoanalysis, history, geography and, gods help us, even economics have begun to think through consumer behaviour. Interest groups within these disciplines increasingly command conference tracks and stand-alone meetings, publish proceedings and newsletters, and post accounts of their members' activities from book writing to reviewing on web sites available for universal consultation. Ironically, many (if not most) of the consumer researchers outside our field who work in the area of 'other stuff' seem unaware of the existence of the *Journal of Consumer Research*, or *Advances in Consumer Research*. Perversely, some who are aware (including august presences such as Danny Miller or Colin Campbell) seem disinclined to import our findings into their own research, or export theirs to ours. For all intents and purposes, the scholarship of consumer research seems safely stored in a disciplinary silo, securely segregated from the basic disciplines, destined to be reinvented rather than discovered and used synergistically.

At the present writing, I tend to read Turner's dénouement with the postmodern grain, rejecting his either-or outcome in favour of an and-both scenario. That is, I believe consumer research will undergo reintegration and schism simultaneously for the foreseeable future. While key figures and their students will maintain a publishing and professing presence on their interdisciplinary flagship home turf, the new freedoms afforded them by both emerging specialist venues and basic discipline niche development will lure them beyond the marketing department pale. Further (as I explore later), the defection of postmodern researchers from the journal article to the book as the preferred mode of publication will increase the visibility of their ideas to new audiences at the same time as it alters the criteria of personnel committees. Concurrently, sponsoring associations of interdisciplinary journals will begin to reassess and realign their allegiances, creating vehicles more in tune with their memberships' needs and interests. More specialized journals will tempt consumer research 'insiders' to publish beyond the walls of the business school. Finally, organizations like *JCR* and *ACR* will be compelled to mount more vigorous and sustained outreach efforts with consumer research 'outsiders' if the hope to stay at the cutting edge of inquiry is to be sustained. Over the long haul, I envision both the rise of a vastly reconfigured multidisciplinary 'spanning' association of scholars interested in consumption broadly construed, as well as the proliferation of specialty associations devoted to the micro-granularities of consumption rooted in local perspectives.

In retrospect, it is clear that the postmodern moment in consumer research is not simply a manifestation of reactance. Our revered elders are still acting out as outrageously as ever. Juniors are emulating their elders in increasing numbers. Hopefully, a simple reinquiry of the Consumer Behavior Odyssey will be considered too trivial an undertaking compared to the launching of an even more provocative enterprise. (Perhaps a virtual Cyberodyssey? A multi-site exploration of lived experience in Temporary Autonomous Zones? An archaeology and psychoanalytic interpretation of Russ Belk's file cabinets?) Nor is the postmodern moment simply a ritual of rebellion, as the ever widening and deepening literature assures that the hegemony of economics and psychology has been a temporal 'blip' on the screen. It seems apparent that the postmodern moment has been the occasion of a revitalization moment. Charisma has been routinized, a new generation of researchers is pushing the field in interesting new directions, and the pioneers continue to innovate even as their earlier contributions are being critiqued by their students.

Perspective Integration Revisited

At the core of my original chapter was a typologized literature review of material emanating chiefly from consumer research – space limitations permitted only a ritual bow in the direction of work outside the discipline (which included perennial usual suspects Campbell, Miller and Wilk) – that I felt fit the 'other stuff' category. Perhaps the most frequent comment I received about the chapter had to do with the sheer volume of work going on outside the mainstream of the discipline. Consumer researchers hadn't realized just how much depth and breadth this emerging field had already attained. I grouped this research into three basic categories: critical, culturological and communicative. With some internal refinement and elaboration, these categories are still structurally sound fifteen years later. However, the literature has since burgeoned. The *Journal of Consumer Research* now relies for 12 per cent of its content (but, recall, 50 per cent of its prizewinners) upon postmodern inquiry. *Advances in Consumer Research* is perhaps even more dependent.[3]

While I will not update the categorization in this chapter, I do think it is useful to revisit and revise some of the suggestions I made at the time for inquiry into issues that an integration of the categories revealed as promising. I thought we'd see more investigation of foundational principles of consumption by now, but the field's major tenets still await systematic rethinking. We have, however, seen exceptional growth in the exploration of extra-economic dimensions of consumer behaviour. We have made some progress in cross-cultural and historical investigations of consumption, but still have a long way to go before escaping the ethnocentric and tempocentric perspectives of American departments of marketing. Discourse-centred and hermeneutic analyses of consumption have flourished over time. Finally, I think our programmes of directed intervention have benefited tremendously from the input provided by these 'other' perspectives, whether at the level of consumer packaged goods or of public policy. Managerial marketing research itself seems to be undergoing something of a qualitative renaissance at the moment, which I believe contributes to consumers being exploited a little less inhumanely, and sometimes satisfied in a more prosocial manner.

Going forward, I am hoping to see a few particular issues emerge from my older categories that will be of special interest to consumer researchers. From a critical perspective, I think renewed attention must be devoted to global-local marketplace dynamics, and to the practices of resistance, accommodation and co-creation consumers adopt in marketplaces around the world. From a culturological perspective, we need comprehensive, nuanced cross-cultural comparative explorations of consumer behaviour, and more precise understanding of virtual marketplaces as experienced by consumers. From a communicative perspective, we still need to field a cultural poetics of desire and convey our research in a manner that addresses the challenges posed by the crisis of representation. At least, I see these imperatives as part of a programmatic package that shapes much of the work I hope to undertake in my own research.

Bringing 'Other Stuff' to Prominence

I was only able to cite two vehicles portending the kinds of change our discipline might expect to weather back when I drafted the chapter Hal had requested in the late 1980s. One was Russ Belk's (1991) *Highways and Buyways,* and the other Beth Hirschman's (1989) *Interpretive Consumer Research.* The former, a multi-site team ethnography emerging from a nominally integrated project, the latter a kitbag of virtuoso exercises demonstrating the range of humanistic inquiry, these volumes proved to be harbingers of the 'other' era. Since their publication, a number of other correctives to conventional consumer research has emerged. These correctives have been multifaceted in nature, and bear some consideration of their own.

John F. Sherry

Conferences are convenient vehicles for launching and nurturing research regimes, for cultivating invisible colleges, and for developing the kind of *esprit* that gives an emerging subdiscipline the kind of immediacy and presence it requires to flourish. Several conferences have stimulated divergent thinking in our field over the past decade and more. The HCR Conference – Heretical Consumer Research – has consistently pushed the envelope on topical and (re-) presentational diversity, adopting the mandate of radical challenge to disciplinary convention. The ACR Gender Conference has continued to explore consumption as it is shaped and reflected by the biocultural forces of masculinity, femininity and its hybrids. Both the ACR International Conferences (Europe and Asia-Pacific) and the Marketing and Development Conference have pushed the discipline to adopt a cross-cultural perspective of consumer behaviour, and have encouraged the critique of dominant views (typically US-centric) of consumption dynamics. Somewhat more idiosyncratic conferences have bracketed this era of postmodern expansion. A pair of early conferences on marketing and semiotics held in Bloomington and Evanston helped set the agenda for the exploration of meaning movement in consumption, while Stephen Brown's Belfast trilogy of marketing 'retreats' has accelerated inquiry into the sacred and utopian dimensions of consumption. While there seems to be no current substitute for place-based conferencing as a mode of stimulating scholarly communal solidarity, I expect we can look forward to Internet-based convocations as technology rapidly improves.

A congeries of programmes and centres has arisen to foster alternative discourse in recent years. Odense University's Doctoral Program in Cultural Dimensions in Marketing, Consumer and Organization Research has trained flights of younger inquirers in the methods and perspectives of nonpositivist research. Bilikent University's Center for Research in Transitional Societies, and Göteborg's Center for Consumer Science promise to build on such a tradition. The University of Utah's Center for Consumer Culture is creating the nucleus of such alternative inquiry in the United States. Russ Belk and Rob Kozinets have just offered the first consumer research videography training under the Center's auspices, in preparation for the first ACR film festival, held in October of 2002. From such programmes and centres may spring the next wave of 'weird scientists' or 'post-Odysseans' to foment change and challenge complacency among the neo-orthodox old guard postmodern researchers.

Institutional changes in professional societies and journals have accelerated the rate of diversification in our discipline as well. To choose just one group, the Association for Consumer Research has offered several important innovations, grounded in democratization, empowerment and inclusion. The ACR Doctoral Consortium has helped initiate young scholars into a heterogeneous research community of peers. The ACR Round Tables have expanded the opportunities for collegial exploration of emerging issues of interest to the discipline. The creation of an ACR Fellows' Bookshelf column of recommendations in the Society's newsletter is expanding the membership's grasp of the complexity and dimensionality of the field exponentially. Finally, the making universally available electronically (at no charge) of the entire body of research published by ACR, will do more to stimulate the growth and diversification of alternative inquiry than any of us can yet imagine. On the journal side, the *Journal of Consumer Research* has evolved to include reflective essays by seminal thinkers inside and outside the discipline, which are designed to stimulate ever greater individuation of the field. Further, *JCR* has established a practice of re-inquiry into 'established' knowledge that promises to challenge some of the foundations of the field, reinvigorating our roots in the bargain.

While space limitations preclude more than a passing nod at the explosion of publications devoted to the 'otherwise-ing' of our discipline, I will single out a few examples suggestive of the trend. Publishers such as Routledge, Sage and Berg have created book series centred on consumption issues. University presses, notably Duke, Minnesota, California and Cambridge, are developing lists that feature consumer behaviour prominently in their numbers. Perhaps no single volume has had such impact on the spread of alternative perspectives in our field than Mike Solomon's (2001) *Consumer Behavior* text, the first to incorporate a systematic sense of the postmodern moment. The recent entry by Arnould, Price and Zinkhan (2001), titled, simply, *Consumers*, builds upon and extends this legacy. Many of the *eminences grises* of postmodern consumer research have begun to release books. The freedom of protracted exploration afforded by books is ever more attractive to scholars whose subject matter grows increasingly granular as it proves ever more pervasive. On a final, complementary note, the circulation of such critical popular periodicals as *Adbusters*, *StayFree!* and *The Baffler* marks the rise of public intellectuals posing a normative, grassroots challenge to the culture of consumption, and the dawn of an era of increased interaction between ivory tower and activist inquirers.

My concluding observations on corrective measures currently at work have to do with the social organization of the discipline. First of all, the longevity of our postmodern pioneers has been remarkable. ACR Fellows such as Wells, Levy, Zaltman, Belk, Holbrook and Hirschman have maintained prolific publishing presences during the postmodern moment. A tier of nearly as prolific, if not as exalted, fellow-travellers – Wallendorf, Sherry, Mick, O'Guinn, Arnould, Stern, Firat and Venkatesh among others – has exhibited similar staying power. Among the heirs apparent to this old guard are scholars such as Thompson, Holt, Peñaloza, Fournier and Schouten, whose output threatens to eclipse that of their elders, as well it might. A fledgling cadre, including scholars such as Kozinets, Ritson and Grayson is currently flexing its wings. The momentum the postmodern moment has generated has been enormous. While many if not most of these researchers have partnered with colleagues in other schools and departments, there has gradually arisen a small set of enclaves around the world where scholars have been able to talk shop and collaborate on projects within their own walls. This handful of schools – Northwestern, Utah, Arizona, Rutgers, Illinois, Harvard, Wisconsin, Penn State, Irvine, London Business School, Ulster, Odense – has become a collective incubator for the postmodern moment. Colleagues and doctoral students at these institutions have formed cottage industries of sorts, and benefited greatly from the ability to dwell together within the research process as it unfolds and meanders. While these enclaves are rare, they are synergistic hotbeds of intellectual activity.

If I were to envision a new era of 'othering', it would be characterized by a few key features. At the populist level, it would begin with the founding of an annual doctoral field school, which in essence would be a travelling workshop or rotating summit. It would meet in different places around the globe, and facilitate both the training of students and the collaboration of faculty on projects of cross-cultural, interdisciplinary scope. At the institutional level, the era would begin with systematic outreach by ACR to other disciplines already actively researching consumer behaviour. Alliances and partnerships across these disciplines could result, at a minimum, in consortia newsletters and websites, and ultimately in joint conferences. At the level of scholarly publication, two initiatives might be undertaken. First, postmodern researchers could become regular contributors to the *Monographs of the Journal of Consumer Research*, while at the same time lobbying vigorously for the recognition of books in the promotion and tenure decisions of their schools; lamentably, while the market for book-length treatments of consumption has expanded rapidly in other disciplines, it is sorely underdeveloped in our own. Secondly, postmodern researchers might be persuaded to adopt, if not found, a flagship journal as their publication outlet of first choice. This journal might resemble a hybrid of *CMC* or *Advances in Consumer Research*, and be modelled along the lines of *Journal of Consumer Psychology* or *Psychology and Marketing*. Perhaps George Ritzer's and Don Slater's *Journal of Consumer Culture* will fulfil this mandate. Ironically, this journal has been launched by an outside initiative, an extramural effort abetted by editorial assistance from a number of ACR members. Should these key features be realized in the new era, I envision a fissioning of ACR and a defection of its postmodern membership to a new society, formed along with the growing confederation of refugee special interest groups from current host disciplines.

Tea Leaf Redux

Recognizing the volatile character of the postmodern moment – indeed it may have already elapsed (marked, perhaps, by the recent special issue of the *Diamond Harvard Business Review* devoted to the subject that was published in Japan) – I made some projections in that early chapter about the avenues emerging research might be expected to follow. These were sociopolitical and disciplinary projections, rather than programmatic prescriptions for particular regime preferences.[4] In reviewing these projections, I realize the research I envisioned has broadened, balanced and balkanized our discipline simultaneously. Our field has finally begun producing the kind of methodological pluralists (Sherry 2000) I hoped would lead to the kind of problem-appropriate inquiry that in turn would lead eventually to a holistic understanding of consumer behaviour. Ironically, that work is not diffusing effectively across disciplinary boundaries. Increasingly, I find the sources that inspire me and the audiences I would like to reach in an orbit frustratingly beyond the one my adopted discipline travels.

Perhaps *E Pluribus Plures* will be the slogan that captures the day, and the dream of a unified field will be so acknowledged. This may be the inevitable legacy of parochial professional societies, if not a business school demesne. Silos and sectarianism seem to characterize that disciplinary moment suspended between fusion and fission, evolution and devolution, efflorescence and decline. In revisiting my earlier projections, I explore the ways our discipline has morphed, and assess some ways a common focus might be retained in the wake of consumption's rise to grace across so many fields of scholarly inquiry.

Approach-avoidance: Marketing

The reverberations of the postmodern moment have produced the most significant change in the discipline of marketing since the experimental psychologists upset the hegemony of the economists. And not only has the academic face of the field changed profoundly. The era has witnessed a global growth in managerial research that is decidedly nonpositivist (Sherry and Kozinets 2000). Cultural critic Thomas Frank (2000), in a contorted exercise in sour grapes and wrist slapping, has lamented the incursion of anthropologists, among others, into the practice of account planning, while Jerry Zaltman (1997) has patented the ZMET® projective tasking procedure he has built into a very successful consulting business. Local practitioner organizations of social scientists engaged in commercial consumer research hold regular regional meetings to network and talk shop, seeking to maintain their intellectual vibrancy as they practise their craft in formerly nontraditional fields. The adaptive radiation of these 'other' or 'alternative' approaches to the commercial sector was inevitable, given both the (insidious if not immoral) overproduction of academic doctorates and the insatiable craving of managers for ever new sources of practical insight. The colonization of the academic discipline has been more of a struggle, but has resulted in some interesting developments.

The study of marketized aspects of consumer behaviour has rapidly accelerated over the past fifteen years. Nothing in the marketing mix has escaped the postmodern purview. Consider just this abbreviated list of topics: branding, advertising and packaging; pricing, merchandising and atmospherics; decision-making, satisfaction and involvement; lifestyle, social class and self; intergenerational transfer, adoption of innovations and category essence; information processing, public policy and service encounters; culture, gender and identity; materialism, socialization and ethnic consumption; technology, mass mediation and ambivalence; fashion, tourism, and gift-giving. Postmodern researchers have continued to pioneer new areas of inquiry, beyond original sacred and profane considerations. Global-local dynamics, cybermarketplace behaviour, consumption subcultures and communities, and methodological innovation comprise a few of these frontier areas.

So also has the study of consumption as a primary, biobasic activity (not as merely an epiphenomenon of marketing) accelerated with a vengeance. This research stream is even more heterogeneous than its parallel cousin. Again, a list is telling: embodiment (adornment, surgery, body image, abortion, gestation, death, etc.) heirlooms and inheritances; desire and authenticity; slavery, propaganda, drug-abuse and illiteracy; feminism, authenticity and ambivalence; ritual, fanaticism and camp; wilderness, homelessness and cosmopolitanism; art, altruism and time; privacy, place and neighbourhood; disability, weddings and STDs. The recent resurgence of interest in community beyond the marketplace – whether positioned as utopia, heterotopia or Temporary Autonomous Zone – among postmodern consumer researchers suggests that this distinctive avenue of inquiry still has great growth potential.

Projecting the approach-avoidance trajectory out into the future, I can imagine the avenues converging in mutual illumination on a nested version of D'Andrade's (1984) meaning systems and material flows. The exploration of material culture under different ideological regimes, as those regimes inexorably interact in the contemporary world, would be a worthy joint venture.

Triangulation

Predictably enough, multimodal studies have proliferated more rapidly within research traditions than across them over the past decade and a half. Postmodern inquiry has combined a number of qualitative methods to produce insight into consumer behaviour. Depth interviews combined with focus groups seems most common. The use of life histories with other personal narrative has also been popular. Archival and historiographic work have been paired effectively. Observation has been combined with interview. Participant observation and interview is an increasingly frequent combination. Ethnography has enjoyed perhaps the greatest elaboration. While participant observation and (individual and group) interviewing provide the baseline, ethnographic interpretations of consumption have also included artefact analysis, photography, videography and projective tasking. Projectives and interviewing comprise a common pairing. Autodriving – the use of photographic stimuli as prompts for depth interviews – has also proven most useful. There has been a fairly gradual trend toward using either photography or videography as a primary representational mode, with ethnography providing important complementary contexting. Both introspection and autoethnography have been incorporated into more conventional ethnographic accounts to interesting effect. Finally, among the most promising new methodological wrinkles on the triangulation frontier is a technique Kozinets (2002) has called netnography, which translates to cyberspace many of the practices ethnographers pursue in physical space.

While fewer in number, multimodal studies across research traditions have exhibited particular promise. Researchers have effectively combined experiment and individual interview, as well as focus group and experiment. Interview and survey is an increasingly common pairing. Focus groups, survey and phenomenological interview have been employed as complements. Statistical context and critical incident analyses have been jointly performed. Focus groups have been combined both with surveys and structural equation modelling. More ambitious studies have combined survey, interview and dyadic analysis. Among the more intriguing of recent efforts at triangulation are those grounded in and sustained by ethnography, but which incorporate statistical analysis into the process. For example, ethnography has been teamed with causal reasoning tasks, network analysis and cognitive mapping to provide comprehensive, nuanced statistically rigorous insight into phenomena. More ambitious still are the longitudinal studies integrating multiple interview and survey vehicles with participant observation. Perhaps the greatest difficulty encountered in such multimodal research is not the reconciliation of different philosophies of science so much as the heroic effort required to recruit experts and coordinate the interdisciplinary teamwork that the enterprise demands.[5]

It may well be that the next wave of triangulated research can best be stimulated through a combination of methodological refinement and serial joint venture. Parsing a project across methods experts in realistic, actionable components, supporting those experts with pluralists who are boundary spanners, and managing the enterprise over its legitimate life cycle could result in a demonstration piece that would serve as an exemplar of multimodality. Such a project might originate most realistically in a proprietary setting, with the sponsoring company gaining real-time access to findings in exchange for the academics' right to publish those findings for the entire research community. A properly ambitious relationship might result in the establishment of long term, ethnographer-friendly consumer panels maintained and mined by doctoral students whose research would be of proprietary interest, but of theoretical significance beyond that demanded by managerial relevance. Of course, these large-scale projects might also be accomplished entirely academically, via consortia of centres, special-issue journal initiatives, or dedicated conference tracks, provided a deadline were enforced.

Outreach and Collaboration

There is no denying the rapid diffusion of inquiry into 'other stuff' over the past decade and a half. In the early 1980s, the fate of some of my own manuscripts in the review process was diagnostic of the era. In the absence of paradigm-appropriate review, I was prepared (somewhat) for *ad hominem* attacks on methodology, but was surprised to learn that reviewers often felt that what I was doing was not consumer research. (This occasionally included Hal Kassarjian, co-editor of *JCR* and eventual commissioner of the chapter on 'other stuff'.) As I now speak, the postmodern moment has touched all of the top tier journals in marketing, as well as those in most of the other tiers as well. The content of that touching has ranged from the outrageously provocative to the yeomanly pedestrian, but the touching is no longer regarded as remarkable. The effort has been given its due, grudgingly or graciously, and the subdiscipline now pursues both normal and frontier weird science in the flagship journals of the field. And, as I noted earlier, a host of new journals has arisen over time to absorb the output of the moment.

Outside our discipline of consumer research[6], the rapid rise of interest in consumption has been just as remarkable. Consumer behaviour has been explored in the flagship journals of anthropology, sociology, geography, psychology and communications, as well in the lower tier journals of those fields. Eric Arnould has even mounted a fifth-column invasion of the *Journal of Contemporary Ethnography*, seeking to diffuse marketing scholarship into contiguous disciplines under a false-flag strategy of sorts. (My own preferred Trojan Horse gambit has involved packaging consumer research into books and exporting them to our bibliocentric cousins. Hopefully both approaches will bear fruit.) Older established journals in the humanities such as *Critical Inquiry* and *Representations* have incorporated consumption into their purview, while newer journals such as *Angelaki* have recognized a consumption mandate from the very start.

While books comprise the principal vehicle of research dissemination outside the field of marketing,[7] there has been an increase in other extradisciplinary channels as well. Danny Miller's Morgan Lectures are an especially visible instance of this growing awareness. Conference tracks at annual meetings in sociology and anthropology are devoted to consumer behaviour. Satellite associations such as the Society for Economic Anthropology have devoted entire conferences to the examination of consumption. Special interest groups within the major fields are served by outlets such as Don Slater's website or Dan Cook's *Consumer, Commodities & Consumption* newsletter. As these channels intersect and as scholars cross pollinate, interpenetrating membership and interlocking directorates are likely to emerge.

I believe the most grossly underutilized but potentially greatest catalyst for multi-and interdisciplinary research into consumer behaviour – a truly ecumenical source of differentiation and individuation – is the Policy Board of the *Journal of Consumer Research*. I also believe the most effective mobilization and exploitation of that Board in the service of scholarly expansion will be directed by the publisher rather than by a visionary Board President, *horribile dictu*. The possibility of ramping up subscription frequency and spinning off carefully cultivated specialist journals is immanent in the Board's design. If each representative of the twelve sponsoring professional associations were charged with cultivating his or her home discipline as a farm club, and empowered not just to prospect for but to develop and recruit talent that would not only reflect the journal's sponsoring base but also lay the groundwork for the apotheosis of consumption in each home discipline, we would experience a golden era, not merely a moment, of the 'otherwise'. Convocation, not just publication, would be stimulated in the bargain.

In lieu of such editorial reconfiguration, outreach and collaboration might best be facilitated by a biennial congress, a kind of 'alternative' exposition of consumer behaviour, to which all disciplines would send delegates, presenters and conventioneers. Again, the venue of this congress might rotate, in an effort to involve as global a constituency as possible.

Critical Views of Consumption

While the postmodern moment has stimulated a tide of empirical investigation, its hallmark may well be the normative positioning it has given consumption. The concepts of moral economy or moral geography have a force that the founding fathers of consumer behaviour may have lauded but never anticipated when they launched their venture in the mid 1970s. Consumer researchers have cast an ever more critical eye on the antecedents and consequences of consumption. Drawing on sources as varied as Marxism, ecology, critical theory, feminism, situationism, media studies, liberation theology, queer studies, anarchism, ecofeminism, legal studies and others, scholars have pursued a critique of consumption that has not only indicted marketing as the engine of planetary immiseration and degradation, but also called (paradoxically? perversely? playfully?) for a marketing solution to problems marketing has ostensibly created. Out of these studies has emerged a renewed interest in consumer agency, as issues of false consciousness, co-creativity, production of consumption, consumer misbehaviour and resistance are unpacked with ever more precise empirical probing. So also is the interest in social engineering seeming to revive, as investigation of Utopian pragmatics accelerates.

I imagine two interesting streams at least will emerge from this critical inquiry. First, the critique of marketing practice must be accompanied by a revision of marketing practice. A simple (if rigorous or comprehensive) audit and exposure of the shortfalls of marketing management (as ideology and practice) is a necessary but insufficient application of the critical perspective. We need to field a variant of Gramsci's engaged intellectual (who, if not willing to work harder, will at least work smarter), committed to translating scholarship into activism. Whether this activism results in the sublation of the global economy (perhaps a variant of the humane capitalism the Swedes have striven to perfect), or the selective disengagement of groups from the system all together (*à la* the bioregionalists, voluntary simplicitarians, gated communitarians or some as yet undeclared monastic or hermetic enclaves), it is a vital component of our professing mission, and one that has been left too long to atrophy. Perhaps Alan Andreasen's Institute for Social Marketing, or Joel Cohen's increasingly aggressive *Journal of Public Policy and Marketing*, are steps in this direction.

The second emergent stream is the relentless, holistic, comprehensive and nuanced empirical investigation of the material conditions of critical counterculturalism itself. We require a thorough understanding of the dynamics of resistance, appropriation or whatever other name by which the strategy of consumer revitalization movement comes to be characterized. The dynamics of populist prosumption or grassroots conduction need to be examined as they unfold, on the ground, in households around the world. Whether ephemeral or long lasting, these instances of wresting autonomy from the system must be understood, harnessed and directed in the service of enhanced quality of life.

New Presentation Modes
As this chapter goes to press, the crisis of representation has finally breached the walls of consumer research. While the tyranny of the journal article has not been deposed, it has been convincingly challenged. As the humanists and artists of our era become bricoleurs of consumer culture (from current permutations of K-Mart realism such as William Gibson's *Pattern Recognition*, Alex Shakar's *The Savage Girl* and Victor Pelevin's *Homo Zapiens*, to the endemic product placement of contemporary cinema and television), and as consumers themselves use the stuff of their consumer behaviour to produce hybrid art forms (I think imme-

diately of the sampling 'mash-ups' that computer technology assists audiophiles in creating), scholars have finally started to represent their understanding in vehicles more emotionally and evocatively attuned to authenticity. Once produced off-the-clock in odd hours and rarely published (perhaps out of fear of the Cornell West rap CD brouhaha potential of their musings), then nurtured in presidential sessions of ACR conferences, and now published in flagship journals, poetry has emerged as a viable vessel of consumer research. Introspective, autoethnographic accounts of consumption experience are finding their way from book chapters to journals as well. Some consumer researchers may find they have more in common with Sundance film-makers than with their information-processing colleagues, as Russ Belk and Rob Kozinets speed the diffusion of videography through our research community.

As more popular cultural biographies of commodities, brands and corporations are produced in trade press book format by writers, journalists and independent scholars, and as academic researchers outside marketing departments generate more scholarly books on consumer behaviour, we are seeing more consumer researchers adopt the book as a vehicle of knowledge dissemination. These books are being produced primarily by senior scholars beyond the reach of promotion and tenure committees, rather than by more junior scholars, who, arguably, might be even more prolific if this option were available to them. I think for this format to flourish, senior scholars must lobby collectively for the adoption of the book as at least the equivalent of the journal article in the evaluation of untenured scholars' productivity. This is especially important for younger researchers whose methods do not include experiment or quantitative data analysis.

One of the most intriguing implications of the crisis of representation is that consumer researchers may be able to reach audiences outside their own narrow domains of specialization. Conveying our understandings in a way that may produce enlightened consumption – that we may have a powerful, provocative, prosocial impact on the lived experience of consumers as they consume – is a heady prospect, and one that is quite edifying. I think of it as a way to take our professing to the streets.

Conclusion

If the legacy of the postmodern moment in our discipline was the exaltation of doubt, the enfranchisement of speculation, and the flourishing of 'alternative' perspectives, it is probably reasonable to state that the passing of that moment has been marked by the routinization of this alterity. Because I assigned dates to certain watershed moments in my original chapter, recognizing at the time the somewhat arbitrary nature of dating in such a fluid intellectual environment, I feel a certain urgency to repeat the effort here, especially in keeping with what I believe to be the ritual auspiciousness that this volume embodies. The 'elusive' consumption we celebrate in this book is both 'illusive' and 'allusive', and we are not so much 'tracking' new perspectives as we are 'releasing' them, if the hunting metaphor be preserved. In deference to the editors, who have extended their ancient tradition of *Allemanstratt* (Gannon 1994) into our discipline, I imagine the summit of 2002 that spawned this book as the threshold of our new era, the suffusion of orthodoxy with otherness, the transformation (not merely the subversion) of our inquiry into complementary holism, the righteous proper became the next ordinary. For now. Let's hope we've witnessed the birth of a discipline we can all recognize simply as 'consumer research'. And that it will henceforth be infused with the egalitarian passion the Swedes call *jamlikhet* (Gannon 1994).

Notes

1. So many of the pioneers of our field - Bill Wells, Joel Cohen, Sid Levy, Jerry Zaltman, Jerry Olsen, Jerry Kernan and others - are interdisciplinary rabble-rousers of the first order, who set into motion changes whose magnitude I'm sure they never imagined. Subsequent instigators whose activities I nominally chronicle in this essay hail primarily from US business schools, a parochial provenance whose circumscription I readily acknowledge. I hope my colleagues will read through the apparently ethnocentric tenor to the situated critique I offer.
2. Which didn't include the rampant rise of alliteration as a persuasive trope, as championed by postmodern marketing's belletrist nonpareil, Stephen Brown (1995).
3. As a proxy measure of this proliferation, the coursepacket for my doctoral seminar, which is drawn principally from intramural sources and winnowed for relevance, now weighs in at 24 pounds, or 12 pounds when duplexed to save trees.
4. For example, my own predilection for such topics as gift-giving, placeways, embodiment and festival were not advanced as vanguard enterprises, despite my passion for them and belief that their importance, especially as unpacked by me, is vastly underrepresented in our journals.
5. For years, my behavioural colleagues at Kellogg and I have nickel-and-dimed a revisionist study of advertising effectiveness, the sole topic we can each agree upon as the requisite whipping boy. We have begun with semiotic analysis of advertisements, initial experimental and survey work, but have never quite made it to the ethnographic study intended to inform future rounds of interview, experiment and survey that would lead to new measures of effec-

tiveness we all could sanction. Alas, more discrete projects have intervened to distract us, and the track has grown cold. Perhaps a project manager would be a wise investment!

6. Each time I use a personal pronoun, I hear a mafioso echo, a clanny, insular, hegemonic reverberation, as if our allegiance to marketing's *cosa nostra* required me to defer to Eric Arnould (a consumer ethnographer in a business school) as a friend of ours and Rick Wilk (a consumer ethnographer in a college of liberal arts and sciences) as a friend of mine. This distinction is a sociopolitical not a personal one. I look forward to an era when we have tunnelled so extensively between silos that erosion produces a common garner.

7. Again, space constraints preclude a cataloguing of this prodigious output, but interested researchers can turn to the *JCR* 'Reflections' and *ACR News'* 'Fellows' Bookshelf' for a running start at the literature. It is a safe bet that the *Annual Reviews* series will include surveys of consumption as regular features among their numbers.

References

Arnould, E., Price, L. and Zinkhan, G. (2001), *Consumers*, New York: McGraw-Hill/Irwin.

Belk, R. (1987), 'A Modest Proposal for Creating Verisimilitude in Consumer-Information-Processing Models, and Some Suggestions for Establishing a Discipline to Study Consumer Behavior', in A. F. Firat, N. Dholakia and R. Bagozzi (eds), *Radical and Philosophical Thought in Marketing*, Lexington, MA: Lexington Books, 361–72.

— (1991), *Highways and Buyways: Naturalistic Research From the Consumer Behavior Odyssey*, Provo, UT: Association of Consumer Research.

— (1995), 'Studies in the New Consumer Behavior', in D. Miller (ed.), *Acknowledging Consumption*, London: Routledge, 58–95.

Brown, S. (1995), *Postmodern Marketing*, New York: Routledge.

D'Andrade, R. (1984), 'Cultural Meaning Systems', in R. Schweder and R. Levine (eds), *Culture Theory: Essays on Minds, Self and Emotion*, Cambridge: Cambridge University Press, 88–119.

Diamond Harvard Business Review (2001), Special Issue on Postmodern Marketing, 6 (June).

Frank, T. (2000), *One Market Under God*, New York: Doubleday.

Gannon, M. and Assocs. (1994), *Understanding Cultures*, Thousand Oaks, CA: Sage.

Gibson, W. (2003), *Pattern Recognition*, New York: Putnam.

Hirschman, E., (ed.) (1989), *Interpretive Consumer Research*, Provo, UT: Association for Consumer Research.

Hunt, S. (1999), *Modern Marketing Theory: Critical Issues in the Philosophy of Marketing Science*, Mason, OH: South Western.

Kozinets, R. (2002), 'The Field Behind the Screen: Using Netnography for Marketing Research in Online Communities', *Journal of Marketing Research*, 39: 61–72.

Lincoln, Y. and Denzin, N. (2000), 'The Seventh Moment: Out of the Past', in N. Denzin and Y. Lincoln (eds), *Handbook of Qualitative Research*, Thousand Oaks, CA: Sage, 1047–65.

Miller, D. (1995), 'Consumption and Commodities', *Annual Review of Anthropology*, 24: 141–161.

Pelevin, V. 2000 *Homo Zapiens*, tr. Arnold Bromfield, New York: Viking.

Shakar, A. 2001 *The Savage Girl*, New York: HarperCollins.

Sherry, J. F., Jr. (1991), 'Postmodern Alternatives: The Interpretive Turn in Consumer Research', in T. Robertson and H. Kassarjian, *Handbook of Consumer Research*, Englewood Cliffs, NJ: Prentice Hall, 548–91.

— (2000), 'Place, Technology, and Representation', *Journal of Consumer Research*, 27: 273–78.

— and Kozinets, R. (2000), 'Qualitative Inquiry in Marketing and Consumer Research', in Dawn Iacobucci (ed.), *Kellogg on Marketing*, New York: John Wiley, 165–94.

Solomon, M. (2001), *Consumer Behavior: Buying, Having and Being*, New York: Prentice Hall.

Turner, V. (1974), *Dramas, Fields and Metaphors*, Ithaca: Cornell University Press.

Zaltman, G. (1997), 'Rethinking Market Research: Putting People Back In', *Journal of Marketing Research*, 34(4): 424–37.

Part II
Odysseys in Time and Space

–4–

The Human Consequences
of Consumer Culture

Russell W. Belk

Fernand Braudel (1967) describes the mass luxuries of the seventeenth and eighteenth centuries in Europe as consisting of chairs, woollen mattresses and feather beds. Based largely on paintings and post-mortem inventories, he identifies the typical possessions of the ubiquitous peasants of the day as consisting of a few pots and pans, a chest, straw to sleep on, a set of clothing and a few tools. There was no table and a single goblet and trencher (communal plate) likely sufficed for the household. Pigs or other farm animals might be separated from others in the house by a screen. But meat was a rarity and bread and porridge were typical food staples. No one in such a family could read or write. Light came from candles or oil lamps. And washing and toiletry were done outside with no running water. Cleanliness was not held in high regard and fashion was limited to a few hairstyles and sporting a beard or moustache. More than half of all children died before reaching age fifteen. Disease was rampant and the fire of the family hearth was the sole source of heat for warmth and cooking. Thomas Hobbes's observation that life was nasty, brutish and short accords well with Braudel's reconstructed image of peasant life.

There were some regional variations to these sparse consumption patterns and those who were rich lived a more materially varied life with a few years added to their lives. Nevertheless, Braudel paints a plausible portrait of material life for not only pre-modern Europe, but most of the world at the time. There remains a substantial portion of the world's population today that is materially not much better off than this. But there is one difference. Today there are very few people who are not aware that millions of others are living in consumer cultures far different from the Hobbesian conditions in which they themselves may be surrounded. Few in today's world are out of the reach of global media, tourism, brands and advertising. Thus, even if they are not themselves participants, almost everyone in the world today is living within an increasingly global consumer culture. We see, hear and read about an unprecedented culture of abundance in which others are depicted not so much drowning in an avalanche of unnecessary and burdensome possessions, nor polluting the planet and voraciously devouring its limited resources, as they are portrayed enjoying a pleasurable feast of luxuries that could not be imagined even in the dreams of the most privileged in prior centuries. Cars, computers, cameras, television, travel, theme parks, movies, malls, McDonalds and much more spills from the cornucopia of consumer culture.

Admittedly, consumer culture consists of more than just an abundance of consumer goods. It also involves a personal orientation and a social sanction for desiring and acquiring these goods. It involves a receptivity to satisfying an increasing variety of human needs and desires by acquiring commodities and purchasing experiences. And it involves a social system of status competition through purchased possessions and services. These too are a part of the mind-sets and societies in an increasingly large portion of our global population.

The question addressed in this chapter is whether we truly better off for the arrival of such consumption environments and the behaviours and beliefs they engender. Are those of us who participate and believe most fully in consumer culture any happier, healthier and more fulfilled because of it? And what of the societal consequences of embracing consumer culture? Is the modern subjectivity of illusory consumer choice beneficial to the society that sustains it? How does consumer culture affect human relationships? What of those who remain at the margins of consumer culture, those for whom the department store is a distant museum of glorious but untouchable objects? Are consumer culture and our ecosystem pitted in an inherently antagonistic and increasingly critical battle?

These are obviously impossibly broad questions to attempt to answer on a global level without the essentialism of reducing a complex world to a few glib generalizations. What is true for the rural residents of a sub-Saharan African country may not be true for those who have moved to China's booming urban free-trade zones or for indigenous youngsters in the Arctic. But there has been enough conjecture and study about the effects of consumer culture to examine some cases and aspects of these questions and to try to come to some tentative conclusions. This is what I try to do in the present chapter.

Consumer Culture

We must first agree about what constitutes consumer culture. Rassuli and Hollander (1986) stipulate four conditions necessary for a consumer culture:

1. A substantial portion of a population consume at a level substantially above subsistence.
2. Exchange dominates self-production of objects of consumption.
3. Consuming is accepted as an appropriate and desirable activity.
4. People judge others and themselves in terms of their consuming lifestyles.

While these seem to be reasonable criteria, there are two grounds for objecting to the first criterion. First, in our globalizing consumer culture, economically developing countries are often bifurcated into haves, who participate fully in consumer culture, and have-nots, for whom it is mostly an inaccessible dream. One group lives in a consumer culture and may feel a sense of similarity to those in other consumer cultures, while the other group does not. Secondly, and altering the picture for have-nots, there is ample evidence that even those who cannot participate fully in a consumer culture may sometimes sacrifice 'necessities' in order to acquire the 'luxuries' that are a part of consumer culture. This includes the practice of placing non-functioning television antennas on huts without electricity, forgoing food in order to afford a refrigerator (which cannot then be stocked with food), and selling nutritious milk in order to afford to buy candy for children (Belk 1988b; Ger 1992). This phenomenon has been referred to as Third World consumer culture (Belk 1988b) or leaping luxuries (Belk 1999). While such people may not fully participate in consumer culture, their consumption is nevertheless affected by the consumer culture that surrounds them. As Shrestha (1997) puts it,

> The poor are forced into a situation in which they either have to spend what little money or resources they have on senseless consumer objects rather than basic necessities in order to deflect total social humiliation or face the prospect of being teased and laughed at (26).

When a family forgoes having more children in order to afford more consumer goods, such practices can be seen as a form of human sacrifice. Contrary to Abraham Maslow's (1954) need hierarchy specifying that we seek to satisfy 'lower order' bodily needs for sustenance and safety before we pursue 'higher order' needs for love, self-esteem and self-actualization, there are numerous inversions of this hierarchy, even in the West where it is thought to apply best.

Peter Stearns (2002) offers a related, but expanded, definition of consumer culture as:

> A society in which many people formulate their goals in life partly through acquiring goods that they clearly do not need for subsistence or for traditional display. They become enmeshed in the process of acquisition – shopping – and take some of their identity from a procession of new items they buy and exhibit (ix).

This definition adds identity formation through visible consumption to the formulation of Rassuli and Hollander (1986). However, Rassuli and Hollander's notion of consumption lifestyle is a broader one than Stearns's focus on individual items, since it envisions ensembles of related goods that Solomon and Assael (1987) termed consumption constellations. Rarely does a single acquisition define a consumer lifestyle. However, Stearns's definition usefully calls attention to the process of shopping that is part of the rituals of consumer culture as well as a source of potential pleasure in itself.

Don Slater (1997) offers a still more expansive definition of consumer culture as involving:

1. Values, ideas, aspirations and identities based on consumption.
2. Market-based capitalism.
3. Mass consumption and impersonal exchange.
4. Free private consumer choices.
5. Production of unlimited desires.
6. Status and identity based on consumption of unstable signs.

Here the specification that consumer culture is only a product of market-based capitalism flies in the face of evidence of consumer culture in both pre-capitalist societies (Belk 1988b) and communist societies (Gronow 1997; Davis 2000). Moreover, the fourth criterion may be a Western conceit. There is an argument that consumption in some Asian cultures may sometimes involve being swept up in consumption 'fevers' aimed more at fitting in than standing out (e.g., Hertz 2001). And the fifth criterion indicting marketing and advertising for producing unlimited desires ignores the more active role of consumers as active co-producers of desire and active participant in consumer self-seduction (Belk 2001).

Michael Schudson (1984) offers a more explicitly value-laden definition of consumer culture as,

> A society in which human values have been grotesquely distorted so that commodities become more important than people, or, in an alternative formulation, commodities become not ends in themselves but overvalued means for acquiring acceptable ends like love and friendship (16).

Although the notion of grotesquely distorted values has an elitist ring to it, like the European condemnation of American consumers as lacking the taste and sophistication of Europeans (Ger and Belk 1999), Schudson usefully raises the issue of materialism and its potentially negative consequences for the individual and the society. His view departs from Csikszentmihalyi and Rochberg-Halton (1981), who make an opposite argument about materialism. They distinguish the negative case of terminal materialism involving wanting things for their own sake, from the positive case of instrumental materialism involving wanting things for the sake of what they can help us do. In fairness, however, they are contrasting the existential states of having and doing rather than addressing

Schudson's concern with the attempt to buy intangible states of being through having desirable consumer goods instead of having the goods for their own sake. Still, while Csikszentmihalyi and Rochberg-Halton believe we expect goods to do to little for us, Schudson believes we expect them to do too much.

Although sharing Slater's bias that consumer culture is strictly a product of capitalism and Schudson's concerns with the commoditization of human values, Livingstone (1998) offers some further aspects of consumer culture in his definition of the phenomenon:

> First, consumer demand becomes the fulcrum of economic growth ...
>
> Second, social relations of production can no longer be said to contain or regulate social relations ...
>
> Third, value as such comes increasingly to be determined not by the quantities of labor time required to produce commodities but by the varieties of subject positions from which goods can be appreciated ...Fourth, with the completion of proletarianization under the auspices of corporate management, the commodity form penetrates and reshapes dimensions of social life hitherto exempt from its logic to the point where subjectivity itself becomes a commodity to be bought and sold in the market as beauty, cleanliness, sincerity, even autonomy (415–16).

This neo-Marxist formulation draws our attention to the shift from production to consumption emphasis among members of a consumer society and to the dominance of exchange value over use value or labour value in such a society. Livingstone also emphasizes that consumer culture is not restricted to consumption, but is instead intimately tied to production and economic growth. And he emphasizes the high degree to which production and consumption are interdependent. However, it should be borne in mind that consumer culture is a consumption phenomenon and not a production phenomenon.

Together these definitions of consumer culture offer a good general understanding of what is meant by consumer culture. Even if they are not entirely compatible with one another, it is clear that they are speaking of the same fundamental cultural shift in which consumption becomes a key part of our personal, social and economic life. Still, there are a few further elements of consumer culture that are not addressed by these definitions. One feature emphasized by Campbell (1987) is the role of novelty and fashions in the development of the unlimited desires highlighted by Slater. This flow of new things provides a large and continually changing set of things to wish for, with these wishes escalating into desires when the hope of their realization can be sustained. When desires become compelling enough we may naturalize them as needs, such that we 'need' a chocolate bar or have to have a new coat (Belk, Ger, and Askegaard 2000). At a more societal level, this process results in a shift in our classification of objects from luxuries to decencies to necessities. An endless parade of items has undergone and continues to undergo these classificatory shifts, albeit at different paces in different cultures. At the same time, with our shrinking globe there is an aggregate counterpart to need hierarchy-inverting luxuries described earlier, such that the progression is not necessarily a slow and steady one.

Caveats and Complexities

Before attempting to assess the human consequences of consumer culture, it is important to recognize that as consumer culture has developed, there have been a number of concomitant changes that, while they may seem to be inextricably linked to the development of consumer culture, remain distinct in their impacts. For instance, industrialization and mass production may bring about the endless parade of goods needed for consumer culture, as well as provide wage labour jobs that provide the means for acquiring these goods. But they are not a part of consumer culture per se. If consumer culture is, as I have argued, a personal and cultural orientation toward consumption, we must try to separate its effects from those of industrialization and mass production. Furthermore, consumer culture remains distinct from economic development, urbanization and globalization, even though these too have been concomitant changes as consumer culture has advanced. The same is true of capitalism, colonialism, slavery and neo-colonialism, all of which have also been associated with the rise of consumer culture. In an effort to demonstrate that these historical developments are not essential for consumer culture, I turn to a fictional tale from an old comic book.

Tralla La
Even though money and wage labour may seem necessary in order to sustain consumer culture, they are not. A prescient story by former Disney cartoonist Carl Barks (1980) illustrates this separation. The 1954 story called 'The Land of Tralla La,' begins when Uncle Scrooge McDuck is besieged by various requests for his billions of dollars. When an oil baron threatens to nationalize his oil wells unless he is given a new limousine, Scrooge is driven over the edge and climbs a tree where he begins chattering like a squirrel. When Donald Duck and his nephews find Scrooge and take him to a doctor, the doctor gives him some nerve tonic syrup and tells him he must escape the stresses he is under by finding a place where there is no money. The doctor tells him that there is rumoured to be such a place in a fog-enshrouded volcanic valley in the Himalayas. So Uncle Scrooge recruits Donald, the nephews and a pilot to fly them into the valley. They find the hidden valley and as they prepare to parachute in, Scrooge has one more bottle of his nerve tonic medicine. The bottle cap from the medicine, seemingly innocently, falls out of the plane and precedes them to the Land of Tralla La.

This is a utopian land where people raise sheep and rice, and where there is no money. Greed is absent and friendship is valued most highly. Each person in Tralla La contributes according to abilities and receives according to needs. Scrooge is given meaningful work as a brick mason and for a time all appears blissful. As Scrooge works, a villager finds the bottle cap that has fallen from the plane. In panels that anticipate Jamie Uys' film, *The Gods Must be Crazy*, the bottle cap becomes an object of awe and wonder. Another villager offers the farmer who found it three sheep if it can become his. Others, anxious to have the rare object, offer up to ten years of their rice crops. But the villager who found the bottle cap declines these offers, telling the others that the pride of having 'the only one' is worth more than food. Meanwhile, Scrooge who is blissfully ignorant of these developments, goes to the lake to empty his last five bottles of nerve tonic medicine, since he no longer needs them and now plans to stay in Tralla La forever. When a villager finds Scrooge in possession of five bottle caps, he proclaims that he is the richest duck in Tralla La.

In order to reduce the rampant consumer desire and envy of him precipitated by the bottle caps, Uncle Scrooge sends Donald and the nephews out of the valley in order to have a billion bottle caps dropped on the valley. When the first planeload arrives and showers its cargo on the valley, the villagers dance among them in the ecstatic belief that they are all rich. However they soon realize that the bottle caps are worthless because now everyone has them. Furthermore, as the second planeload of bottle caps rains down it becomes clear that the bombardment is destroying the rice crops and covering the grass so that the sheep cannot eat. A serpent has appeared in this Garden of Eden. On threat of losing their lives, the ducks agree to leave the Land of Tralla La in order to stop any further planeloads of bottle caps from being dropped. As they are leaving the valley, the Nephews demand their wages of 30–cents an hour and it is clear that Uncle Scrooge is heading back to the stresses of a greedy world.

Although there are some Adam Smith-like assumptions about human nature in this comic book tale, it does outline a plausible scenario under which the key elements of consumer culture can arise without wage labour, money, slavery, colonialism, industrialization or mass production. That the fashionable goods that breed the envy, materialism and desire that characterize consumer culture have been precipitated by the introduction of a foreign good, is perhaps not all that different from the situation of many cultures in today's less economically developed world, where people are faced with numerous global consumer goods.

Further Provisos

It should also be recognized that adopting consumer culture is neither a dichotomous yes/no choice nor a one-time event. Consumer culture is an ongoing ever-changing phenomenon. And despite globalization and the co-reflexivity of various consumer cultures, what constitutes consumer culture at one time and place is not identical to what consumer culture means in another time and place.

Despite humanitarian inclinations to condemn consumer culture on its face, the phenomenon is neither inherently good nor evil. The intent in the analysis that follows is to hold such judgments in abeyance in order to consider the consequences of consumer culture more openly and completely. Furthermore, what is good in one time and place may be bad in another time and place. This is all the more true because the effects of consumer culture are not evenly distributed nor equally positive or negative within a given moment and locale. Rich and poor, young and old, male and female, and other segments within society are all likely to be differentially impacted by consumer culture.

Finally, we cannot take a unidimensional approach to assessing the impacts of consumer culture. Its effects are individual, social, cultural, economic, political, moral and much more. Consumer culture is a way of looking at and seeking to derive value in the world that has far reaching implications. To attempt to tally up its effects on a single register is folly.

Effects of Consumer Culture

The necessity for the last proviso can be seen clearly by considering some of the multiple dimensions on which we might evaluate the impact of consumer culture. One area of human well-being that may be impacted by certain of the things desired and acquired within a consumer culture is health. Nearly twenty years ago Kenneth Boulding (1985) demonstrated that indices of health around the world tend to rise, along with consumer culture, as income grows to a level that was then about US$2000 per capita. After that the health indices seem to plateau or grow very slowly. The growth in health and life expectancy is likely due to better food, better housing, better sanitation and better access to medicine and medical care. No doubt this figure would be higher today, but it seems certain that there is still a finite limit in the ability to buy better health. In the explosion of consumption that followed the Second World War in the USA, along with cars and televisions, Americans were most apt to buy such health-related goods as houses, refrigerators, washing machines and stoves, rather than more personal luxuries (May 1988). While it may be difficult to imagine today – at least in the affluent West – such goods were imbued by advertising with a mythical status that made them the embodiment of luxury, status and happiness (e.g., Strasser 1998). The suburban homes that were a part of this flourishing consumer culture likely also provided a sense of safety and security that may have contributed to both physical and psychological health.

A second likely effect of consumer culture is raised by Schudson (1984): increased materialism. Materialism has been defined as 'The importance a consumer attaches to worldly possessions. At the highest levels of materialism, such possessions assume a central place in a person's life and are believed to be the greatest sources of satisfaction and dissatisfaction in life' (Belk 1985: 265). Evidence of the association of materialism and consumer culture is seen in a study by Ger and Belk (1996) which found that of a dozen countries examined in the early 1990s, measured materialism levels were highest not only in the widely acknowledged consumer culture of the United States, but also in the rapidly changing consumer cultures of Romania, Ukraine, Turkey and reunified Germany. Materialism has been conceptualized as involving possessiveness, nongenerosity and envy (Belk 1985), beliefs that having things represents success, happiness, and a central focus in life (Richins and Dawson 1992), and aspirations for financial success, social recognition and an appealing appearance (Kasser and Ryan 1996). Results have consistently shown that despite the materialistic belief that things bring happiness, materialism is negatively related to happiness and feelings of well-being (Belk 1985; Kasser and Ryan 1993; Richins and Dawson 1992).

We might look at the relationship between consumer culture and happiness in a different way by comparing income gains to feelings of well-being. Myers and Diener (1996) note that although Americans' income had doubled since 1957, their level of happiness actually declined. Richard Easterlin (1973) found that absolute gains in personal income do not influence feelings of happiness unless there is also a relative gain relative to the others against whom we may compare ourselves. According to one argument, having to choose between more alternative consumer goods is a burden and actually makes us less satisfied (Waldman 1992). Similar arguments have been made about the effect of having more possessions due to the burden of care and maintenance that owning these things imposes. Robert Putnam (2000) marshals evidence suggesting that the increasing physical capital of having things in a consumer culture causes the social capital of rewarding human relationships to decrease dramatically. That is, as Karl Marx suggested, the vivification of our relationship with commodities may lead to a commodification of our relationship with people. These too are reasons that the costs of consumer culture may outweigh its benefits.

There are, however, arguments that consumer culture can be beneficial. Schudson (1998) argues that there is a certain 'dignity and rationality in people's desire for material goods'. Possessing useful and beautiful objects may enrich our lives, Schudson suggests, although making such consumption our sole purpose in life is surely destructive. The signifiers that stand out in a consumer culture may also be motivators, as suggested by Wilson (1972):

It is a grand, well-furnished home, well equipped with modern appliances, fine furniture, china and linens, good stylish clothes, an expensive education, manners and deportment. These signifiers are also the foci of ambition for the populationas a whole (226).

For those who would quibble with the hedonism of such pursuits, Marty (1999) relates a Hasidic tale of the ascetic:

A world-denying Jew heard the call to asceticism. He thought it a part of the command-ments that he must do without good food, good wine, and the company of good women and friends in general. He took no place at their festive tables; he heard no good music and did without great art. All of this he did with an eye onthe promise of paradise for the renouncer.

He died. He did indeed find himself in paradise. But three days later, they threw him out because he understood nothing of what was going on (184).

As with posing voluntary simplicity as a lifestyle of sacrifice, such asceticism is a difficult and largely impossible cause to sell within a consumer culture.

A part of what makes the acquisition of unnecessary consumer goods pleas-urable may be the extended sense of self that may come from our possessions (Belk 1988a). We potentially feel bigger, more important, and more efficacious through our possessions. This can be seen in two accounts of feelings derived from possessions: the first a nineteenth century parlour organ and the second a contemporary Porsche automobile.

Buying a prominent object like a parlor organ [in 19th century America] might initiate a new chapter in a set of lives, not only by providing a new way to use time but also a new tool to measure time. In later years the object would serve to remind its owners of the day it first entered their home and of the time that had passed since then. It would not only structure their present but also their perceptions of their own past. They knew from experience that purchasing a major object could be a significant and momentous occasion in itself, a time of heightened positive emotions and feelings of well-being and importance ... a major purchase would transform them in their own eyes and in the eyes of others. They would become worth more ... and acquire greater status. By doing so they would receive more respect and deference from others which would, in turn, make them feel better about themselves. Buying a parlor organ would make them something they were not before. (Ames 1984)

Sometimes I test myself. We have an ancient, battered Peugeot, and I drive it for a week. It rarely breaks, and it gets great mileage. But when I pull up next to a beautiful woman, I am still the geek with glasses. Then I get back into the Porsche. It roars and tugs to get moving. It accelerates even going uphill at 80. It leadeth trashy women ... to make pouting looks at me at stoplights. It makes me feel like a tomcat on the prowl. Nothing else in my life compares – except driving along Sunset at night ... with the sodium vapor lamps reflecting off the wine-red finish, with the air inside reeking of tan glove-leather upholstery and the [stereo] playing ... so loud it makes my hair vibrate. And the girls I will never see again pulling up next to me, giving the car a once-over, and looking at me as if I were a cool guy, not a worried, overextended 40–year-old schnook writer. (Stein 1985)

Although we may ask as Fromm (1976) did, 'If I am what I have and what I have is lost, who then am I?' (76), very likely the feelings in these accounts resonate with most of us. As I have argued elsewhere (Belk 1991), few of us are without some self-extending, 'magical,' treasured possessions such as perfume, jewellery (a wedding ring perhaps), favourite clothes, favourite foods, transitional objects (not just a childhood security blankets but the photos in our wallets and purses, for example), homes, vehicles, pets, various amulets, talismans and good luck tokens, drugs and medicines, gifts we have received, souvenirs of our travels, art, relics, antiques, heirlooms and so on. Within global consumer culture, possessing a minimal set of luxuries may also come to be perceived as necessary for a feeling of decency. As the former Yugoslavian writer Draculić (1991) poses the issue:

What is the minimum you must have so you don't feel humiliated as a woman? It makes me understand a complaint I heard repeatedly from women in Warsaw, Budapest, Prague, Sofia, East Berlin: 'Look at us – we don't even look like women. There are no deodorants, no perfumes, sometimes even no soap or toothpaste. There is no fine underwear, no pantyhose, no nice lingerie. Worst of all, there are no sanitary napkins.' What can one say except that it is humiliating (31).

The comparison here, 'we don't even look like women', reinforces the social nature of consumer culture. Once a culture has become a consumer culture, former luxuries come to be seen as decencies or even necessities. For a feeling of dignity in such circumstances, these consumer goods are requisite. In Leach's (1993) terms, desire has been democratized. Twitchell (1999) sees consumer culture as liberating for the majority who participate in such developments.

Douglas (1994) labels this same liberation as narcissism. We might also question to what degree the consumption that is the aim of consumer desire has also been democratized. The gap between the rich and the poor is growing as never before, not only between North and South, but also within virtually all nations of the world. Most of Africa and South America have become marginalized by globalization, while China and India are prime examples of the polarization of wealth within nations with growing consumer cultures. Current WTO, IMF and G8 protests target only the former between-nation gaps. But while millions of Chinese are becoming rich, millions of Chinese workers are impoverished by the closing of factories and a declining social welfare system.

It is also necessary to consider the toll of the spectacle and waste of a consumer culture on the physical environment. Our forests, fisheries and finite fossil fuel resources are diminishing while our emissions produce global warming, acid rain and polluted air (Taylor and Tilford 2000). Species are dying out and waste is piling up. The more we succumb to global consumer culture, the worse these problems become, despite growing concern and efforts to lessen the damage. The recent rage for fuel-hungry and dangerous 'sport utility vehicles' in the USA is a dramatic evidence that consumer culture trumps the environment. With attention to our natural environment, we can consider the trade-off we are making in our consumption between the promise of present pleasures and the threats of future catastrophe.

Two Test Cases: Christmas and Collecting

Two practices of consumer culture that may be telling in assessing its effects are the increasingly global secular celebration of Christmas (Miller 1993), and the increasingly popular activity of collecting something. Collecting has been called 'consumption writ large' (Belk 1995b) because it involves the perpetual pursuit of luxury goods, usually purchased in the market. And because Christmas celebrations have come to involve lavishly decorated homes and buildings, abundant feasting and the exchange of costly consumer goods, it too can be regarded as the embodiment of consumer culture.

Christmas is an ambivalent holiday, not only because of the co-presence of its religious and secular rituals, but also due to the tension between its familial and material aspects. On one hand it is regarded as a time of peace and goodwill. Charitable contributions peak at this time of year and increasingly far flung family come together, at least in the West. In Christmas we celebrate the joys of childhood, the unity of the family, home, altruism and gifts of love (Carrier 1993). But at the same time, Christmas means a time of family tensions (Löfgren 1993), commercialism, using Santa Claus to elicit children's material wishes and teach them to be desirous consumers (Belk 1987), a time of placing heavy burdens on women to shop for gifts and prepare feasts (Fischer and Arnold 1990), and, generally, a time of eating, drinking and spending to excess.

We can see these Christmas tensions in Charles Dickens's 1843 story, *A Christmas Carol* (Belk 1993). This tale in commonly interpreted in terms of the miserly, selfish, joyless, avaricious, workaholic pre-transformation Ebenezer Scrooge (the model for Scrooge McDuck, whom we encountered earlier) versus the generous, loving, happy and home-focused Crachit family. But consider the consumerism message here. The Crachits, though poor and suffering (including young Tiny Tim who will die without an operation), nevertheless spend funds they can ill afford on a Christmas goose and plum pudding. Similarly, the post-transformation Scrooge starts throwing money around like there was no tomorrow. He turns from a frugal utilitarian to a free-spending hedonist. Perhaps Boorstin (1973) and Lévi-Strauss (1963) were not far off in calling Christmas 'the National Festival of Consumption' and 'a giant potlatch'. Within this festival potlatch, Santa Claus can be seen as the god of materialism and his myth can be seen as a secular echo of the story of Christ (Belk 1987). So Christmas embodies both the joys and problems of being a part of a consumer society.

Collecting behaviour can also be seen in two very different lights in terms of consumer culture. As noted above, it involves the endless pursuit of superfluous luxuries. Even if the objects were once useful objects like salt and pepper shakers, when they enter the collection they are no longer used for their original purpose and become decorative trinkets. What collectors describe as the thrill of the hunt for collectible objects (Belk 1995b) is little more than an exercise of acquisitiveness and subsequent possessiveness in an often highly competitive game of status-seeking and one-upmanship. The spending that collectors engage in for their collections is often a guilty pleasure, as is the time they spend with their beloved collectibles rather than with their families. It is little wonder that family members are often loathe to take on the collection bequest, because it had been a rival for the collectors' affections (Belk 1995a). And like obsessive compulsives, collectors gradually narrow their sphere of satisfactions toward the point where only fellow collectors and collecting produce pleasure. At the extreme, the things they collect matter more than the people around them.

But this same narrowing of focus and single-minded pursuit of the collection can have, for the collector, a romanticism in which they often see themselves as noble saviours of objects that few others appreciate. They are heroic saviours pursuing a noble passion, even if the objects collected are humble beer cans, nutcrackers or ceramic elephant replicas. It is not unusual for collectors to feel they are sacrificing for a great cause that they vaguely relate to contributing to art or science (Belk 1998). As such, the objects pursued are precious above price and ideally no sacrifice of time or money is too great. For many collectors there is at the same time a nostalgic retreat to the pleasures and objects of childhood, whether they are comic books, trading cards, toys, or once popular and desired old automobiles. And rather than succumbing to commercialism and commodi-fication, collectors often see themselves as resisting the forces of the market (Belk 1995). The objects that enter their collections are not for investment or profit as much as enshrinement in a sacred temple or private museum where they will be honoured in a strictly non-utilitarian fashion. In this respect objects in a collection parallel objects given and received as gifts. As with collectibles, the gift is above price (we carefully remove price tags and any evidence of the item's commercial origins), we ritually bestow it on others, and we hope the recipient will keep and treasure it forever. Far from being an exercise in consumerism and materialism, for collectors their action is an antidote to the uncaring market with its cheap loyalties toward possessions that are ultimately disposable.

Conclusion

We seem to have shaken centuries of concern about the debilitating effects of living a life of luxury (Berry 1994) in favour of a full frontal embrace celebrating our love affair with luxury (Twitchell 2001). The world seems struck by a luxury fever (Frank 1999). Traditional modesty in consumption in order to avoid making others envious has largely been replaced by a desire to make material status claims and incite the envy of others (Belk 1988b). Concern for others and the safety of truly social security has increasingly been supplanted by individualism and feelings of impersonal financial security. We have learned to value things more than people. William Whyte (1956) once observed that 'thrift is now un-American'. Americans were reminded of this in the wake of the September 11 terrorist attacks when we were told to strike back by going shopping (e.g., du Lac 2001; Reich 2001). Not only is thrift un-American, but deficit financing has become the norm.

The more affluent citizens of the world worry what will happen when there are a billion cars in China. But the consumption of the Chinese consumer is still only a fraction of their own. Meanwhile, global tourists flock in search of authenticity in Third World cultures and in the process they become walking advertisements for global consumer culture. Our personal sense of identity has been externalized and made more temporary and tenuous by being vested in our fashionable branded possessions. We grow fat by consuming more than we can use.

Our children are pampered with possessions that come to be seen as the coin of caring and love. By age eight children not only understand the symbolism inherent in children's products (Belk, Mayer and Driscoll 1984), but for adult products like houses and cars as well (Belk, Bahn and Mayer 1982). Children can identify about a dozen local plants and animals, but more than 1000 corporate logos (Orr 1999). This is true not only in the West. The children of the world are leading the way in the march of consumer culture, although they have plenty of adult role models to emulate.

Despite all of this, there is no denying that our lives are better than the non-consuming peasants described by Braudel at the beginning of this chapter. And while we show little indication of having reached saturation with consumer culture, perhaps some of us will some day be sated by our surfeit of things. In this regard it seems appropriate to recall the narrator of a chapter called 'The Dream' in Julian Barnes' (1990) *A History of the World in 10½ Chapters.* He awakes one morning to find that he is in heaven, fully embodied, and able to have anything he wishes. He is served his favourite breakfast, which he repeats a number of times. He then goes shopping for more delicacies. He plays golf, has sex and meets famous people. The newspaper was full of good things, including a championship by his favourite soccer team. He does more shopping, has sex with famous people, gets his golf score down to 18, eats more fabulous food, goes on cruises, explores the jungle, paints, falls in love many times, learns canoeing, mountaineering, and ballooning, tries performing surgery, drinks, does drugs, has fast cars, wins all the tennis and soccer championships, runs the New York marathon in 28 minutes, and has every want and whim gratified. And when he becomes bored with it all he chooses, as have those who preceded him, to have one last wish gratified: to truly die off so he can cease all this play and consumption.

Perhaps one day we too will grow tired of it all and seek an escape from consumer culture. But with an ever-expanding treasure house of things to want, it seems we are not likely to call it quits any time soon.

References

Ames, K. L. (1984), 'Material Culture as Nonverbal Communication: A Historical Case Study,' in E. Mayo (ed), *American Material Culture: The Shape of Things Around Us*, Bowling Green, OH: Bowling Green University Popular Press, 25–47.

Barks, C. (1980), 'The Land of Tralla La,' *Uncle Scrooge*, 183, Poughkeepsie, NY: Western Publishing Company (original 1954, Walt Disney Productions).

Barnes, Julian (1990), *A History of the World in 10½ Chapters*, London: Picador.

Belk, R. W. (1985), 'Materialism: Trait Aspects of Living in the Material World,' *Journal of Consumer Culture*, 12 (December): 265–80.

— (1987), 'A Child's Christmas in America: Santa Claus as Deity, Consumption as Religion,' *Journal of American Culture*, 10 (1): 87–100.

— (1988a), 'Possessions and the Extended Self,' *Journal of Consumer Research*, 15 (September) 139–68.

— (1988b), 'Third World Consumer Culture,' in E. Kumcu and A. F. Firat, (eds), *Marketing and Development: Broader Dimensions*, Greenwich, CT: JAI Press, 103–27.

— (1991), 'The Ineluctable Mysteries of Possesions,' *Journal of Social Behavior and Personality*, 6 (6): 17–55.

— (1993), 'Materialism and the Making of the Modern U.S. Christmas,' in D. Miller (ed.), *Unwrapping Christmas*, Oxford: Clarendon Press, 75–104.

— (1995a), 'Collecting as Luxury Consumption: Some Effects on Individuals and Households,' *Journal of Economic Psychology*, 16 (September): 477–90.

— (1995b), *Collecting in a Consumer Society*, London: Routledge.

— (1998), 'The Double Nature of Collecting: Materialism and Antimaterialism,' *Etnofoor*, 11 (1): 7–20.

— (1999), 'Leaping Luxuries and Transitional Consumers,' in Rajiv Batra (ed.), *Marketing Issues in Transitional Economies*, Norwell, MA: Kluwer, 38–54.

— (2001), 'Specialty Magazines and Flights of Fancy: Feeding the Desire to Desire,' in Groeppel-Klein A. and Esch, F. R. (eds), *European Advances in Consumer Research*, Berlin: Association for Consumer Research, 197–202.

—, Bahn, K. D. and Mayer, R. N. (1982), 'Developmental Recognition of Consumption Symbolism,' *Journal of Consumer Research*, 9 (June): 4–17.

—, Ger, G. and Askegaard, S. (2000), 'The Missing Streetcar Named Desire,' in Ratneshwar, S., Mick, D. G., and Huffman, C. (eds), *The Why of Consumption: Contemporary Perspectives on Consumer Motives, Goals, and Desires*, London: Routledge, 98–119.

—, Mayer, R. N. and Driscoll, A. (1984), 'Children's Recognition of Consumption Symbolism in Children's Products,' *Journal of Consumer Research*, 10 (March): 286–397.

Berry, C. J. (1994), *The Idea of Luxury: A Conceptual and Historical Investigation*, Cambridge: Cambridge University Press.

Boorstin, D. (1973), *The Americans: The Democratic Experience*, New York: Random House.

Boulding, K. (1985), *Human Betterment*, Beverly Hills, CA: Sage.

Braudel, F. (1967), *Capitalism and Material Life, 1400–1800*, New York: Harper & Row (original *Civilisation Matérielle et Capitalisme*, Librarie Armand Colin).

Campbell, C. (1987), *The Romantic Ethic and the Spirit of Modern Consumerism*, Oxford: Basil Blackwell.

Carrier, J. (1993), 'The Rituals of Christmas Giving,' in D. Miller (ed), *Unwrapping Christmas*, Oxford: Clarendon Press, 55–74.

Csikszentmihalyi, M. and Rochberg-Halton, E. (1981), *The Meaning of Things: Domestic Symbols and the Self*, Cambridge: Cambridge University Press.

Davis, D. S. (ed.) (2000), *The Consumer Revolution in China*, Berkeley: University of California Press.

Douglas, S. J. (1994), *Where the Girls Are: Growing Up Female with the Mass Media*, New York: Time Books.

du Lac, J. F. (2001), 'Red, White and Green: Many Entrepeneurs are Rushing to Capitalize on America's Wave of Patriotism,' *Sacramento Bee*, October 11, http:www.sacbee.com/lifestyle/news/lifestyle01_20011011.html.

Draculić, S. (1991). *How We Survived Communism and Even Laughed*, New York: Norton.

Easterlin, R. A. (1973), 'Does Money Buy Happiness?,' *The Public Interest*, 30: 3–10.

Fischer, E. and Arnold, S. (1990), 'More than a Labor of Love: Gender Roles and Christmas Gift Shopping,' *Journal of Consumer Culture*, 17 (December): 333–45.

Frank, R. H. (1999), *Luxury Fever: Why Money Fails to Satisfy in an Era of Excess*, New York: Free Press.

Fromm, E. (1976), *To Have or To Be*, New York: Harper & Row.

Ger, G. (1992), 'The Positive and Negative Effects of Marketing on Socioeconomic Development: The Turkish Case,' *Journal of Consumer Policy*, 15 (3): 229–54.

— Belk, R. W. (1996), 'Cross-Cultural Differences in Materialism,' *Journal of Economic Psychology*, 17 (1), 55–78.

— (1999), 'Accounting for Materialism in Four Cultures,' *Journal of Material Culture*, 4 (July): 183–204.

Gronow, J. (1997), *The Sociology of Taste*, London: Routledge.

Hertz, E. (2001), 'Face in the Crowd: The Cultural Construction of Anonymity in Urban China,' in Chen, N. N. (ed), *China Urban: Ethnographies of Contemporary Culture*, Durham, NC: Duke University Press, 274–93.

Kasser, T. and Ryan, R. M. (1993), 'A Dark Side of the American Dream: Correlates of Financial Success as a Central Life Aspiration,' *Journal of Personality and Social Psychology*, 65, 410–22.

— (1996), 'Further Examining the American Dream: Differential Correlations of Intrinsic and Extrinsic Goals,' *Personality and Social Psychology Bulletin*, 22: 280–7.

Leach, W. (1993), *Land of Desire: Merchants, Power, and the Rise of a New American Culture*, New York: Vintage.

Lévi-Strauss, C. (1963), 'Where Does Father Christmas Come From?,' *New Society*, 63 (December): 6–8.

Löfgren, O. (1993), 'The Great Christmas Quarrel and Other Swedish Traditions,' in D. Miller (ed), *Unwrapping Christmas*, Oxford: Clarendon Press, 217–34.

Livingstone, J. (1998 , 'Modern Subjectivity and Consumer Culture,' in Century, Strasser, S.,

McGovern, C. and Judt, M. (eds), *Getting and Spending: European and American Consumer Societies in the Twentieth Century*, Cambridge: Cambridge University Press, 413–29.

Marty, M. E. (1999), 'Equipoise,' in R. Rosenblatt (ed), *Consuming Desires: Consumption, Culture, and the Pursuit of Happiness*, Washington, DC: Island Press, 173–91.

Maslow, A. H. (1954), *Motivation and Personality*, New York: Harper and Row.

May, E. T. (1988), *Homeward Bound: American Families in the Cold War Era*, New York: Basic Books.

Miller, D. (ed) (1993), *Unwrapping Christmas*, Oxford: Clarendon Press.

Myers, D. and Diener, E. (1996), 'The Pursuit of Happiness,' *Scientific American*, May, 70–72.

Orr, D.W. (1999), 'The Ecology of Giving and Consuming,' in R. Rosenblatt (ed), *Consuming Desires: Consumption, Culture, and the Pursuit of Happiness*, Washington, DC: Island Press, 137–54.

Putnam, R. D. (2000), *Bowling Alone: The Collapse and Revival of American Community*, New York: Simon and Schuster.

Rassuli, K. M. and Hollander , S. C. (1986), 'Desire – Induced, Innate, Insatiable?', *Journal of Macromarketing*, 6 (Fall) 4–24.

Reich, R. B. (2001), 'How Did Spending Become Our Patriotic Duty?,' *Washington Post*, September 23, http://www.washingtonpost.com/ac2/wp-dyn/A7904–2001Sep22.

Richins, M. and Dawson, S. (1992), ' A Values Orientation for Materialism and Its Measurement: Scale Development and Validation,' *Journal of Consumer Research*, 19: 303–16.

Schudson, M. (1984), *Advertising, The Uneasy Persuasion: Its Dubious Impact on American Society*, New York: Basic Books.

— (1998), 'Delectable Materialism: Second Thoughts on Consumer Culture,' in D. A. Cocker and Linden, T. (eds), *The Good Life: Justice and Global Stewardship*, Boston: Rowman and Littlefield.

Shrestha, N. R. (1997), *In the Name of Development: A Reflection on Nepal*, Lanham, MD: University Press of America.

Slater, D. (1997), *Consumer Culture and Modernity*, Cambridge: Polity Press.

Solomon, M. R. and Assael, H. (1997), 'The Forest or the Trees: A Gestalt Approach to Symbolic Consumption,' in Umiker-Sebeok, J. (ed), *Semiotics: New Directions in the Study of Signs for Sale*, Berlin: Mouton de Gruyter, 189–218.

Stearns, P. (2002), *Consumerism in World History: The Global Transformation of Desire*, London: Routledge.

Stein, B. (1985), 'The Machine Makes This Man,' *Wall Street Journal*, 205 (June 13): 30.

Strasser, S. (1998), '"The Convenience Is Out of This World,': The Garbage Disposal and American Consumer Culture," in Strasser, S., McGovern, C., and Judt, M. (eds), *Getting and Spending: European and American Consumer Societies in the Twentieth Century*, Cambridge: Cambridge University Press, 263–79.

Taylor, B. and Tilford, D. (2000), 'Why Consumption Matters,' in Schor, J. B. and Holt, D. B. (eds), *The Consumer Society Reader*, New York: The New Press, 463–87.

Twitchell, J. B. (1999), *Lead Us Into Temptation: The Triumph of American*

Materialism, New York: Columbia University Press.

— (2001), *Living it Up: Our Love Affair with Luxury*, New York: Columbia University Press.

Waldman, S. (1992), 'The Tyranny of Choice,' *New Republic*, January 27.

Whyte, W. H., Jr. (1956), 'Budgetism: Opiate of the Middle Class,' *Fortune*, May, p. 133.

Wilson, P. (1972), *Crab Antics: The Social Anthropology of English Speaking Negro Societies of the Carribean*, New Haven, CT: Yale University Press.

5

Multiculturalism in the New World Order: Implications for the Study of Consumer Behaviour

Lisa Peñaloza

And of course, the ideal form of ideology of this global capitalism is multiculturalism, the attitude which, from a kind of empty global position, treats each local
culture the way the colonizer treats colonized people – as 'natives' whose mores are
to be carefully studied and 'respected.'

Slavoj Žižek, 'Multiculturatism'

Introduction

This paper initiates an inquiry into the complex interfaces between multiculturalism, capitalism and democracy. I come to these issues having worked over
fifteen years with Latinos/as in the USA, at first focusing on Mexican immigrant
consumers (Peñaloza 1994), and now exploring their similarities and differences
with Mexican Americans, an ethnic consumer subculture of which I am a part.[1]

Mexican immigrants, like many other immigrant groups, demonstrate tremendous agency and operate according to strong market logic, as they move from one
nation to another seeking better work as labourers, a better lifestyle as consumers
and, for some, a better opportunity for investment of their capital. Mexican
Americans, like other groups of ethnic consumers who are the descendants of
immigrants and colonized peoples, express tremendous agency as well, in
etching out an identity and community within the country where they were born.

Together, immigrants and ethnic subcultural consumers are changing the face
of the USA and many other nations all over the world (Stalker 2002), and in their
careful study I am able to bring to the fore key contradictions between capitalism
and democracy. Particularly acute is the movement of people from developing to
developed nations. In this sense, the movement and residence of people from
Mexico into the USA is similar to other consumer diaspora; for example, people
moving from the former colonies in Algeria to the nations of their former colo-
nizers in France, and the immigrant worker settlements of Turks in Germany or

Denmark. Notably, most attention has been directed to those subcultural groups comprised predominantly of labourers. Their differences from mainstream cultural groups in appearance, language, social class, and cultural values and practices foster conflicts related to housing, schools, social services (Peñaloza 1995) and even mainstream withdrawal from school systems and cities (Lasch 1995).

Yet immigration and colonization account for but part of the multicultural tensions at issue in the new world order. Ethnic groups comprised of owners of capital have commanded less attention in the literature, yet they are a major source of tension in the world today. As these ethnic minorities have come to dominate their nations' resources, anti-market and anti-democratic sentiments and violence are the result as the majority retaliates against the elite minority, and as the latter often mobilize police to safeguard their privilege (Chua 2003). Examples include the Chinese in Indonesia or the Philippines; Whites in many Latin American nations, such as Venezuela and Bolivia, and African nations, such as Angola or Zimbabwe; and Jews in Russia.

In dealing with multiculturalism in the global economy, this paper is primarily concerned with Mexican immigrants and Mexican Americans in the USA, an ethnic subcultural group comprised predominantly of labourers, although, in developing implications, I also consider elite minority groups. I begin by reviewing briefly the literature on consumer socialization, consuming communities, and market culture in developing the research questions to be addressed using a combination of historical and ethnographic methods. Findings are presented as a historical and contemporary mosaic of the Latino/a experience in the USA, with attention to political and market incorporation.

Discussion focuses on multiculturizing the study of consumer behaviour. First, I extend consumer socialization studies beyond comparing differences in the consumer behaviour of various groups, to focus on their interrelations and how these cultural relations impact fundamental concepts of consumer behaviour. I then distinguish between ethnic consumer subcultures and brand communities. While these two types of consumer groups have characteristics in common, they differ in ways important in distinguishing the respective challenges of each in building community. Also important is examining consumption crossovers, i.e., the consumption of the artefacts of one culture by members of other cultures, as these play a role in the maintenance of cultural difference in society. I then reconceptualize the market as a culture in its own right. I arrive at this reconceptualization having questioned the degree to which Mexican immigrants assimilate market culture versus Anglo culture in the USA. My argument is that market culture and Anglo culture are combined in research and in the discourses of free trade currently proliferating the globe, yet only by separating them are we able to examine the effects of the market on various cultures.

Finally, implications return to the complex interrelations of multiculturalism, capitalism and democracy. The global economy is defined by trade within and between increasingly diverse nation states, hence the importance of under-standing the social and economic implications of market interactions within and between borders. People increasingly express their free choice to live and work where they want and express who they are. Among its advocates, globalization is promoted as better for everyone, yet its manifestations may be seen to challenge ideals of the nation-state and market.

Regarding US-Mexican relations, it is ironic that officials in the USA have built a wall separating the USA from Mexico in the aftermath of what many proclaimed to be the 'triumph of capitalism' in bringing down the Berlin wall. For those groups large enough and with enough spending power, like Latinos/as, the market responds with specially tailored marketing campaigns. This special-ized target marketing reflects and informs the group members' sense of them-selves and what they stand for. Yet such target marketing can inflame intergroup tensions by violating the traditional position of the mainstream at the centre of culture, and in doing so, challenging modernist national hopes and dreams for unity.

At the core of the discussion is an examination of the ways multicultural rela-tions may be seen to put to the test economic ideals of free markets and political ideals of democratic participation. These dynamics are visible in comparisons of the intersections of market hierarchies with social hierarchies, and of market enfranchisement with more traditional political enfranchisement. As we shall see, market hierarchies will sometimes converge with social hierarchies, while at other times, they work against each other. When they work together, the resulting market enfranchisement renders minority groups visible, yet reinforces the priv-ileges of some over others, hence conflicting with the tenets of traditional polit-ical enfranchisement. In contrast, their disjunction and the resulting blurring of these hierarchies will be seen to move society towards democratic ideals of equality.

Multiculturalism in the Marketplace

Market multiculturalism is defined as the array of cultures within a nation, with an emphasis on relations between various cultural groups as they impact consumer behaviour and market practice and structure. This paper touches on ethnic, racial, national, social class and lifestyle cultural difference in the USA. Yet these dimensions are not exhaustive. Other cultural differences that impact consumer behaviour and marketing include age, life-cycle stage, religion, and gender and sexuality (Peñaloza 1996).

Theorists have noted that specialized market targeting efforts reflect and reproduce the paradox of greater cultural homogeneity and heterogeneity across the globe (Inda and Rosaldo 2002; Costa and Bamossey 1995). Homogeneity is found in similar consumption patterns across nations of the world and a blurring of styles across cultural groups; heterogeneity is recognized in the presence of distinct cultural consumption patterns within and across nations.

Scholars accounting for the simultaneous presence of similarities and differences in markets feature such factors as increasing mobility, technological advances, the increasing centrality of consumption in social life, and the stepped up marketing efforts of corporations targeting specialized groups of consumers with increasingly specialized, diverse media (Firat and Venkatesh 1995). The increasing prevalence of cultural differences in the marketplace raises many questions for consumer behaviour scholars. Bodies of literature useful in exploring these differences with attention to larger community issues impacting multicultural societies include consumer socialization, consumption communities and market culture.

Consumer Socialization

Consumer socialization is a foundational topic in the field of consumer behaviour, as it seeks to understand the processes by which people become consumers (Moschis 1987). In a comprehensive review of the studies, Roedder John (1999) noted a range of topics including acquisition of consumption symbolism and its use in negotiating identity and social relations with parents and peers; knowledge and attitude formation regarding products, brands and shopping; and decision-making heuristics.

Regarding cultural differences, the first generation of work compared various cultural groups. As examples, when compared to Whites, Latinos/as were noted to be more family oriented and more brand loyal (Strategy Research Corporation 1991), and to prefer Spanish language media (O'Guinn and Meyer 1984). While useful in documenting differences in consumption behaviours, this work has tended to reproduce the very distinctions it purports to measure in maintaining mainstream cultural dominance, as the result of a disturbing tendency to view minority cultures according to the standards of the mainstream (Venkatesh 1995).

In multiculturizing this work, I seek to go beyond measuring differences between the groups to focus on the significance of group interrelations in the marketplace. Thus, the market is recast as the terrain upon which cultural relations are negotiated, and research attention is directed at how these differences are employed by consumers and marketers. For consumers inhabiting a multicultural social domain, the abilities to know codes of more than one group, and use them in communicating with, and distinguishing themselves from, members of other cultural groups are highlighted.

Consumption Communities

This second body of work focuses on the social formations consumers make around product usage and meanings. For example, Muniz and O'Guinn (2001) used the term 'brand community' to describe Saab car owners and Apple computer users, in yet another indication of the increasing expression of human agency and subjectivity in the market. Examining the structure and activities of communities of Salomon snowboarders, Cova (2003) emphasized their shared passion, positioning apart from the mainstream, and loose and volatile organizational form.

These studies provide a valuable contrast for the present study of Latino/a consumers, as this latter group is exemplary of social groups that unite around the social categories of race, ethnicity or gender. My questions relate to the bonds these groups of consumers make around consumption, and how they relate their consumption and that of members of other groups to the development of the communities in which they live.

Markets, Cultures, Communities

The third body of work I draw from is cultural studies in marketing.[2] Culture appears most often in the discipline of marketing as a characteristic of consumers, such that research is sanctioned to assist marketers in targeting them, as intimated in the opening quote. In bridging this work with the previously mentioned literature, I put forward a view of the market as a culture (Hefner 1998) to understand better its impact on the Latino/a community. Specifically, I reconceptualize the market as a distinct semi-autonomous sphere of discourses and practices that overlaps and disjoins various cultural groups in various ways. Further, in viewing the market as a culture I direct attention to its organizational forms, as well as its practices, agents and values.

Market cultures are characterized by a shared subjectivity, group interactions, a loose organizational structure and a complex positioning vis-à-vis the social hierarchy. Historically, the bourgeoisie has occupied a foundational position in market culture. Historians have amended earlier views of the French and the American Revolutions to grasp better the convergence of market liberty and personal freedom animating the formation of bourgeois subjectivity (Lefebvre 1971; Wood 1991). Historians lay an important part of the foundation for the formation of subjectivity at the heart of market culture that continues to the present.

Yet further work is needed to get to the intersection of markets and cultures impacting ethnic minority communities. While not explicitly referring to them as separate cultures, scholars have demonstrated that markets have their own prerogatives, practices and values (Weber 1958; Marx 1906; Costa and Bamossey 1995), through which they impact cultures of consumers at a number

Lisa Peñaloza

of levels: globally, that of the nation-state, region and city. Markets are semi-autonomous from national culture, in the sense that market customs stem from particular socio-historical trajectories, but are informed by the economic logic of multinational companies (Callon 1998; Slater and Tonkiss 2001). This is evident in the marked contradictions between the market and religious (Weber 1958) and political institutions (de Tocqueville 1832), and small town and agrarian communities (Bell 1976; Peñaloza 2001). Yet while culture most typically is operationalized at the level of the nation, it is experienced most directly by consumers at the level of the city, and for this reason I pay particular attention to this level of analysis in this research.

Consumption Politics within the Multicultural Marketplace
The first point to glean from the previous discussion is that notions of identity and community are profoundly *relational*, in the sense that each is defined in terms of other groups (San Juan, Jr. 2002). Regarding Latinos/as in the USA, of interest is their socio-demographic profile in relation to that of the White US mainstream and in relation to the market. Latinos/as are the majority of the population in the cities studied; one third of the population of the states of California and Texas; and 12 per cent of the USA population. How Latinos/as are represented in business, how they relate to other cultural groups and to the market, and how they behave as consumers are all important research questions in themselves and in relation to the vitality of their community.

Second, patterns of wealth distribution impact the respective vitality of cultural groups over time. Drawing from early work by W.E.B. DuBois and Booker T. Washington, Malcolm X (1971) urged African Americans to invest their money and activities in their community to develop it. He was responding to the outflow of dollars from Black consumers to White merchants, which he sought to redirect to Black businesses, neighbourhoods, schools and other social organizations.

Then and now, cultural dimensions of markets are much more difficult to comprehend than the above call for separation implies. Notably, in the days of segregation, laws enforced racial divisions with economic ones. In this sense, Jim Crow laws preventing Black and Latino/a consumers from frequenting White businesses may be seen as the mechanics by which Whites limited severely the economic development of minorities. The result of this segregation was uneven, as many Black businesses and institutions of higher learning thrived, while countless individuals were limited restricted access to employment. In response to the latter, not the former, Black, Latino/a and White Civil Rights activists fought for access to mainstream White-owned establishments as labourers and consumers. Such access would disrupt the enforcement of racial/ethnic hierarchies by economic ones.

Of particular interest in this paper, then, are relations between social hierarchies composed of race/ethnicity and gender, and market hierarchies composed of capital versus labour classes. As we will see, at times the two hierarchies collapse into one in reinforcing each other; yet they can also work in opposite ways, blurring the boundaries between the subgroups and breaking down embedded power relations between them.

In the USA the minority of people who have the majority of the nation's wealth are White, the same race as the majority of population. Thus, classism and racism come to the fore in constituting and maintaining the market dominance of upper and middle class Whites over working class Whites and other ethnic/racial groups of Latinos/as and Blacks. For Whites, issues of class are most relevant; for Latinos/as and Blacks, ethnic and racial distinctions conflate with class. Yet, as Lipsitz (2001) notes, Whiteness is fraught with problems in the maintenance of its power amidst a larger national discourse of equality and merit. He describes a complex web of institutional and interpersonal discourses and practices that convey and support the normalcy of Whiteness, and in doing so, constitute its power. Paradoxically, many of the laws and institutions supporting the group in power do so by directing attention to the margins, such as the above example of Jim Crow laws which leave the position of the mainstream invisible, even as they constitute its privilege.

Investigating the interweavings of market and social dynamics in the USA is challenging. Yet while these two social domains overlap, reproducing their convergence compromises our ability to understand the effects of the market on subcultural groups, Latino/a as well as Anglo. The institutional and social discourses and practices that Lipsitz points out are likely to play out in consumption behaviours and market practices as well. For example, product and service symbolism is an important means of validating identity and community. Such symbolic consumption behaviours may be influenced by the politics of invisibility, such that products and services not specifically coded as 'other' – Latino/a or Black become White by default.[3]

At first glance, it seems multiculturalism is celebrated in the marketplace. People of colour are increasingly common in the media and in advertising, especially in specialist media targeting them. Even so, socio-economic indicators for Latinos/as and Blacks remain dramatically below those of Whites. The increased market visibility raises the final question to be addressed in this research, namely, how market enfranchisement, i.e., the rights and benefits markets afford, compares to more traditional political rights. While this may appear to be a strange comparison, I suggest that market legitimacy is an increasingly important form of social validation in capitalist societies, and as such, examining these market dynamics in relation to political dynamics is useful in appreciating the strengths and limitations of each domain.

Market beliefs in economic liberty and meritocracy have evolved in tandem with the democratic ideals of equal opportunity and participation. Yet, at times they are diametrically opposed. Democracy is inherently inclusive, egalitarian and founded on the principle of personal liberty and brother- and sisterhood, while capitalism is inherently hierarchically organized on the basis of distinctions of capital, labour, socio-economic power, and endowment (Peñaloza 1995: 92). Further, democratic institutions favor the universal rights of the individual (Taylor 1992), while marketing institutions appear to have less problem with using the cultural group as segmentation target of marketing and advertising efforts. Perhaps this is because the role of business in social formation is considered more fair and less manipulated by particular interests than government, as illustrated in the popular adage that the dollar is colour-blind. At any rate, group versus individual concerns and the beliefs of freedom and merit vis-à-vis the practices of social distinction are important in understanding the nature of the challenges multicultural societies pose to capitalism and democracy.

Methods

This paper draws from historical work on Latinos/as in the USA, previously published ethnographic work with Mexican immigrant consumers in Pueblo, California (Peñaloza 1994) and the multicultural marketers who do business with them (Peñaloza and Gilly 1999), and a current ethnographic study of Mexican American consumers and business people in Mission, Texas.[4] Historical work traces Latinos/as in the continental USA through subsequent periods of colonization, segregation and assimilation, and resistance and cultural assertion, to the present political and economic incorporation. This historical account provides a useful backdrop for understanding contemporary Latinos/as.

The previously published work with Mexican immigrants was conducted over an eight-year period, from 1989 to 1997. The 1994 paper focused on the consumer adaptation processes of sixteen immigrant families from Mexico living in Southern California, noting how they maintained Mexican customs in the USA, assimilated aspects of the US way of life, resisted both US and Mexican cultures, and lived in fairly segregated neighbourhoods consisting primarily of other Latinos/as. The 1999 paper documented how retailers learn to do business with another culture, in familiarizing immigrants with US market artefacts and customs, brokering Mexican products in their stores, and incorporating a mix of US and Mexican market customs.

The current study in South Texas, carried out from 1999 to present, explores whether Mexican Americans, those like myself, born in the USA of Mexican descent, are *still crossing borders*. By this I mean, are Mexican Americans still maintaining Mexican culture, still fostering Mexican customs in the marketplace, and still living somewhat apart from the Anglo mainstream? As before, I interview and interact with a range of people who vary by age, social class, gender, life-cycle stage and language abilities. However, number of generations in the USA becomes a key issue. Questions relate to family background, consumption experience, influential agents and institutions, cultural identity, social relations, understandings of market popularity, market/non-market locations of culture and community formation.

As appropriate to qualitative data, interpretative analyses are carried out consisting of data coding and pattern analysis in deriving categories and themes. Particular attention is directed to relations between data units, patterns, and themes; and to triangulating the analysis across types of data, and examining counter examples and outliers. Also critical is situating these data within their socio-historical contexts.

Historiographic Account: Still Crossing Borders

From Mexican to Mexican American, Chicano/a, and Latino/a
In January 2003 Latinos/as became the nation's largest minority in the USA, numbering approximately 38 million persons (Armas 2003). Recently this subculture has garnered attention for its tremendous market growth and future potential, yet this has not always been the case. For each of the following historical periods I identify critical incidents and discuss their role in contemporary identity and community formation. Note the changing use of terms over time from Mexican and Mexican American, to Chicano and its feminine counterpart Chicana, to Hispanic, and most recently to Latina and its male counterpart Latino.

Spanish Colonization to Mexican Independence to US Conquest
Foundational parts of Mexican American culture today are language and customs dating to the Spanish colonization of Native Americans in the early sixteenth century. Mexican rule was short-lived, dating from the Mexican Revolution for independence from Spain in 1810 to the 1948 signing of the Treaty of Guadalupe Hidalgo ceding the territory to the USA (Montejano 1987). However, this short time duration contrasts with the strong impact of this period in the consciousness of many Mexican Americans today, which is likely due to the strong agency of people in gaining their independence.

The period from the 1830 to 1860 was characterized by violence and a dramatic change in land ownership, from roughly two-thirds Mexican ownership to two-thirds Anglo ownership. A common lament among Mexicans at the time was that there was not a Texas Ranger without Mexican blood on his boots (Acuña 1988). As notable as the violence is the legacy of land theft for many

Mexicans and Mexican Americans (Acuña 1988). For them, the taking of the Southwest by the USA resonates with meanings vastly different from the freedom and democratic triumph celebrated in US accounts.

To this day many older Mexican Americans refer to themselves as *Mexicanos/as* (Mexicans). For them, the use of this term reflects the customs of their formative years, as Anglos and Latinos made little distinction between those born 'on this side' or 'on that side' (of the Mexican-US border). Mexican immigrants continue to use this term as well, expressing their primary identity with their nation of birth (Peñaloza 1994).

Segregation and Assimilation characterized the 1940s to the early 1960s. The term *Mexican American* comes into use at this time, reflecting a budding consciousness of cultural duality. The GI Forum (literally Government Issue, a term used in reference to soldiers), a prominent Mexican American organization, came of age in response to the refusal of an Anglo funeral home director to bury the bodies of Mexican American troops killed overseas (Montejano 1987). Mexican Americans who fought in The First World War and the Korean Conflict reasoned that if they were good enough to fight and die for *their* country, they were good enough to receive its full benefits.

A second group, the League of United Latin American Citizens (LULAC) was also founded at this time. This group consisted primarily of upper and upper-middle class Mexican Americans, and was social and service in orientation, although members also engaged in some political activity. Informant Hope Casanova recalls riding with others in a bus to the 'whites only' swimming pool in an area just north of Mission. Segregation was the order of the day. Informant Sister Helena recalls not being served ice cream on her ninth birthday. The shop-keeper took her and her mother outside where a sign on the door posted the words, 'No Dogs, No Mexicans and No Niggers'. While chicano/a activists would later blast LULAC and the GI Forum for being too conservative, they were perhaps less sensitive to the violence and separationist practices experienced by this early cohort.

Resistance and Cultural Assertion marked the mid 1960s to the late 1970s. A major thrust of El Movimiento (the Civil Rights movement for Latinos/as) was to reverse over a century of violence and discrimination (Acuña 1988; Montejano 1987). Prominent leaders included Corky Gonzales, Jose Angel Gutierrez, Reies Lopez Tijerina, César Chavez and Dolores Huerta. Activists coined the word *Chicano* at this time, mobilizing an ethnic movement primarily organized around labour and a working-class identity that transformed into La Raza Unida (The United Race) political party, and a student group, Movimiento Estudiantil Chicanos de Atzlan (MECHA), which still operates on many college

campuses. Inside the movement, feminists asserted their position in the community as *Chicanas*. Notably, many of the demonstrations were held at consumption
venues: lunch counters, city buses, retail stores and educational institutions. The
Civil Rights legislation of 1965 is a response to these calls for democratic
enfranchisement and inclusion, and resulted in marked gains in tolerance and
acceptance, although the laws were enforced unevenly.

Political and Market Incorporation   characterizes the period from 1980 to the
present. The first official tabulation of *Hispanics* was conducted by the US
Census Bureau in 1980.[5] This term remains in use among highly assimilated
Mexican Americans and other Latinos/as, and by others as deemed appropriate
in White social contexts.

The discovery of the *Latino/a* market begins roughly five years later.
Dramatic population growth and a strong identity and community bolstered by
years of civil rights gains for Latinos/as, in contrast to stagnant growth rates
and intense competition for the mainstream Anglo market convince major
firms to tap into this 'sleeping giant'. The irony of their discovery does not go
unnoticed by movement activists, who remain oriented towards labour, and
sceptical of what big business attention would do for the community, even as
small businesses continue to be a vital part of Mexican and Mexican American
community.

Today the term, Latino/a, has many connotations, some more and some less
political, and is favoured by subsequent generations who do not identify with
their parents' home countries. Latinos/as are increasingly visible in the USA, in
what could be called the *mainstreaming* of the culture that consists of a more
widespread geographic presence that has extended to suburban areas and small
towns from urban areas, and media representations that consist predominantly of
celebrities and an emerging middle class. Yet despite two decades of market
attention, the socio-economic status of most Latinos/as in Mission has remained
stagnant or actually lost ground. Gaps persist such that Anglos earn roughly 50
per cent more than Latinos/as here. It is a tale of *dos gente Latina* (two Latin
people), the working classes and an emerging huppie class (Hispanic upwardly
mobile professionals).

Still Crossing Borders
Mexican Americans differ from Mexican immigrants; they are born in the United
States, and as US citizens are entitled to all rights and privileges thereof. That
said, more subtle similarities and differences unfold between them. Like
Mexican immigrants, Mexican Americans are at once inside and outside US
culture, as they produce Mexican culture at home, in their neighbourhoods, at
school, at leisure and in the market.

Generational differences in language and socio-economic differences distinguish family members, as does residence in the working-class barrios (Latino/a neighbourhoods) in the West and South as compared to the middle-class North side. A smaller, counter trend is notable, as some middle-class Chicanos are returning to the barrios. Further, language differences noted previously between immigrant parents from Mexico and their children, such that the latter carry out prominent roles in the market, in using their English skills to translate for their parents and act in their behalf (Peñaloza 1994), are less common in the current study, as these subsequent generations of Mexican Americans speak English.[6] Even so, observational data reveals a marked change in the marketplace, such that Spanish language is now prominently spoken by store personnel and is readily apparent in advertisements in the media and on billboards, as firms cater to the Spanish-speaking segment of the Latino/a market, which is continually invigorated by immigrants from Mexico, as well as Central or South American countries.

Thus, crossing borders continues for subsequent generations of Mexican Americans, as they negotiate relations with friends, shopkeepers, teachers and at church. While permeable, these cultural boundaries continue to be manifest between Latinos/as and Anglos in language and other cultural and market practices. Ironically, each group, Latinos/as and the Anglo mainstream, is becoming at once more like the other. Two-thirds of all Mexican Americans claim families dating several generations in the USA, so for them life in the USA comes easily. 'It's all we've known,' they say, alternately taking for granted and aware of the bicultural skills they employ. Those more political are quick to note that 'The border crossed us,' noting mainstream adaptation to them and keeping alive the cultural memory that this US territory was once Mexico.

Significantly, many Mexican Americans/Chicanos/as say they most experience their culture at home and in their neighbourhoods, in foods, music and holiday celebrations. For some, this is a conscious activity, done as much for the pleasure as the politics. In contrast, many Mexicans who have moved up socio-economically and out of the barrio, experience their culture in marketplaces like El Mercado, a four block area of Mexican restaurants, stands and shops selling items imported from Mexico, and The River Walk, a tree-lined canal of bars, restaurants, hotels and specialist shops, or to local Mexican American organizations like the Guadalupe Center or Esperanza.

Finally, the mainstream market is changing as well, as Anglos assimilate Mexican American culture. This is harder to see, partly due to a national ideology that looks in the opposite direction for change and recoils from alarming sentiments of what Rodriguez (2002) calls the 'Browning' of America. Today Anglos eat more Mexican food, and play more Mexican music or the hybrid, Tex-Mex than do Latinos/as in the USA! They are adopting elements of our language and cultural ways, like amistad (friendliness), valores de familia (family values), closer social proximics, and a looser time orientation focused on social relations and activities in the present. Moreover, Anglo residents of the city of Mission and tourists from all over the country are the majority of consumers at El Mercado and The River Walk on any given day. Here they consume a very different form of Latino/a culture than that produced in the barrios by Mexican Americans, with most of the proceeds going to the owners of the establishments, although some tax revenues are distributed to Latino/a organizations through city institutions.

Discussion and Implications

> But what is the different/other if not the dominated? To constitute a difference and to control it is an act of power, since it is essentially a normative act. Everybody tries to show the other as different. But not everybody succeeds in doing so. One has to be socially dominant to succeed in it.'
>
> Faugeron and Robert, 'La justice et son public'

The impacts of multiculturalism in the marketplace are global, cutting across consumer behaviour, employment, public policy, media and social relations. Over time, with continued immigration and subsequent generations of ethnic group members, long-term trends are changing formerly homogeneous countries into heterogeneous ones, and making those that were heterogeneous, even more so. Important in recovering the elusive nature of consumption is sidestepping our discipline's fixation on cultural universals to redirect attention to the wide range of lived social groupings of consumers and how these groups interact within the marketplace.

From Consumer Socialization to Acculturation

In these data, Mexican Americans and Mexican immigrants display a type of consumption literacy that goes beyond economic knowledge and psychological activities to encompass knowledge of their own and other cultural groups. Consumers' expressions of Latino/a identity take place in and outside the marketplace, and are impacted by internal dynamics in relating to the social group(s) to which they belong and do not belong, and by external dynamics regarding relationships between the various cultural groups. Further, increasingly crucial in navigating multiple cultures and identities in the market is understanding knowledge of relations of power between cultural groups so as to be able to maintain their own amidst social constraints. Language for Latinos/as in the USA is a good example. After roughly a century of forced English assimilation, Latinos/as gained some cultural power in the form of Spanish language programmes in the schools. However, bilingual programmes are under attack today, and their loss portends a dangerous cultural barrier potentially limiting the future development of Latino/a children in the USA who only speak Spanish.[7]

Distinguishing Consuming Communities from Communities that Consume

I use the term 'communities that consume' for Latinos/as to differentiate this work from previous work on brand communities (Muniz and O'Guinn 2001), consumer subcultures (Schouten and MacAlexander 1995) and consuming tribes (Cova and Cova 2002) in terms of the relative importance of consumption to identity and community, and location vis-à-vis the market and other cultural groups.

Significantly, I locate Latinos/as' primary agency in community identity, and not in consumption. Although consumption plays a significant role in community development, the latter is not reducible to the former. Many Latinos/as develop their community in various sites outside the market, as in the case of those least acculturated and most political who experience their culture most at home and in the neighbourhoods. When they employ products acquired in the market, they use these items not as ends in themselves, but as the means towards their own individual and community ends. Even those more acculturated Latinos/as who have moved away from the barrios and experience their culture primarily in the marketplace, maintain a cultural identity that exceeds the market.

Yet, while Latinos/as' identity stems from their ethnicity and colour, it is important to note that it is not determined by these characteristics any more than product ownership determines brand community involvement. This is evident in the range of expressions of identity and community displayed by informants that mirrors the range of expressions of community emanating from the larger subset of product owners. Thus, interaction in the two types of communities varies, from 'professional', very active Latinos and Latinas, to those less intensely involved in the communities; and very active to casual users of products and services, and their meanings.

Further, since their identity is located primarily outside consumption, communities that consume may be more autonomous than brand communities, consumer subcultures, and consumer tribes, although this is partly the result of their wilful separation from others and others' policies of segregating them. Both communities that consume and brand communities retain some autonomy from the market, and should not be reduced to it, even as they are implicated in it, in needing to work and consume, not only to live, but also because these are increasingly the terrain of identity and community.

Consumption Crossovers

As previously discussed, community development happens as the result of the consumption activities of cultural members and non-members. Market transactions that entail the consumption of the artefacts of one culture by members of another culture are referred to as *consumption crossovers*. Anglos consume Latino/a culture in Mission in many ways, as noted in their consumer behaviours at El Mercado and The River Walk. Upon initial examination, these cross-overs appear as benevolent as they are widespread. After all, in capitalist society, what could be more profitable than to have your culture consumed by another? Yet further analysis reveals mixed impacts on the local Latino/a community, as a function of who owns elements of the culture and how or whether these elements are brought into the marketplace.

While it is likely that not all Anglos consuming Latino/a cultural elements do so with the specific intention of validating this group, I argue that these consumption crossovers have profound reality effects. Whether intended or not, consuming artefacts identified with particular cultural groups functions to validate them, as tempered by the degree to which the validations are contested. Thus, the significance of consumption crossovers in community development is best understood with these dynamics in mind.

Ultimately crossovers are unavoidable in the global economy, as products are increasingly manufactured and assembled away from the nation in which they are consumed due to dramatic differences in labour rates in developing as compared to developed nations. In making sense of them I emphasize consumers' attributions of cultural association over geographical site of production. Consumption crossovers increase in the new world order as a function of non-members' knowledge of other cultures, and their interpretation and usage of the meanings of these products and services in the growing lexicon of multicultural society.

Market Culture and Formation

Markets display culture in their values and practices. Notable are the ways market hierarchies resonate with social hierarchies in multicultural society, with implications affecting community development and intergroup relations. In the current study in Mission, a major cultural entertainment event, Fiesta de la Cultura (Party of Culture) is presented by a German organization that not only historically precluded Latino/a members, but continues to be composed predominantly of Anglos. Latinos/as participate in the show as a choreographer, many dancers, stage hands, concession vendors and cleaning crews. That these cultural brokers supply philanthropic resources, some of which go back to Latino/a community organizations and causes, does not shield them from informants' criticisms that Anglos are making money off Latino/a culture.

As noted in these data, market practices selectively incorporate some aspects of Latino/a culture, even as they ignore other aspects of this community that consumes. In doing so, these market practices render increasingly private cultural knowledge and skills previously manifest as collective goods, and through economic principles of capital accumulation, resources accrue to agents offering cultural products who are not necessarily members of the culture.

Notable are the ways markets recognize diversity within a culture and work against its incorporation, and this happens at various levels of nation and city. Earlier in this paper I described the increasing geographic and media visibility of Latinos/as; the former is important in bringing about increased market targeting, the latter its result. Yet while Latinos/as are more visible in some ways, they remain outside the imagined US national identity, which remains predominantly White as consistent with a long-standing race hierarchy. In previous generations White hegemony was more blatant, initially implemented by violence, and later by more subtle, but no less effective socialization in key institutions such as the police, government agencies, schools, stores and churches. Today, some differential treatment remains, yet Latinos/as are more visible in neighbourhoods, cities and the media. Regarding the latter, representations of Spanish speaking, middle-class Latinos/as predominate (Dávila 2001), just as upper middle-class Whites predominate in mainstream Anglo media (Goad 1997). In contrast, incorporation of Latinos/as has gone the furthest for employees in governmental agencies and businesses, likely the result of Civil Rights legislation.

To get a better understanding of the ways the market impacts culture, I reorient the national unit of analysis typically used for both culture and markets in our discipline with that of the *city*. Insights regarding market formation are generated with attention to the profile of marketing and consuming communities, which may then be related to business activity, infrastructural concerns, municipal service allocations, schools and community centres (Jacobs 1969).

Significantly, because Latinos/as are the majority of consumers in Mission, Texas, and in Pueblo, California, numbering approximately 65 per cent, this alternative mainstream is integrated even in the very up market, White shops and neighbourhoods, but it is a slow process. Nevertheless, politically Latinos/as retain a minority presence in positions of power such as the city council, school boards and state legislatures.

Business is an important engine of community development, especially given current trends of government budget cuts. This research shows business to be a small presence in both communities, with cultural activities centered around community organizations and tourism. In Mission and Pueblo there are emerging segments of Latino/a professionals and large and small business owners within both of the communities under study. Yet, these groups are relatively small in both areas; the larger concentration by far is in the working classes, with some small business owners. The two cities differ markedly in composition, and in the magnitude of dollars flowing out. In California there are more small businesses and more money recirculates within the Latino/a community. Tourism is scarce except on holidays. In contrast, in Texas there are fewer small businesses, and most of the money flows outwards. Its absence is only partially made up in terms of community support by large scale Anglo tourism in the form of taxes, and much of this business is located in the tourist areas, rather than in the barrios.

Two other obstacles to market development within the Latino/a community are noteworthy. Like Native Americans, Latinos/as have notions of common 'property' public spaces and cultural traditions. Further, El Movimiento (Civil Rights activism) was oriented primarily to labour, and its legacy remains three decades later in a lack of trust in business, and the view that business is something done to them rather than something they can do and benefit from. Yet there is some indication that the younger generation sees market culture less as a threat, and more as a necessary means of cultural survival. Unlike their parents and grandparents, they see no forced choice between Latino/a and Anglo cultures, and this is the message echoed in social and market institutions since the 1960s. Many draw from both cultures as they see fit.

In sum, the cultural heterogeneity that appears as market fragmentation and cultural erosion from the perspective of those in the mainstream can entail validation and social legitimation from the perspective of consumers within minority subcultures (Peñaloza and Gilly 1999; Peñaloza 1995, 1996). Yet for minority consumers market visibility and representation is a mixed blessing. Views of market incorporation as the source of enhanced social legitimation are countered by a lack of trust in business and doubt that it will contribute substantially to their community development.

Capitalism and Democracy

Increasing cultural difference in the marketplace raises a number of questions regarding the nature of the enfranchisement that comes with market visibility, and how it compares to more traditional, political forms of enfranchisement. First, while a similar logic appears to underscore recent multicultural market inclusions with earlier political forms, there are key differences. Market rights do not stop with fair treatment in transactions, as market inclusion brings some social legitimation to communities that consume. Yet there are notable limits to such market enfranchisement. There is no question that it is easier to be a Latino/a in the USA than ever before in history. Yet this recent market inclusion came *after* decades of political activism and enfranchisement, and continues to rest on law enforcement by local and national government within the larger context of a more subtle, yet continuing White hegemony.

In the imagined Whiteness of the USA, multiculturalism is a threat (San Juan, Jr. 2002; Lipsitz 2001). The strong negative reactions among some elements of the mainstream to multicultural market targeting and inclusion are a curiosity given their dominant position. It may be that mainstream contestations are in direct proportion to the efficacy of the legitimacy accorded to minority groups in the marketplace. If so, the dynamics of power may be changing such that the market increasingly functions as social arbiter. Laufer and Paradeise (1990) noted that marketing practices including polls, focus groups and press releases are increasingly used in building political legitimacy.

However, as previously mentioned, while governments enfranchise individuals, markets enfranchise groups. Taylor (1992) argues compellingly for the need for governments to provide political legitimacy to groups, but notes strong resistance that group rights are not necessary because *all individuals are covered* in a nation's Bill of Rights or Constitution. This resistance comes in many other forms; particularly resonant in the USA is a concern against state-sponsored favouritism.

The tests for democracy in market societies remain equal access to opportunity and participation in the political process. Constitutional guarantees of life, liberty and the pursuit of happiness are compromised somewhat by persistent socio-economic differences. Regarding Latinos/as, socio-economic differences in comparison with Anglos are rendered more extreme by market culture in the joint workings of social and market hierarchies, as noted in this research. Yet market multiculturalism could herald a system more inclusive system than what currently exists, by incorporating to a greater degree all cultural groups (Dallmayr 1996), with attention to a more equitable distribution of resources and status (Malveaux 2003), and with more elements of community intact, such as compassion, mutual understanding, and reciprocal obligations (Cova and Cova 2002; Ger 1997). Ironically, these are precisely the elements of their community that informants view the market as compromising.

A welcome extension to our knowledge comes from studying how markets and cultures interact, i.e., the ways social hierarchies are played out in the market, and markets reproduce socially coded differences. Given that cultural and market imperatives split particular subgroups from the larger society – for example commonfolk from elites, Black and Latino/a from White, and developed from developing nations – institutional mechanisms are vital in maintaining democratic political systems. Notes Taylor (1985: 309), 'The basic error of "liberal" atomism in all of its forms is that it fails to take account of the degree to which the free individual with his own goals and aspirations … is only possible within a certain kind of civilization; that it took a long development of certain *institutions and practices*, of the rule of law, of rules of equal respect, of habits of common deliberation, of common association, of cultural development, and so on, to produce the modern individual,' (italics added).

There are historical reasons why economic freedom initially was conflated with political freedom in the USA, but we must question the legacy of their conflation today. This is not a new question; concern with the violation of political freedoms by economic liberties dates to the nation's inception (Wood 1991), and for good reason. When market transactions and values overrule democratic rights, the effects are demoralization, resentment and, sadly, violence in the short term; with severe challenges to the legitimacy of democracy and capitalism likely in the long term. Yes, markets are needed to develop communities. Yet if we have learned anything from the accounting scandals and stock market losses of yesterday and today, it is that markets require political oversight to be fair. A growing number of people in the world also believe markets should be just. They are calling for democratic participation and more equitable distribution of resources in the International Monetary Fund and World Bank (Danaher 2001). To hold markets to the highest political and economic ideals is the most radical act of all. My hope is that more consumer researchers will take an active part in this struggle. Last year Daniel Kahneman received the Nobel Prize in economics for demonstrating psychological aberrations in markets. It is not far-fetched that one day a consumer researcher will receive it for demonstrating their equally important *multicultural aspects*. Cultures and markets will be better for it.

Conclusions

Distinctions between market enfranchisement and its counterpart, political enfranchisement are increasingly important distinctions as freedoms of the market conflate with political freedoms in the global economy. In terms of the economy, popular sentiments put forward a 'free' market unfettered by social distinctions and hierarchies. Yet Latinas/os' testimony and experiences both historically and at present challenge these ideals. Technically the free market entails unrestricted movements of capital, products and services, as well as people. Yet even when they are citizens, Latinos/as experience the workings of social and economic boundaries, at times together and at times apart in refusals of service and social restrictions in currency allowances, tariffs and immigration controls.

At the same time market participation allows people social mobility, the economic enfranchisement it provides pales in comparison to the rights and benefits won by minority groups through more traditional forms of political activism. While capitalism and democracy evolved historically in tandem in the USA, and the two concepts continue to be conflated in popular rhetoric, their coexistence is not guaranteed for future generations in this country or the many others throughout the world which continue to emulate it.

Becker and Becker (1997) argued that democracy is good for capitalism, as the freedom of expression and agency this political body of ideals affords encourage production and consumption behaviours in the market system. Yet there are equally compelling arguments that capitalism compromises democracy. The alignment of market hierarchies with social ones results in unequal distributions of wealth and access to economic and political power that potentially undermines and curtails democratic participation. Only with attention to the ways these disparate social domains overlap and disjoin can we understand why market multiculturalism tests political and economic ideals, and work to reproduce more desirable social conditions in the future.

Notes

1. Regarding terms, I use Mexican immigrant for persons living in the USA born in Mexico; Mexican American for persons living in the USA of Mexican descent. Latino/a is a broader term, referring to those persons living in the USA born in Latin American countries and those born in the USA whose descendants came from Latin American nations. Mexican Americans and Mexican immigrants are by far the largest group of Latinos/as, comprising over 60 per cent nationally (Armas 2003).
2. While a major disciplinary break divides studies of consumers from markets, I suggest that we must position consumers within the market to adequately understand them.
3. One could substitute other cultural dimensions here, such as gay versus heterosexual, feminine versus masculine, or even rural versus urban (Peñaloza 2001, 2000). In each case the subordinate group is marked.
4. City names are pseudonyms.
5. Prior to the 1980 the Census Bureau relied on Spanish surname and use of Spanish language to designate Latinos/as.
6. This sad legacy of legislation making English the official language of the USA prevents Mexican Americans from being qualified for the many jobs emerging with the growth of the Latino/a market in the USA and in Latin America. Instead, companies prefer to hire foreign born Latinos/as educated in Spanish in their home countries (Dávila 2001).
7. Interestingly, bilingual programmes are supported more by non Latinos/as wanting an edge for their children in the global market, and subsequent generations of Mexican Americans seeking to maintain their culture, than recent immigrants striving to adapt and thrive in the USA.

References

Acuña, Rodolfo (1988), *Occupied America: The Conquest and Colonization of the USA Southwest*, New York: Harper Collins.
Armas, Genaro C. (2003), 'Hispanics largest U.S. minority: New status may translate into political clout,' *Boulder Daily Camera*, Wednesday, January 22, Section A, Page 1–2.

Becker, Gary S. and Guity Nashat Becker (1997), 'Democracy is the Soil Where Capitalism Flourishes Best,' in Becker & Becker *The Economics of Life*, New York: McGraw-Hill, pp. 243–4.

Bell, Daniel (1976), *The Cultural Contradictions of Capitalism*, New York: Basic Books.

Callon, Michel, ed. (1998), *The Laws of Markets*, Oxford: Blackwell.

Chua, Amy (2003), *World on Fire: How Exporting Free Market Democracy Breeds Ethnic Hatred and Global Instability*, New York: Doubleday.

Costa, Janeen Arnold and Gary J. Bamossy, eds. (1995), *Marketing in a Multicultural World*, Thousand Oaks, CA: Sage.

Cova, Bernard (2003), 'Analyzing and Playing with 'Tribes Which Consume,'' working paper, European School of Management, Paris.

— and Véronique Cova (2002), 'Tribal Marketing: The Tribalisation of Society and its Impact on the Conduct of Marketing,' *European Journal of Marketing*, 36: 595–620.

Dallmayr, Fred (1996), 'Democracy and Multiculturalism,' in Seyla Benhabib, (ed.), *Democracy and Difference: Contesting the Boundaries of the Political*, Princetown, NJ: Princeton University Press, p. 278–94.

Danaher, Kevin (2001), *Democratizing the Global Economy*, Monroe, ME: Common Courage Press.

Dávila, Arlene (2001), *Latinos, Inc.: The Marketing and Making of a People*, Berkeley, CA: University of California Press.

Faugeron, C. and P. Robert (1978), *La justice et son public et les représentacions sociales du système pènal*, Paris: Masson.

Firat, Fuat and Alladi Venkatesh (1995), 'Liberatory Postmodernism and the Reenchantment of Consumption,' *Journal of Consumer Research*, 22(December): 239–67.

Ger, Guliz (1997), 'Human Development and Humane Consumption: Well-Being Beyond the Good Life', *Journal of Public Policy and Marketing*, 16(1): 110–25.

Goad, Jim (1997), *Redneck Manifesto: America's Scapegoats, How We Got that Way, and Why We Aren't Going to Take it Anymore*, New York: Simon and Schuster.

Hefner, Robert W. (1998), *Market Cultures: Society and Morality in the New Asian Capitalisms*, Boulder, CO: Westview Press.

Inda, Jonathan Xavier and Renato Rosaldo (eds) (2002), *The Anthropology of Globalization*, Oxford: Blackwell.

Jacobs, Jane (1969), *The Economy of Cities*, New York: Vintage Books.

Lasch, Christopher (1995), *The Revolt of the Elites and the Betrayal of Democracy*, New York: Norton.

Laufer, Romain and Catherine Paradeise (1990), *Marketing Democracy: Public*

Opinion and Media Formation in Democratic Societies, New Brunswick, NJ: Transaction Publishers.

Lefebure, Georges (1971), *The Coming of the French Revolution*, first printing 1939, translated by R.R. Palmer, Princeton, NJ: Princeton University Press.

Lipsitz, George (2001), *The Possessive Investment in Whiteness: How White People Profit from Identity Politics*, Philadelphia, PA: Temple University Press.

Malcolm X (1971), 'The Black Revolution,' *The End of White World Supremacy: Four Speeches*, New York: Arcade Publishers.

Malveaux, Julianne (2003), 'Shared Status: A Global Imperative,' invited lecture, University of Colorado, Boulder, February 21.

Marx, Karl (1906), *Capital: A Critical Analysis of Capitalist Production*, translated by Samuel Moore and Edward Aveling, and edited by Frederick Engels, London: Swan Sonnenshein and Co.

Montejano, David (1987), *Anglos and Mexicans in the Making of Texas, 1836–1986*, Austin, TX: University of Texas Press.

Moschis, George (1987), *Consumer Socialization: A Life-Cycle Perspective*, Lexington, MA: Lexington Books.

Muniz, Albert M. and Thomas C. O'Guinn (2001), 'Brand Community,' *Journal of Consumer Research,* 27(March) 412–32.

O'Guinn, Thomas C. and Timothy P. Meyer (1984), 'Segmenting the Hispanic Market: The Use of Spanish Language Radio,' *Journal of Advertising Research*, 23(December) 9–16.

Peñaloza, Lisa (1994), 'Atravesando Fronteras/Border Crossings: A Critical Ethnographic Exploration of the Consumer Acculturation of Mexican Immigrants,' *Journal of Consumer Research*, 21(1 June): 32–54.

— (1995), 'Immigrant Consumers: Marketing and Public Policy Implications,' *Journal of Public Policy and Marketing*, 14(1 Spring): 83–94.

— (1996), 'A Critical Perspective on the Accommodation of Gays and Lesbians in the USA Marketplace,' *Journal of Homosexuality*, 31(1/2 Summer) : 9–41.

— (2000) 'The Commodification of the American West: Marketers as Producers of Cultural Meanings at the Trade Show,' *Journal of Marketing*, 64(October 2000): 82–109.

— (2001), 'Consuming the American West: Animating Cultural Meaning and Memory at a Stock Show and Rodeo', *Journal of Consumer Research*, 28(December): 369–8.

— and Mary Gilly (1999), 'Marketers' Acculturation: The Changer and the Changed ' *Journal of Marketing*, 63(3July): 84–104.

Rodriguez, Richard (2002), *Brown: The Last Discovery of America*, New York: Viking.

Roedder John, Deborah (1999), 'Consumer Socialization of Children: A Retrospective Look at Twenty-Five Years of Research,' 26(December):

183–213.

San Juan, E. Jr. (2002), *Racism and Cultural Studies: Critiques of Multiculturalist Ideology and the Politics of Difference*, Durham, NC: Duke University Press.

Schouten, John and James Mac Alexander (1995), 'Subcultures of Consumption: An Ethnography of New Bikers', *Journal of Consumer Research*, 22(June): 43–61.

Slater, Don and Fran Tonkiss (2001), *Market Society: Markets and Modern Social Theory*, Cambridge: Polity Press.

Stalker, Peter (2002), 'Migration Trends and Migration Policy in Europe,' working paper, Centre for Development Research, Oxford, UK.

Strategy Research Corporation (1991), *1991 U.S. Hispanic Market*, Miami: Strategy Research.

Taylor, Charles (1985), *Philosophy and the Human Sciences: Philosophical Papers*, Vol. 2, Cambridge: Cambridge University Press.

— (1992), *Multiculturalism and the Politics of Recognition*, Princeton: Princeton University Press.

de Tocqueville, Alexis (1832), *Democracy in America*, New York: Mentor Books.

Venkatesh, Alladi (1995), 'Ethnoconsumerism,' in Janeen Costa and Gary J. Bamossy, (eds), *Marketing in a Multicultural World*, Thousand Oaks, CA: Sage.

Weber, Max (1958), *The Protestant Ethic and the Spirit of Capitalism*, tr. Talcott Parsons, NY: Charles Scribner's Sons.

Wood, Gordon S. (1991), *The Radicalism of the American Revolution*, New York: Vintage Books.

Žižek, Slavoj (1997), 'Multiculturalism, Or, the Cultural Logic of Multinational Capitalism,' *New Left Review*, 225(September-October): 28–51.

Part III
Performing Identities

6

The Little Black Dress is the Solution, but what is the Problem?

Daniel Miller

Introduction – 'Leached on the Beach'

Salman Rushdie's wonderful children's book *Haroun and the Sea of Stories* is based on the premise that there is some evil mechanism that is taking away the vital stream of stories that course through the veins of our world. My paper is based on a kind of adult equivalent to this story. During my lifetime I have been witness to a similar dreadful loss and in this paper I want to don the mantle of the anthropologist as detective and see if I can locate the culprit. The crime is evident all around us. There has been a gradual leaching out of colour and print from the world of Western women's clothing. Just like in Rushdie's story it is as though somewhere there is a vast hole through which colour and print is leaking out leaving an increasingly grey and black world of clothing that makes for a drab colourless environment, only partly compensated by a few exceptions such as sportswear and the little red dress (Steele 2001). I feel personally affronted by this assault on my own world and the threat that my sense of colour is being atrophied by my environment, since I too suffer from this same affliction. When I started lecturing I was still wearing a bright orange jersey and a necklace of shells retained from my fieldwork in the Solomon Islands. But already I was already looking the anachronistic 'hippie'. Of course being a hippie was itself merely conventional to that time and I have shifted with all the subsequent movement towards the colourless. Today I have adopted the general conventions of male clothing based around indigo and black, which is constructed along a vague polarity with 'classic' Armani emulating cuts for more formal wear, and jeans materials for the more informal. About the most exciting possibility left to me is to discover a new shade of grey.

Furthermore I am particularly sensitive to this shift having just completed (along with Mukulika Banerjee) a book about the sari in India (Banerjee and Miller 2003), a garment which retains a glorious rainbow of colour and an effusion of print. Recalling my life as a sartorial hippie, the last major explosion of colour in women's clothing is probably precisely that time now lovingly recalled in the Austin Powers movies which pay proper homage to the clothing of the 1960s and 1970s. It was a time when as a child I earned holiday money working in a 'Carnaby Street' style boutique and was enthralled by the coral sea of clothing, while festooned in my own purple flared trousers, beads and floral shirt. Since then it seems that each year has seen a gradual reduction in permitted levels of colour and print.

It was men's clothing that declined most precipitously. The decline in women's clothing while slower, now looks pretty much as deep. I write this having just been on a shopping expedition for Christmas 2002 with some female friends, which really did consist entirely of a discussion about shades of grey, in a shop called 'Muji' which seems to thrive essentially on a kind of Western amalgamation of the minimalism associated with stereotypes of the Japanese, now manifested almost entirely in grey. In the clothing sales following New Year I sat in the younger women's section of Selfridges in London faced by rows of grey to black, facing off against white to cream, with various shades of red seeming to stand in for 'colour' in general. It seemed to me as though an extraordinary number of the shoppers passed by in almost interchangeable combinations of blue denim jeans and black tops.

The title of this paper is in essence a reflection of the role of the little black dress in particular as the vanguard of these developments. This is not a work in any sense on fashion history. Edelman (1998) provides such a history defining a starting point for that dress with the designer Chanel in 1926 and examining the role of different influential women that have worn these dresses as much as the designers, women such as Wallis Simpson, Audrey Hepburn and Jacqueline Kennedy (see also Ludot 2001, and, for black fashion more generally, Mendes 1999). If the term little black dress is used colloquially rather than as it is employed in more academic circles of fashion history then it evidently plays a major role as a cliché for women talking about clothing generally. As noted there are several books concerned with the little black dress, there is even a book called *The Little Black Dress Diet* (Van Straten 2001). Similarly the Internet reveals sites called thatperfectlittleblackdress.com, littleblackdress.co.uk and even lbdtogo.com.

The literature provides various psychological theories for the popularity of the dress, but as a social scientist my concern is rather with this dress in its specific aspects as a vanguard for the dominance of the colourless costume, that which speaks to this issue of leaching. So it is the contemporary black dress that is the issue here and I will not assume that it is necessarily popular for the same reason as in earlier times. I have represented it as iconic in my title as much in relation to this history as to my own encounter with the problem of leaching. My material comes largely from the ethnographic work carried out by myself and Alison Clarke in London. Although the title refers to one exemplification of this trend, this paper is actually concerned with the trend as a whole and as it appears in the ethnography. Quite apart from this dress, grey and black have marched to the fore. Indeed black itself is equally iconic as the backdrop to modern dress. If by chance any other colour tries to get a look in, the fashion magazines will say 'brown is the new black' or 'green is the new black', though it has now become pretty clear that for most of the time black is the new black.

It was, however, specifically the little black dress that started my own ruminations upon the topic. I guess my desire to write such a paper started when as a parent I organized my daughter's birthday parties. If you have a 12–year-old girl and you are organizing some kind of party or disco in London you can pretty much bet that they will all, and I mean all, turn up in very similar little black dresses. This might simply be a reflection of how 12–year-olds are very anxious about getting embarrassed and lack confidence. But are these the factors that apply also to the degree to which other older women seem to rely upon this foundational garment? Certainly when it comes to wearing black more generally, there are days when colleagues, friends and other groups of older women seem almost as beholden to this colour as do these children.

But what finally prompted the writing of this paper was a further extension of these observations. Having become reconciled to the evidence that both men and women had collapsed into drabness for everyday wear I still expected a kind of 'Hawaiian shirt' lifting of these constraints when on holiday, with the expectation that here at least people would relax their sartorial codes and embrace a more adventurous field of colour. Well for a while this seemed true, but then I was starting to find that my fellow tourists were bringing out the same dull drab clothes on holiday that they were wearing at home – just more interesting messages on the T-shirts. But at least I felt that if holiday clothes had also become drab, the last refuge of colour would indeed be the beach and the swimsuit, with at least some desire to 'fit in' when snorkelling over a coral reef. So the decision to write this paper can be precisely timed. It came when taking a family holiday on a beach in Mexico. I had my novel and my drink, and was relaxing under a beach umbrella. This was quite a European resort and the people around me were probably Dutch, Swedish and English with a few Americans. Anyway, after a while, I started looking around me and what actually caught my eye was that every single bikini or swimsuit as far as my eye could see was – you guessed it – black. At that point I decided that, if the anthropologist could turn detective, while I might not be able to stem this tide, I might at least find the culprit.

Interrogating the First Suspect – Capitalism

The vast majority of books on clothing are concerned with fashion, and thereby with the fashion industry. So the history of fashion is often collapsed into the

Daniel Miller

history of the industry itself. The model underlying such works is made clear in the general argument of Fine and Leopold (1993: 93–137, 219–37). Each major commodity, such as food or clothing, exists within a vertical system so that in order to understand consumption we must also understand production. In the clothing system, fashion is the primary link between them, driving both demand and supply. Books certainly exist on the industry itself as a commercial form (e.g. White and Griffiths; 2000 Rath 2002), but by far the largest group of writings is based on the history of the fashion designer as an influence again on both production and consumption. This is where the 'little black dress' is hunted down and attributed to the influence of key individuals, usually from Paris, or seen as part of some particular trend such as simplicity (e.g. Arnold 2001: 17–22).

The problem with this argument is how to establish its credibility other than as simplistic conclusion based upon déjà vu? That is to say, having seen that the world has gone black, we simply locate particular designers who promoted this trend and assume they are responsible for it. The problem is that this does not allow for the possibility that this trend developed despite rather than because of design. A more credible way of examining this question is to acknowledge that we are indeed looking at a huge business, a major element of modern capitalism, and that to make the case a convincing one we have to find some logic that links the interests of this industry with black as a result or effect of this trend. This is precisely where the argument starts to look much less plausible. Indeed the evidence against it can be seen on every high street. If the fashion business was a largely monopolistic concern and if there were efficiency gains to be had by simplifying the products themselves then one could envisage such a logic, analogous to the famous claim of Henry Ford for his model T cars 'they have any colour they like as long as its black'. But irrespective of whether this quote is apocryphal, it simply doesn't reflect the fashion industry today. So far from being monopolistic, this is one of the most diversified industries of the modern world, and it is relatively easy for small outfits with limited capital to start up either as producers or retailers. The main chains and designers may dominate, but there are quite a few of them, and they exist in a state of clear competition one with another.

In such a distributed and competitive market the struggle for each is to find some niche, some element, that will give them a particular character. It is fine for one or two firms such as Armani to establish themselves with a certain ideal of the classical that is indeed largely grey to black, but precisely because companies such as Armani occupy this niche, it is necessary for others to find alternatives. On the whole the high street is full of companies, ranging from the 'united colours of Benetton' to the creative and provocative mix that festoons a shop such as Morgan or Zara. In short, the fashion industry has to be based on difference rather than homogeneity. From haute couture to *prêt-à-porter* to the smallest independent producers and retailers there is a desperate desire to find something, preferably different and novel, that can capture the market and lead to shoppers feeling there is missing from their wardrobes an item of clothing that this company can supply. So the primary evidence for this industry not being the culprit here is simply a comparison between what is on sale and what is being worn. I have not met anyone as yet who would disagree with the general qualitative assessment that the styles and colours being worn as one goes to work each day, or looks around the street, or even goes out in the evening are far more homogenized that what is available in the shops. The shops have become more homogenized over the years, as in the retailscape at Selfridges mentioned above. But this seems to follow rather than force the trends in what people wear. It is simply that attempts to create distinction in colour and print do not sell sufficiently over the long term.

I just can't see any commercial logic in the clothing business as a whole which makes black the way to profit – the industry needs a diversity of niches to exploit, not just homogeneity. If anything the entire population going into black is more likely to put business finances into the red! Sure, they can probably cope with it, Armani does pretty well out of grey, but if this is some kind of business plot, it is not an obvious one. The problem in decoding clothing is that it is simply too easy to argue that what people wear must follow from what commerce supplies. We have to be dragged into the opposite corner of seeing what is supplied as a surrender to what people are prepared to wear, but the logic of modern women's clothing with respect to its ever increasing homogenization represented in the decline of colour and printing certainly seems to imply that the driving force has been the customer not the couturier.

Interrogating the Second Suspect – History

So it looks like the simplest and most deterministic theory, that a shift in consumption merely reflects a shift in production will not do. We need to find some other candidates in the literature. Is there perhaps some historical precedent, some other period in which clothing leached out colour and print? Fortunately there has recently been published a volume which seems as though it could be a clear precedent for our current situation. The book is called *Men in Black* and was published by John Harvey in 1995. Firstly this is useful because it discusses some other theoretical accounts. Flugel (1976) it seems had already argued that the move to black was a kind of egalitarian, democratic response rejection of the *Ancien Régime* by the bourgeois of the period. This sounds credible, but unlikely to work for the contemporary case. If anything the colourful years of the 1960s and 1970s were a genuine repudiation of traditional class hierarchies, and in parallel with this earlier case led by the bourgeois middle class rather than the working class of the time. In general we have seen a return to a political conservatism since then and more recently a return to greater inequalities in countries such as the UK and USA. There is a more subtle version of this argument, in which we can see men through the eighteenth and nineteenth centuries giving up the overt display of wealth and power and adopting the measured and perhaps more menacing uniform of a generic power that does not need to be specified. Once again, however, there is little reason to see the little black dress and subsequent general adoption of black by women as related in any way to this. There might be a few 'power suits' within the black genre but those little girls at their parties, and the adults at theirs neither seem to desire nor achieve this sense of menacing empowerment.

These are not, in any case, the theories that Harvey uses for the period of his concern. His book is devoted to the rise of black amongst men in Victorian Britain. Just as we might finger key designers today as having a certain influence, the dandies of that time seem to have adopted a certain ascetic and minimalist appearance which made black fashionable, the elaborations being in style rather than colour. But Harvey also rejects the idea that the mass adoption of black by the middle class was particularly influenced by the stylistic antics of the elites. He sees a greater legacy in the centuries of adoption by the church of an association between black and sobriety and seriousness, that gave black a certain gravitas, which is reflected in Shakespearean characters such as Hamlet and Othello and evident in the sobriety of the male figure in Dutch art. In effect there is a kind of Durkheimian movement whereby the social norms of the middle class take on in a secular version the values of the church (Harvey 1995: 147). But the catalyst that really brought about this association with black was, according to Harvey, the bridge between the secular and the religious that emerged in the Victorian cult of the funerary. This is evident in the obsessions of Tennyson and other cultural 'spokespersons' of the period, but importantly these reflect a genuine social pressure. It was men who were expected to attend funerals with some frequency, so that funerals came to occupy a significant place in many people's lives at that time.

The concern in this book is largely with men rather than women, since he argues for this period that in general 'in the protestant countries especially, it appears, strains of asceticism were liable to blanch women as they darkened men' (Harvey: 1995: 211). Thanks to many television reconstructions of novels written during this period we have become increasingly familiar with scenes from this time composed of men in black dancing with women in white who appear, in general, rather cold embodiments of a certain wifely virtue. Although this white has a rather ghostly aspect, at least in funerary custom the genders blend, since Victoria herself embodied the vision of endless mourning that gave rise to that quintessence of black we think of as 'jet black' as jet dominated as an accessory for mourning. What this book demonstrates is that there are clear precedents for the phenomenon this paper is concerned to explain. There are indeed other periods in which clothing leached and bleached.

What does not follow, however, is the conclusion that these precedents give us the key to explaining the current example of these shifts in acceptable sartorial codes. To take the specific instance of Harvey's book, this obsessive funerary concern is an unlikely candidate for the little black dress today. I doubt that the women I meet at parties are trying to dress as though for a funeral – some of the parties I go to are bad, but not usually that bad! Rather what we have to learn from these works is that there are likely to be some quite specific factors at play in any particular instance of this phenomenon and that we should not assume that there is anything in common between any two such instances as separated by time and space. One legacy of the extensive writings that once dominated the anthropology of clothing based on semiotic theory (e.g. Barthes 1985; Sahlins 1976) has been the acknowledgment that in a world in which some societies adopt black for funerals and others white, it is the internal logic of the clothing system that has to be accounted for, and not at all some deep 'psychological' predilection based on the property of any colour for humanity as a biological species. It is perhaps more sensible to recognize that black is a colour that is going to have many diverse connotations and periods of ascendancy. There is not necessarily going to be a strong link between the sartorial habits of Dickens and of the modern teenage Goth, even if both do favour black.

Interrogating the Third Suspect – Modernism

For my third candidate I want to turn to the wonderful title of what unfortunately turns out to be a slightly disappointing book *Chromophobia* by David Bachelor (2000). The great thing about the title is it makes a direct case for a recent decline in colour, a leaching out of colour from the world that can apply to the rise of both white and black, and also that it points the finger at one clear culprit, which is the rise of modernism and modernist minimalism. It provides a number of instances both in literature and art which seem to suggest this pervasive fear and dislike of colour and its increasing condemnation as vulgarity. The book also does a useful job of noting that there exists an opposing tendency, a Chromophilia, that can be found for example in a certain film tradition stretching from the *Wizard of Oz* to the recent *Pleasantville*. Beyond this, however, the volume lacks the convincing scholarship that can be used to explain the phenomenon.

Fortunately, in contrast to *Chromophobia,* there is a book with a less succinct title, but quite excellent in its substantive content, called *White Walls, Designer Dresses* by Mark Wigley (1995). This makes precisely this argument for the centrality of leaching to the modern movement, but does so with considerable and impressive scholarship and through making an unexpected, but convincing, link between the histories of clothing and of architecture. Wigley starts from the pervasive presence of white walls in modern architecture. His argument is that these are supposed to be neutral and silent but actually speak volumes about the attempt to assert certain hegemonic values through modernism. He shows how white, and I think we can add black, is not a neutral absence but often an assertive presence. Tracing back its source, he sees a powerful influence upon architects such as Le Corbusier to be found in earlier dress reform movements. It was in dress reform that there developed a clear ideal of rationalism applied to aesthetic form. Rationality seen as both the ends and means of civilization itself proclaims white as a form of purity, the hygienic, the pristine. This allows for a pure utility, that which is assertively functional, to emerge from mere decoration. But behind this in turn lies another set of oppositions. The dress reform movement proclaimed an opposition that was repeated in the architectural literature between decoration and function.

While this is common to both genres, there are also specific associations within the field of clothing. Decoration in dress is associated by the reformers with the phenomenon of fashion, and this in turn with superficiality and with women. These associations formed part of a larger logic by which rationalism as the civilizing tendency is seen as a robust male endeavour that needs to overcome a whole series of what in contrast are seen as primitive and superficial tendencies. Indeed in its more extreme forms, colour and print become associated not only with a kind of non-civilized and irrational world, as illustrated in naïve or primitivist art assumed to be analogous with the pre-modern, but also with the dangerous, the uncontrolled, the images of the drugged and the bestial (also in Batchelor 2000). Women are seen as the conservative force retaining a less civilized and superficial fascination with colour and the decorative.

So the key modern thinkers and writers within modernism such as Loos, Gropius and Le Corbusier all claim function as precisely that which fashion is not. Function is deep and universal and impervious to the frippery of the decorative 'the Modern movement is the architectural equivalent of the masculine resistance to fashion' (Wigley 1995: 119). So both by direct influence and by analogy modernism is seen as the nineteenth-century dress reform movement applied to architecture. It was the modern movement as applied to architecture that consolidated a certain minimalist aesthetic, an aethhetic whose emphasis upon white, black and appearance reduced to its basic elements seemed to speak to this functionalism; an aesthetic which seemed to promise a means by which to escape the transience and vulgarity of mere fashion.

How then does this apply today? Well so far from being explained by this account, in some ways the little black dress seems to be an ironic mockery of the pretensions of modernism. The greatest fear of the modernists would be that their ideals would themselves be turned into mere fashion. Yet today the minimalism associated with modernism no longer retains its connotations of science, universalism and rationality, rather it has become almost entirely identified with style. As Wigley points out, the modernists were simply unable to see that white walls are also a form of decoration, that architecture is also dress, is always also the production of surfaces (Wigley 1995: 362). The little black dress, though not white, certainly does exploit the stylistic cool of modernism. But it does so unashamedly as surface, as fashion and as female, in complete repudiation of the now failed quest for scientific modernism. Unlike the arguments from historical precedents such as Harvey, we can acknowledge a considerable direct impact of modernism on the instance of colour leaching that is the subject of this paper. The success of the modern movement through the twentieth century has surely considerably impacted upon the acceptability of the little black dress as stylish. The sense of Italian cool that may have helped in the vanguard of these developments was one of a number of variants of the modern movement's impact upon popular culture.

So we need to tease out here a complex effect; accepting that modern leached clothing is experienced as stylish partly through the influence of modernism in general, but at the same time clearly distancing ourselves from some of the possible correlates of this trajectory. What we have is clearly modernism in its aspect as style and fashion and not at all an expression of the values of the modernist theorists, such as rationality and utility. Furthermore we have to be careful of the dating here. The modernist movement was established as an architectural style from the 1920s. In furnishing, for example, we see a rapid manifestation of these ideals in the kind of chrome and glass functional look that remains largely unchanged as the style of 'modern' furniture in the high street today. When we turn to clothing, by contrast, we can see a whole series of changes and shifts over the last eighty years, all of which had modernism available in the background. So it is not at all clear why the specific changes that are the subject of this chapter, that is developments in the last thirty years, which were preceded by a riot of colour and decorative form in clothing, should have occurred at this particular time. There is nothing in the links to modernism that account for it. So with modernism we have a relevant background applied in an almost ironic and unexpected manner, but one that does little to explain the specific questions posed by this paper.

Interrogating the Final Suspect – the Ethnography of Consumption

It was important to interrogate these earlier suspects because it was otherwise quite plausible that what we see today should best be understood as the outcome of certain deep historical transformations, the expression of some clear set of values, or simply an outcome of the interests of industry. But what if none of these suspects seem sufficiently guilty? If they all have alibis that suggest they are largely, though perhaps not completely, innocent, then we need instead to focus upon the phenomenon itself. Instead of looking elsewhere, we need to encounter the phenomenon directly and see if this encounter provides insights that can be the foundation for a more satisfactory explanation. As is commonly the case if we want to understand some aspect of contemporary consumption, it is that activity itself we need to explore. Most of my own work on consumption has been centred upon this larger argument for the benefits of an ethnographic approach to the topic

In a recent article in the journal *Fashion Theory* (Clarke and Miller 2002), Alison Clarke and myself presented some findings based on an ethnography that we carried out in North London during 1994–5. The fieldwork was conducted for a year mainly around a single street (called here Jay Road) in North London (for the setting see Miller 1998, 2001; Clarke 2000, 2001). The research methodologies included participant observation relating to both formal shopping (Miller) and informal provisioning (Clarke) and supplementary interviews. In this more recent paper we focused upon the specific topic of shopping for clothes. We argued that the starting point for accounting for contemporary clothing seemed to be an experience common to most of those we worked with, which was a considerable anxiety with regard to selecting them; best expressed by the image of a woman confronting a well-stocked wardrobe before getting dressed, with a despairing sense of 'not having a thing to wear'.

One of the extended examples presented in Clarke and Miller 2002 was a woman – Charmaigne – who sets out to buy a floral dress, in a deliberate attempt to expand out of her conventional wardrobe and to try and associate herself with this other genre of clothing. By following her around the shops we can actually watch her increasing anxiety when it comes to making a choice that will lead to her expressing a more distinct sartorial identity in public outside the arena of what are experienced now as simple and safe minor variants upon the core of printless and colourless clothing. What emerges from cases such as this is that there remains a considerable desire to wear different colours and prints, and yet at the moment of purchase women seemed unable to bring themselves to fulfil their own desires. The general anxiety about what to wear increases to the degree to which the clothing appears at all distinctive and thereby unconfirmed by all the other clothing being worn by one's peers or even the strangers that form the crowd.

So the paper starts by presenting the ethnographic evidence for this state of a pervasive anxiety with regard to selecting clothing and the conclusion that the more women departed from this core safety net of jeans and black clothing the more anxiety and lack of confidence emerged. Secondly, the paper followed through the various forms of support that women find in order to give themselves confidence in making their particular selections of clothing. These start from intimate family support such as the opinions of sisters or within mother-daughter relations, and extend to taking a friend shopping and getting advice from peers. The ethnography suggested that where these were not available or sufficient, women might turn to the development of semi-institutional support, such as catalogues and companies. An extended illustration is given of the reliance upon one such company 'Colour Me Beautiful' (see also Grove-White 2001), which claims to have developed a kind of science of colour that tells an individual which colours it is appropriate for them to wear and how to construct a wardrobe based around mixing and matching these specific colours and not others.

So based on an ethnographic encounter we come to a perhaps not terribly surprising result, that the increasing emphasis upon black, grey and plain unadorned clothing at the expense of colourful, decorated or printed fabrics is based on considerable anxiety about making any kind of fashion statement that strays too far out of what have become conventionally accepted norms. Red seems the only colour 'robust' enough to survive this decline since other colours leach or bleach to form either dark versions such as brown or grey that shades off into black, or pastels that shade off into white. But in a way this tells us more about how these changes have come about than why. Finding anxiety at the root of this refusal to be distinctive does not tell us anything about why women are so anxious, and why this might be more the case now, than say thirty years ago.

For this reason the conclusion to that paper turns to a much more general trend that may properly constitute an explanation of the phenomenon. We argue that what we have uncovered is the combination of two forces; one long-term and one short term. The long-term trend could be identified, not so much with modernism, as with modernity. The condition of modernity as analysed by Habermas (1987) is one in which we become decreasingly convinced by the authority of institutions and rules that previously determined how we should act. We can no longer say simply that this is our 'custom' or our 'religion'. Instead we have to face up to the degree to which we are making up our own moral rules. We become, as individuals, increasingly burdened with the task of creating normativity for ourselves. This is even more difficult given our increasing self-awareness, that this is what we are engaged in. All this pressure to create our own normativity in turn produces a tremendous desire for self-reassurance (for details of this argument see Miller 1994: 58–81).

In other words, where we can no longer rely on conventions to tell us what to do, and have to decide this for ourselves, we turn increasingly to each other for reassurance and support that we are making the right choices. The more these choices are important to us, the more we seek this support. Parents, for example, can be seen to spend a considerable amount of their time and energy trying to find out what other parents do in similar circumstances to themselves, and therefore to see if their actions as parents are typical. They may then decide to do something different, but it is almost always with reference to a norm that they have established exists. In some countries such as Norway this is particularly clear, as in Gullestad's (2001) ethnography of this activity. In other countries where social appropriation of previous moral forces such as religion are less evident, there is a more individual quest for support over choices to be made, often using commercial sources such as magazines and media representation to shore up one's individual decision making in the absence of sufficient social networks.

With respect to the recent world of fashion and clothing, we can see all these general trends and their consequences exemplified in microcosm. The last three decades have seen a clear decline in what had become the traditional form of fashion authority that is an authoritative claim as to what fashion is, for a given year, in terms of lengths of skirts or colours of the season. This went together with a democratizing of individuals' relationship to fashion and greater freedom to create particular niches by the population of consumers rather than merely the industry; a trend manifested in punk and other subcultural movements. This has coincided for women with the period in which feminism has become gradually accepted as a movement by which women feel entitled to reflect upon and reject assumed authority, particularly male authority, as a determinant of who they should be and what they should do. Feminism asserts the right to determine for oneself the choices to be made about one's life as an individual woman.

These more recent struggles for freedom and emancipation are very much in the tradition of the whole modern movement as a child of the Enlightenment which has had at its core the constant struggle for emancipation from customary authority and an assertion of the rights of the individual as found in liberal philosophy. As is commonly the case, however, such positive movements tend to have unexpected and unintended consequences and in this case the more recent freedoms of the feminist movement exacerbate the effects of longer struggles which can be characterized as the condition of modernity. This brings us back to Habermas's point about the increasing dependence upon ourselves to make up the criterion by which we live and the burden of this freedom in increasing anxiety about whether we are doing this right, given the loosening of previous forms of authority that we relied upon to take such decisions for us.

So the evidence accumulated from the ethnography when appraised in the light of certain theoretical and philosophical writings lead us to what is taken to be the final suspect and indeed the culprit behind the particular crime that is being solved. Surprisingly, the culprit is the possibility and experience of freedom. For older women it was particularly the 1970s to 1990s that brought a new consciousness of freedom with feminism's assault on traditional ideas of femininity and gender roles. As one might expect, this new freedom that feminism created about who you want to be inevitably brought with it a huge increase in that particular form of modernist anxiety, of just not knowing who you want to be.

This is why the shoppers are less and less confident about making a clear choice. They want to buy something strong and bright, but they just can't bring themselves to do it. We live not in a risk society, but in what we might better call the no-risk society. What we do is pretend that choosing shades of grey is more subtle and sophisticated – an intelligent choice. We say to each other we are all very cool and sophisticated. But of course this is nonsense. We would much rather be making bold choices, but (speaking now as a man) we just don't have the balls actually to do so, because of the burden of freedom; because we are defensive about being held responsible for the sartorial statement we have thereby made. We simply have no way of knowing if this was actually the right choice. We can only hope for social or institutional support, or otherwise rely upon conventionality itself. This is not really a moral issue, it is the corollary of a necessary contradiction. You cannot have democratic liberty and equality without a concomitant sense of anxiety that is the precise result of that experience of freedom. It is above all the emancipation that was achieved through feminism that has left women with this huge burden of freedom and this further accentuation of much older fears and concerns over social embarrassment. But if the alternative is a return to those older forms of authority – of the constraints of officially sanctioned sartorial codes, and an unwarranted respect for the voice of industry elites about what fashion 'is' – then it may well seem that an anxiety that requires still more shops to be visited before making a choice, or that makes a full wardrobe appear to have 'nothing in it', may, on reflection, be a price worth paying. Contrary to the expectations of the 1960s and 1970s we have excavated a logic which explains why a free world is likely to be a drab world.

Conclusion

What conclusions does this case-study of the anthropologist as detective have for contemporary studies of consumption more generally? The various candidates that were put forward as possible 'villains' in the line-up from which, as fashion victim, I have tried to identify the culprit, could be also described as a round up of 'the usual suspects'. In most examples of contemporary consumption they are likely to make their appearance in similar identification parades. While capitalism was relatively innocent on this occasion there are countless other crimes of causation in which it stands properly convicted. History is another hardened criminal properly held responsible for all sorts of contemporary practices. In recent times, modernism has become almost the archetypical villain, accused of a whole battery of crimes, many of which I suspect it is innocent of, so perhaps we are not surprised to see its association with black today as somewhat natural. Other disciplines such as psychology and consumer behaviour studies have their own 'police files' of common culprits.

The argument of this chapter is that, while becoming more common, a particular method of investigation is still not nearly as routine as one might expect, given that it is often invoked as important. One of the most effective means of rounding up suspects accused of crimes of consumption is surely that of ethnography. It is rather more time-consuming and difficult than taking culprits that are already well documented from previous convictions. Of course we might have located 'freedom' lurking in the background somewhere without resource to this particular methodology, but somehow, I think it is much more likely that clues will emerge that will set us on the right trail when we are prepared to walk the streets looking for them. Of course, whichever criminal we finger will have had accomplices. The ethnographic evidence needs to be considered in the light of other contributions. Commerce has some influence, the history of black in fashion with respect to mourning and modernity may still have some bearing on the case. The more specific and recent history traced by Edelman (1998) and others with regard to the factors that made black appear mature, chic, serious and seductive are still more relevant. But while the original move to black from the 1920s to 1950s may have been a repudiation of the 'merely pretty' there are other factors behind the popularity of grey and black in our new century that cannot be understood from past and precedent, but only through direct encounter.

In this case, the main evidence came from direct confrontation with forms of anxiety that needed to be accounted for first – and are simply not the same anxieties that were prominent prior to modern feminism – before the larger questions could be answered. This is often the best way to proceed. If we want to understand the major trends in consumption, it often won't be from the easy and obvious suspects. Mostly it won't be from studying commerce, or modernism, or some force that determines what we buy. The understanding of consumption will come from the experiences of the population and the kind of generalizations that social science can make about those experiences and what underlies them. We can only understand consumers through coming to see the world from their point of view as a social body. Surely we have seen enough movies to know that good detectives cannot just work from an office – we have to hit the street.

References

Arnold, R. (2001) *Fashion, Desire and Anxiety: image and morality in the twentieth century.* London: I.B. Tauris.

Bachelor, D. (2000) *Chromophobia.* London: Reaktion.

Banerjee, M. and Miller, D. (2003) (in press) *The Sari.* Oxford: Berg.

Barthes, R. (1985) *The Fashion System.* London: Cape.

Clarke, A. (2000) 'Mother Swapping: the Trafficking of Second Hand Baby Wear in North London' in Jackson, P. Lowe, M. Miller, D. and Mort, F. (eds), *Commercial Cultures: Economies, Practices, Spaces* Berg: Oxford.

— (2001) 'The Aesthetics of Social Aspiration' in Miller, D. (ed.), *Home Possessions: Material Culture and the Home.* Oxford: Berg.

— and Miller, D. (2002) 'Fashion and Anxiety', *Fashion Theory* 6: 191–213.

Edelman, A. (1998) *The Little Black Dress.* London: Aurum Press.

Fine, B. and Leopold, E. (1993) *The World of Consumption.* London: Routledge.

Flugel, J (1976) *The Pyschology of Clothes.* New York: AMS Press.

Grove-White, A. (2001) 'No rules, only choices? Repositioning the self within the fashion system: a case study of colour and image consultancy', *Journal of Material Culture* 6: 193–211.

Gullestad, M. (2001) (first edition 1984) *Kitchen-Table Society.* Oslo: Universitetsforlaget.

Habermas, J. (1987) *The Philosophical Discourse of Modernity.* Cambridge MA: MIT Press.

Harvey, J. (1995) *Men in Black.* London: Reaktion.

Ludot, D. (2001) *Little Black Dress: vintage treasure.* Paris: Assouline Press.

Mendes, V. (1999) *Black in Fashion.* London: V&A Publications.

Miller, D. (1994) *Modernity: an Ethnographic Approach.* Oxford: Berg.

— (1998) *A Theory of Shopping,* Cambridge: Polity/Cornell: Cornell University Press.

— (2001) *The Dialectics of Shopping.* Chicago: Chicago University Press.

Rath, J. (2002) *Unravelling the Rag Trade.* Oxford: Berg.

Sahlins, M. (1976) *Culture and Practical Reason.* Chicago: University of Chicago Press.

Steele, V. (2001) *The Red Dress.* New York: Rizzoli.

Van Straten, M. (2001) *The Little Black Dress Diet.* London: Kyle Cathie.

White, N and Griffiths, I Eds (2000) *The Fashion Business: theory, practice, image.* Oxford: Berg.

Wigley, M. (1995) *White Walls, Designer Dresses: the fashioning of modern architecture.* Cambridge, MA: MIT Press.

7

Making Up People:
Consumption as a Symbolic Vocabulary for the Construction of Identity

Richard Elliott

Introduction

Within sociology and cultural studies there is a widely held assumption that identity is a social construction and that the development of individual self-identity is inseparable from the parallel development of collective social identity. This problematic relationship has been described as the 'internal-external dialectic of identification' by Jenkins (1996), who maintains that self-identity must be validated through social interaction and that the self is embedded in social practices. Endeavours to create the consumer's self-identity often involve the consumption of products, services and media; and there is always a tension between the meanings we construct for ourselves and those we are exposed to socially, and this dialectical tension requires active negotiation of meaning. Although McCracken (1988) suggests that ritual is the prime means for the transfer of symbolic meaning from goods to the person, the complex social practices of consumer culture extend far beyond the concept of the ritualistic, and entail a reciprocal, dialectical relationship between the individual and her/his cultural milieu. This chapter explores this tension and builds a synthetic model of consumption as a symbolic vocabulary and resource for identity construction and maintenance through 'communities of practice'.

Self and Identity in Consumer Research

Many of the conceptualizations of self and identity used in consumer research are psychological in their ontology and epistemology and individual in their methodology. Identity is often conceptualized as a cognitive construct accessed through structured questionnaires. For example, Kleine et al.'s Social Identity model of mundane consumption (see Kleine, Kleine & Kernan 1993; Laverie, Kleine & Kleine 2002) treats identity as a stable set of self-definitions that can be accessed through self-completion questionnaires, the social aspect being derived from symbolic interactionism and operationalized as the extent (number) of a person's interpersonal relationships. For Aaker (1999) the self-concept is a set of relatively stable self-conceptions or self-schemata which can also be accessed via self-completion questionnaires, the social aspect here being addressed by experimental subjects 'imagining' themselves being in a social situation. Interpretative approaches to identity have typically used phenomeno-logical interviews (e.g. Thompson & Haytko 1997) or narrative interviews (e.g. Holt 2002) together with attempts at abstraction from the micro to the macro level via such approaches as Burawoy's extended case method (Burawoy 1998).

Identity Is Not Just Cognitive and Narrative

The focus on language has lead to what Gergen (1999: 85) calls 'linguistic reduc-tionism' where concentration on the foreground of discourse has blurred the significance of the background, the 'non-verbal signals – facial expression, gaze, gestures, posture'. Language as social action includes all our gestures, dress, bodily markings and personal possessions. Goffman's (1969) dramaturgical metaphor for identity points to the need for identity to be performed, and that bodily gestures are part of how we communicate identity. Performances always implicate an audience: 'When an individual plays a part he implicitly asks his observers to take seriously the impression that is fostered before them' (17) and there are different levels of skill in that performance. Thus we can be good or bad at communicating our identity, for example, where having the right clothes doesn't convince the audience. Shortly after the Berlin Wall fell in 1989, classes were being advertised for 'Ossies' (East Berliners) to learn the skills of looking like a West Berliner. The emphasis being on not just buying Western clothes but in learning the skill of wearing them.

Recent social and cultural theory has paid much attention to the 'aestheticiza-tion of social life', this is because it is widely assumed that the techniques involved in the performance of self-identity concern aesthetic or cultural prac-tices and that these performative aspects of the self increasingly constitute cultural resources (Adkins and Lury: 1999). Featherstone (1991: 187) maintains that within consumer culture a new conception of self has emerged: 'The Performing Self' which places greater emphasis on 'appearance, display and the management of impressions'.

The Embodied Self

This leads us to the concept of style, a combination of dress and the way in which it is worn, where the body has become the site for identity (Entwistle 2000).

Studies of youth subculture have shown the importance of the body in defining membership of a group and communicating it both within and outside the group. Brake (1985) suggests that style – composed of possessions, postural expressions, and argot and its delivery – communicates the degree of commitment to the group and opposition to the dominant cultural values. Hebdige (1979) describes how the 'cool' body style of the Mods distanced them from their lower-class environment of high-rise flats and low-status jobs. Similarly, Willis (1975) describes how the identity of 'hard' masculinity sought after by motorbike Rockers was articulated not just by the display of tough leather clothes but by a body posture of 'toughness'. Thus subcultures produce their own particular social practices 'which are in part bodily orientations or ways of moving, walking and talking which are worn like a second skin on the body of the skinhead, punk, raver' (Entwistle 2000: 138). Thornton (1995) draws attention to the importance of 'authenticity' in the performance of identity in what she calls 'taste cultures', where people can develop 'subcultural capital' through authentic displays of 'cool'. The vital role played by authentic performance was identified in Nancarrow, Nancarrow and Page's (2002) study of 'style leaders' which drew on Pountain and Robins' (2000) analysis of cool as requiring the bodily expression of 'ironic detachment'.

Although there has recently been a renewed interest in the role of the embodied self in the sociology of consumption this has rarely been supported by empirical data (Goulding, Shankar & Elliott 2002). Ironically, one of the few works which connects what people actually do with their bodies with cultural theory is Mauss (1979) who more than half a century ago showed that even the fundamental act of walking was influenced by nationality, gender and age. However, the individuals in the Goulding et al. study of rave/dance culture in the UK demonstrate consciousness and agency in relation to their utilization of the body to structure and communicate self-identity in their consumption of popular culture.

Identity is Socially Constructed and Socially Maintained

The investigation of identity in consumer research has usually been based at the individual level. Although it is often argued that micro-level data can provide macro-level insights, the construction of identity at the social level has rarely been studied. What has been studied extensively are discourses of identity, where the medium of both data and interpretation is language. Pujol and Montenegro (1999: 84) refer to the 'naturalization' of discourse as an object of research and point out that 'trying to study the social world with language as its only metaphor' ignores the need for extra-discursive concepts, particularly the influence of the social and of material objects. As Bhaskar (1989: 4) maintains, 'social practices ... are not exhausted by their conceptual aspect. They always have a material dimension.'

A profoundly social approach to identity is to conceive of identity as situated social practices: 'who we are lies in the way we live day to day, not just in what we think or say about ourselves' Wenger (1998: 151). Locating identity within 'communities of practice' integrates the self with the social and the material and identifies the emergence of a repertoire of resources for the negotiation of meaning.

A Situated Social Action Perspective on Identity

The following outline of the theory of 'communities of practice' is adapted from Wenger (1998). A community of practice is defined by two key dimensions: mutual engagement and shared repertoires. A community of practice is not a synonym for a group, a team or a network. Membership is not just a matter of social categorization, declared allegiance or personal relations. A community of practice is not defined merely by communication through a network of interpersonal relations. Membership is a matter of mutual engagement, which requires a group of people who are engaged in actions whose meaning they negotiate with one another. Membership requires the work of 'community maintenance' because it is a kind of community that does not entail simple homogeneity. Rather, it encompasses both diversity and homogeneity as members find a unique place and gain a unique identity. These identities become interlocked and articulated through mutual engagement, but they do not fuse into one. It is the practice of meaning negotiation necessary for mutual engagement which constitutes the community. This definition has similarities with Cova's (2003) analysis of consumption tribes, where he argues that a neo-tribe involves 'shared experience, the same emotion, a common passion'. But the tribe is characterized by a 'volatility of belonging' which means that homogeneity of behaviour and formal rules are eschewed.

Over time, maintaining community coherence involves the development of a shared repertoire. The shared repertoire of a community of practice includes words, ways of doing things, stories, gestures, symbols, actions or concepts that the community has produced or adopted in the course of its existence. It includes both the discourse of members as they make sense of the world as well as the styles by which by which they express their forms of membership and their identities as members. Thus communities of practice would include the 'style communities' and subcultures discussed above, and also accords with Cova (2003): 'Belonging to a tribe is not the result of individual characteristics, but the result of a common experience of reality.'

Trajectories of Identity

Displays of social competence in a particular community of practice become reified into language labels we use ourselves, and the experience of being labelled is the experience of being the situated self. So identity is not an object but a constant process, as we travel along trajectories of identity as we move between a variety of social communities with multi-membership across family, work and culture. As we go through a succession of forms of participation, our identities form trajectories both within and across communities of practice. Trajectories have a coherence through time that connects the past, the present and the future and so they are fundamentally temporal. Because it is constructed in social contexts the temporality of identity is more complex than a linear notion of time, not a foreseeable path but a continuous motion as we are constantly negotiating our identity through social practices.

Identity as Multi-membership of Communities of Practice

We all belong to many communities of practice, some past, some current, some as full members, some in more peripheral ways. Some communities may be central to our identity and some more peripheral. Whatever their nature, all forms of participation through practice contribute to the production of our identities. I am a father, a husband, a son, a manager, a colleague, an Englishman. Some of the trajectories are inbound, some outbound and some peripheral but all are constituted by displays of competence in the social practices in each community. In particular, the work of reconciliation necessary to maintain our identity across boundaries gives rise to a profoundly social form of identity work. Through the negotiation and maintenance of social competencies across boundaries we build a cohesive person who can engage in different practices in each of the communities to which we belong, yet resist the tensions of fragmentation of the self described in contemporary social theory (e.g. Giddens 1991).

Structural and Positional Sources of the Self

Consumption as a social practice is a dynamic and relatively autonomous process which involves the symbolic construction of a sense of self through the accumulation of cultural and symbolic capital. However, to paraphrase Marx: although we make our own history, we do not do so in circumstances of our own choosing. Symbolic freedom is severely constrained by social structure and by ideological limits to that which we are able to imagine. Discourse is socially determined through relationships of power extending through class and society.

Language can be viewed as both reflecting reality and constituting reality in a dialectic dynamic. This entails the assumption that the self is produced across a range of discursive practices where meaning is a constant site of struggles for power (Weeden 1987). Although individuals 'imagine' that they are the authors of their discourse and in control of its meaning (Weeden 1987), discourse is largely socially and ideologically constructed. However, the social practices of discourse are in a dialectical relationship with social institutions and although individuals are constrained by their position in orders of discourse, they are also enabled to act creatively within the discursive frame (Fairclough 1989). Social practices draw upon discourse types but do not mechanically reproduce them, so there is a gap between objective social space and representations of that space, which become 'a site for symbolic struggles that transform the real by renaming it' (Collins 1993). In their social practices individuals are faced with 'ideological dilemmas' as to how to categorize information into the multiplicity of alternative schemas they possess (Billig, Condor, Edwards, Gane, Middleton & Radley 1988). This indeterminacy of meaning and relative freedom of the individual to escape from 'regimes of truth' has been related to consumption through Bourdieu's theory of social practice as 'necessary improvization' in symbolic fields (including consumption) (Bourdieu 1977).

While the individual brings his or her own subjective repertoire to a particular interpretative act, it is a repertoire shaped in 'particular social-historical contexts' (Thompson 1990). The social nature of interpretation 'delimits' the heteroglossic potential of a reading in much the same way as open and closed texts exercise a degree of limitation on a polysemic text. The readers' connection to their 'social position' ensures that their subjective interpretation will often match or correspond with other readers' interpretations of the same text, and thus 'interpretative communities' are formed.

Lived and Mediated Symbolic Resources

The symbolic resources available to the individual for the construction of the self can be distinguished as being either lived experiences or mediated experiences (Thompson 1990; Gadamer 1989). Lived experience refers to the practical activities and face-to-face encounters in our everyday lives. It is situated, immediate, and is largely non-reflexive, in that we take it for granted as 'reality'. Mediated experience is an outcome of a mass-communication culture and the consumption of media products and involves the ability to experience events which are spatially and temporally distant from the practical context of daily life. It is recontextualized experience, in that it allows the experience of events that transpire far away, and will vary widely in its relevance to the self.

The individual can draw selectively on mediated experience and interlace it with lived experience to construct the self. The life history and social situation of individuals will lead to differential valorization of forms of experience, varying between those at one end of the continuum who value only lived experience and have little contact with mediated forms, and others at the opposite end of the continuum for whom mediated experience has become central to the project of the self. However, central to the postmodern condition is a growing range of opportunities for the use of mediated experiences in the project of the self, countless narratives of self-formation, countless visions of the world such that we may be encountering 'symbolic overload'. However, 'for most individuals, as they move along the time-space paths of their daily lives, lived experience continues to exert a powerful influence on the project of self-formation' (Thompson 1995: 233).

The Role of Ritual

Ritual can be seen as a means of 'locking in' meaning through repetition of embodied performances and as such valorizes lived experience against the mediated symbolic overload of consumer culture. For Lévi-Strauss (1977) the value of ritual resides primarily in physical action (a paralanguage) and secular ritual is often an arena of contradictory and contestable perspectives where individuals 'make it up as they go along' (Gerholm 1988). I wish to emphasize here the personal level of ritual (Rook 1985) where social symbolism via public performance may be absent, and the form of ritualized behaviour which may be enacted in private (Tetreault & Kleine 1990). For example, daily grooming rituals can have 'mystico-spiritual qualities' where individuals who reject romantic and magical effects in other realms of life 'appear quite able to suspend their disbelief and fantasize about magical lotions, elixirs, and other forms of social war paint' (Rook & Levy 1983: 331). Thus even low-level repetitive consumption behaviour enacted in private has the potential to play an important role in the construction and maintenance of the self.

Consumption as a Symbolic Vocabulary

In this perspective, consumption is but one element of identity practice, but it is a rich resource for social action and shared interpretations. An explosion of consumption choices threatens current identity trajectories and necessitates the development of new social competencies as a member of new communities of practice. Consumption of the symbolic meaning of goods plays a central role in supplying meanings and values for the performance of social practices (Elliott & Wattanasuwan 1998) and advertising is recognized as one of the major sources of these symbolic meanings. These cultural meanings are transferred to brands and it is brands which are often used as symbolic resources for the construction and maintenance of identity (McCracken, 1987; Mick & Buhl 1992). However, a wider definition of consumption practices implicates popular culture as a major source of meaning, for example, the consumption of TV programmes has been identified as helping consumers learn how to perform the social practices of drinking coffee (Hirschman, Scott & Wells 1998). Meanings also emerge in the interpersonal communication among consumers and may later become socially shared meaning: 'Shared meanings involving media content will arise among participants in the social action performances of reception and subsequent accommodation' (Anderson & Meyer 1988: 47).

The rich symbolic vocabulary used in advertising is a prime resource for identity construction and maintenance. Ritson and Elliott (1999) describe the important role of advertising in providing verbal and behavioural resources that are used by young people in the expression of the self, as a source of metaphoric meaning, in the maintenance of group membership and the development of new rituals. But this vocabulary is not a one-way meaning transfer. The meaning of a particular advertisement is not given within the advertisement itself, for as Anderson and Meyer (1988) point out: 'meaning is not delivered in the communication process, rather it is constructed within it.' But the meaning that consumers construct from advertising is viscous in nature, and signification through the media is likely to be much less potent than signification through actual behavioural experience (Elliott, Eccles & Hodgson 1993). Certainly, there is considerable empirical evidence that attitudes formed through direct experience are stronger, more accessible, held more confidently and are more predictive of behaviour than those derived from mediated experience through advertising (e.g. Fazio & Zanna 1978; Smith & Swinyard 1988). Thus lived experience with a brand, through purchase and usage over the life cycle, will tend to dominate the mediated experience of advertising, and both forms of experience will be validated through social interaction.

Narrative identity theory (Ricoeur 1984, 1992) suggests that in order to make time human and socially shared, we require a narrative identity for our self, that is, we make sense of ourselves and our lives by the stories we can (or cannot) tell. Thus we come to know ourselves by the narratives we construct to situate ourselves in time and place. This task can be greatly aided by symbolic resources, the main one articulated by Ricoeur (1977) is literature which gives structure and meaning to the complexity and confusion of life by providing a causal model for the individual by linking disparate life events into a coherent sequence. However, advertising can also be used as a symbolic resource for the construction of narratives to give sense to our life history and personal situation: the soap opera is still a mainstay of advertising executions which situates the brand and the consumer in a powerful representation of narrative sequence.

Consumption Practices and Identity

We can model the tension between our ability to construct identities through social practices, drawing partly on resources from consumption, and the limitations on our freedom to escape our material history and social position. While we can learn ways of being and develop social competencies across our various communities of practice, our ability to escape the structures of culture is limited. Thus the self in action as we travel on trajectories of identity is constantly being developed and re-developed as we make consumption choices and perform consumption practices, always within historical constraints.

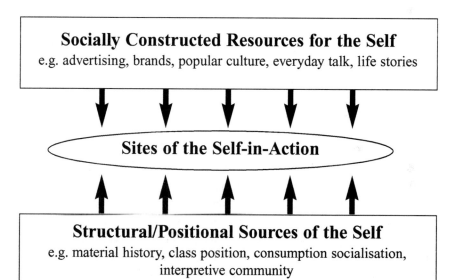

Figure 7.1 Consumption Practices and Identity

Some Methodological Issues Arising From A Social Action Perspective

We can now explore the implications for consumer research of this approach to identity as a situated social practice. As the self is constructed and maintained along trajectories of identity across various communities of practice, meaning is always in contest, contradictory and under negotiation. As meaning is negotiated between self-identity and social identities, between embodied performance and cognitive elaboration, between reason and emotion, between mediated and lived experience, between language and materiality, so we can expect that it is not a simple matter to study these phenomena. Two key issues are the extent to which people are able to report fully and accurately on their behaviour: the 'limitations of asking' (Mariampolski 1999) and the problem that 'people don't always do what they say', (Fellman, 1999). The limitations of asking are illustrated by a recent meta-analysis of 100 survey studies comparing how well data on purchase intentions actually predicted subsequent sales, which concluded that 'people are generally not reliable predictors of their own long-term purchasing behaviour for any type of good' (Ovans 1998).

The distance between saying and doing is illustrated by a study of the consumption practices of a group of very religious Buddhist teenagers in Thailand (Wattanasuwan & Elliott 1999). It became clear that their actual behaviour was in stark contradiction with their expressed beliefs and descriptions of their actions. When discussing their belief systems in group discussions and individual interviews they were adamant in their contemptuous rejection of brands and other manifestations of consumer culture. Yet when accompanied on shopping trips the teenagers dropped their anti-materialist values when they saw famous brands on sale and went ahead and made purchases with apparent glee.

Quasi-Ethnography

A step towards tackling these issues is the use of quasi-ethnographic methods which utilize a wide range of different approaches to the study of contextualized consumption practices (Elliott & Jankel-Elliott 2003). Extending beyond the conventional ethnography of participant and non-participant observation, quasi-ethnography uses anything that can get us closer to people's lived reality. For example, in a study of the mobile consumer, we gave the individual and one member of their family a dictaphone and a credit-card-sized prompt to carry around for a week responding to questions regarding feelings, consumption and unmet needs as they perceived them within various contexts. This method was particularly important for accessing thoughts and emotions 'on the move' as pilot work made it clear that people could not remember what they did let alone how they felt about it.

In studying the concept of 'flow' in addictive consumption, as well as accompanied shopping and other traditional approaches, Eccles and Elliott (1995) used an experience-sampling method which entailed informants recording their current mood into dictaphones at predetermined times of the day. Now with the availability of text messaging this approach is being updated and promises to yield new insights into emotion and lived experience.

The availability of low-cost digital video-recording technology has made it feasible to issue informants with a digital camera and ask them to record episodes from their life without the presence of the researcher. In a study of the dynamics of symbolic brand communities and their consumption of fashion brands, we were interested in authentic and inauthentic identity performance and asked our informants to keep a video-diary where they recalled instances of when they observed people who 'got it right or just got it wrong' (Elliott & Davies 2003).

Cooperative Inquiry

A further step towards dealing with the complexities of human life is the use of cooperative inquiry (Reason 1994; Heron 1996). This approach takes seriously the humanistic idea that human beings are self-reflexive agents who can contribute fully to a research project, ideally at all stages. This involves recruiting an 'inquiry group' which will work as a team with the researcher to investigate a particular issue. For example, in order to study the role of personal conversations in the development of trust in brands, Edwards, Davies and Elliott (2002) recruited a team of friendship-pairs who recorded their everyday talk and reflected on the role of brands in maintaining their friendships over time. This allowed the researchers to access 'naturally occurring speech' in a personal context, a task that had presented an extremely difficult challenge to other research methods.

Conclusion

By widening the focus of research into identity and consumption to include embodied performances, communities of practice and ritual; by recognizing the historical limitations on the social construction of reality and therefore on the self; by acknowledging the negotiated and contested nature of meaning, we problematize the study of the consumer. By adopting cooperative approaches to inquiry along with a wide range of quasi-ethnographic methods we can increase, a little, our ability to cope with the complex social practices of consumer culture.

References

Aaker, J. (1999), 'The Malleable Self: The Role of Self-Expression in Persuasion', *Journal of Marketing Research*, 36 (Feb): 45–57.
Adkins, L. and Lury, C. (1999), 'The Labour of Identity: Performing Identities, Performing Economies'. *Economy and Society*, 28(4): 598–614.
Anderson, J. and T. Meyer (1988), *Mediated Communication: A Social Action Perspective*. London: Sage.
Bhaskar, R. (1989), *Reclaiming Reality: A Critical Introduction to Contemporary Philosophy*, London: Verso.
Billig, M., Condor, S., Edwards, D., Gane, M., Middleton, D., & Radley, A.

(1988). *Ideological Dilemmas: A Social Psychology of Everyday Thinking.* London: Sage Press.

Bourdieu, Pierre (1977), *Outline of a Theory of Practice*, Cambridge: Cambridge University Press.

Brake, M. (1985), *Comparative Youth Culture*, London: Routledge and Kegan Paul.

Burawoy, M. (1998), 'The Extended Case Method', *Sociological Theory*, 16(1): 4–33.

Collins, J. (1993). 'Determination and Contradiction: An Appreciation and Critique of the Work of Pierre Bourdieu on Language and Education'. In C. Calhoun, E. LiPuma, & M. Postone (eds.), *Bourdieu: Critical Perspectives.* Cambridge: Polity Press.

Cova, B. (2003), 'Analyzing and Playing with 'Tribes Which Consume'', *Finanza, Marketing & Produzione.*

Eccles, S. & Elliott, R. (1995), 'Addictive Consumption & the Experience-Sampling Method', *Proceedings of the Marketing Education Group Annual Conference*, University of Bradford.

Edwards, H., Davies, A. and Elliott, R. (2002), 'Consumers and Their Personal Conversations: Where Brand Equity is Built', *Proceedings of The British Academy of Management Annual Conference*, London: University of Middlesex.

Elliott, R. and Davies, A. (2003), 'Symbolic Brand Communities and the Authenticity of Identity Performance.' Discussion Paper, *Centre For Consumer Research, University of Exeter.*

— and Jankel-Elliott, N. (2003) 'Using Ethnography in Strategic Con-sumer Research', *Qualitative Marketing Research: An international journal*, 5(4). 215–233.

—, Eccles, S. and Hodgson, M. (1993) 'Re-Coding Gender Representations: Women, Cleaning Products, and Advertising's "New Man"'. *International Journal of Research in Marketing*, 10: 311–24.

— and Wattanasuwan, K. (1998), 'Brands as Resources for the Symbolic Construction of Identity' *International Journal of Advertising*, 17 (2): 131–44.

Entwistle, J. (2000), *The Fashioned Body*, Cambridge: Polity Press.

Fairclough, N. (1989). *Language and Power*. London: Longman.

Fazio, R. and Zanna, M. (1978) 'On the Predictive Validity of Attitudes: The Role of Direct Experience and Confidence'. *Journal of Personality*, 46: 228–43.

Featherstone, M. (1991), 'The Body in Consumer Culture', in M. Featherstone, M. Hepworth and B. Turner (eds.), *The Body: Social Process and Cultural Theory*, London: Sage.

Fellman, M. (1999), 'Breaking Tradition', *Marketing Research*, 11(3): 20–5.

Fiske, J. (1987). *Television Culture*. London: Routledge.

Gadamer, H. (1989), Trans. J. Weinsheimer, *Truth and Method*, London: Sheed and Ward.

Gergen, K. (1999), *An Invitation to Social Constructionism*, London: Sage.

Gerholm, T. (1988), 'On Ritual: A Post-Modernist View', *Ethnos*, 3–4: 190–203.

Giddens, A. (1991) *Modernity and Self-Identity: Self and Society in the Late Modern Age*. Cambridge: Polity Press.

Goffman, E. (1969), *The Presentation of Self in Everyday Life*. London: Allen Lane.

Goulding, C., Shankar, A. and Elliott, R. (2002), 'Working Weeks, Rave Weekends: Identity Fragmentation and the Emergence of New Communities', *Consumption, Markets and Culture*, 5 (4): 261–84.

Hebdige, D. (1979), *Subculture: The Meaning of Style*, London: Methuen.

Heron, J. (1996), *Co-operative Inquiry: Research into the Human Condition*, London: Sage.

Hirschman, E., Scott, L. and Werlls, W. (1998), 'A Model of Product Discourse: Linking Consumer Practice to Cultural Texts', *Journal of Advertising*, 27(1): 33–50.

Holt, D. B. (2002) 'Why do Brands cause Trouble? A dialectical theory of consumer culture and branding', *Journal of Consumer Research*, 29(1): 70–90.

Jenkins, R. (1996) *Social Identity*. London: Routledge.

Kleine, R. E., III, S. Kleine and J. B. Kernan (1993), 'Mundane Consumption and the Self: A social identity perspective', *Journal of Consumer Psychology*, 2(3): 209–35.

Laverie, D., R.E. Kleine III and S. Kleine (2002), 'Reexamination and Extension of Kleine, Kleine and Kernan's Social Identity Model of Mundane Consumption: The Mediating Role of the Appraisal Process', *Journal of Consumer Research*, 28(4): 659–70.

Lévi-Strauss, C. (1977), *Structural Anthropology 2*, London: Allen Lane.

Mariampolski, H. (1999), 'The Power of Ethnography,' *Journal of the Market Research Society*, 4(1): 75–92.

Mauss, M. (1979), 'Body Techniques' in *Sociology and Psychology*, tr. B. Brewster, London: Routledge and Kegan Paul.

McCracken, G. (1987) 'Advertising: Meaning or Information?'. In M. Wallendorf and P. E. Anderson (eds.) *Advances in Consumer Research* XIV. Provo, UT: Association for Consumer Research.

McCracken, G. (1988) *Culture and Consumption: New Approaches to The Symbolic Character of Consumer Goods and Activities*. Bloomington: Indiana University Press.

Mick, D. G. and C. Buhl (1992) 'A Meaning-Based Model of Advertising Experiences'. *Journal of Consumer Research*, 19: 317–38.

Nancarrow, C. Nancarrow, P. and Page, J. (2002), 'An Analysis of the Concept of

Cool and its Marketing Implications', *Journal of Consumer Behaviour*, 1(4), 311–22.

Ovans, A. (1998), 'The Customer Doesn't Always Know Best', *Harvard Business Review*, May/June, 76, 3,

Pountain, D. and Robins, D. (2000), *Cool Rules: Anatomy of an Attitude*, London: Reaktion Books.

Pujol, J. and Montenegro, M. (1999), 'Discourse or Materiality? Impure Alternatives for Recurrent Debates', in D. Nightingale and J. Cromby (eds.), *Social Constructionist Psychology: A Critical Analysis of Theory and Practice*, Buckingham: Open University Press.

Reason, P. (1994), 'Three Approaches to Participative Inquiry', in N. Denzin and Y. Lincoln (eds.) *Handbook of Qualitative Research*, Thousand Oaks, CA: Sage.

Ricoeur, P. (1977) *The Rule of Metaphor: Multi-disciplinary Studies of the Creation of Meaning in Language*, tr. R. Czery, London: Routledge and Kegan Paul.

Ricoeur, P. (1984) *Time and Narrative*, Vol. 1. tr. K. McLaughlin and D. Pellar. Chicago: Chicago University Press.

Ricoeur, P. (1992) *Oneself as Another*, tr. K. Blamey. Chicago: Chicago University Press.

Ritson, M. and Elliott, R. (1999), 'The Social Uses of Advertising: An Ethnographic Study of Adolescent Advertising Audiences', *Journal of Consumer Research*, 26(3): 260–77.

Rook, D. (1985), 'The Ritual Dimension of Consumer Behaviour', *Journal of Consumer Research*, 12: 251–64.

Rook, D. and Levy, S. (1983), 'Psychosocial Themes in Consumer Grooming Rituals', *Advances in Consumer Research*, 10: 329–33.

Smith, R. and Swinyard, W. (1988), 'Cognitive Response to Advertising and Trial: Belief Strength, Belief Confidence and Product Curiosity', *Journal of Advertising*, 17(3): 3–14.

Tetreault, M. and Kleine, R. (1990), 'Ritual, Ritualized Behaviour, and Habit: Refinements and Extensions of the Consumption Ritual Construct,' *Advances in Consumer Research*, 17: 31–8.

Thompson, C. J. and D. L. Haytko (1997), 'Speaking of Fashion: Consumers' uses of fashion discourses and the appropriation of countervailing cultural meanings', *Journal of Consumer Research* 23: 15–42.

Thompson, C. J. (1990). *Ideology and Modern Culture*. Cambridge: Polity Press.

— (1995) *The Media and Modernity: A Social Theory of the Media*. Cambridge: Polity.

Thornton, S. (1995), *Club Cultures: Music, Media and Subcultural Capital*, Cambridge: Polity.

Wattanasuwan, K. and Elliott, R. (1999), 'The Buddhist Self and Symbolic

Consumption: The Consumption Experience of Teenage Dhammakaya Buddhists in Thailand,' *Advances in Consumer Research*, 26: 150–5.

Weeden, C. (1987). *Feminist Practice & Poststructuralist Theory.* Oxford: Blackwell.

Wenger, E. (1998), *Communities of Practice: Learning, Meaning, and Identity*, Cambridge: Cambridge University Press.

Willis, P. (1975), 'The Expressive Style of a Motor-Bike Culture', in J. Benthall and T. Polhemus (eds.), *The Body as a Medium of Expression*. London: Allen Lane.

8

Gender, Technology and Computer-Mediated Communications in Consumption-Related Online Communities

Pauline Maclaran, Margaret K. Hogg, Miriam Catterall and Robert V. Kozinets

Introduction

Gender is a much more elusive concept than we often realize. Whilst many people think of it as a homogeneous category, it is not.[1] Rather, it is heterogeneous, involving 'status, identity and display' (Lorber 1999: 417) and these vary across different groups of men and women. Thus gender, being derived from socialization and social context, is potentially at once multiple, fluid and context-dependent (Lorber 1999).

This chapter focuses on the intersections between gender, technology and computer-mediated communications (CMC) in consumption-related online communities and proposes a methodology that enables researchers to explore better the nuances of gender effects online. First we discuss the relationship between gender and technology, including how this impacts on communications technologies. Then we detail the many issues surrounding the study of gender in relation to CMC before going on to outline how online ethnography, termed 'netnography' by Kozinets (1997), can be combined with discourse analysis to study the ways in which gender is performed online. We draw on findings from an online consumption-related community, a digital camera discussion forum, to illustrate how the consumption of CMC may exhibit important gendered and gendering effects. Often online community consumption related topics tend to skew discourse towards particular masculine or feminine styles that reflect the gendered nature of many production and consumption practices (Auslander 1996). Within these communities a range of discursive strategies is employed that relate to a variety of gendered and gendering positions. Our chapter concludes by suggesting a research agenda for future gender research in relation to online consumption-related communities.

Gender and Technology

Early feminist work in this area focused on how technology impacted on women at home and at work. Women were often portrayed as the passive victims of technology, which was seen as embodying patriarchal and capitalist interests (Lubar 1998; Wajcman 2000). By the end of the 1980s the emphasis in technology studies and in feminism had shifted towards a less deterministic and a more social constructionist view of technology and gender. Studies that examined how technologies are developed and used emphasized how various groups of people involved with a technology (designers, users and so on) can understand and interpret it differently. Similarly, gender was increasingly conceptualized as a performance, 'gender is not fixed in advance of social interaction, but is constructed in interaction' (Wajcman 2000, p. 456). As a result, recent and current studies of the relationships between gender and technology emphasize 'a two-way mutually shaping relationship between gender and technology in which technology is both a source and consequence of gender relations and vice-versa' (Faulkner 2001: 81). Research focuses on three interlinked aspects of gender and technology relationships: structures; gender symbols; and identities (Wajcman 2000; Faulkner 2001).

In respect of structural aspects, there are strong divisions of labour around technology both in its production and consumption (Cockburn 1992; Hocks 1999). The consumption of technology can become gendered by association. For example, few household technologies are used equally by males and females. White goods, such as washing machines and those employed in routine domestic tasks are more commonly used by women and associated with femaleness. By contrast, technologies for less routine household tasks, such as power drills, and black/brown goods, such as music centres, are more commonly used by men and associated with maleness (Cockburn 1997).

By contrast there are comparatively few studies of the gender-technology production relationship. This is largely because few women are involved in the early stages of technology innovation and design, (although they are, of course, involved as production workers). Cockburn (1997) and Cockburn and Ormrod (1993) showed how unequal gender relations can shape the design and development of new technologies. Product engineers (largely male) consider housework technology to be simple and uninteresting whereas working on leisure and entertainment technology is seen as challenging state-of-the-art work (Cockburn 1997). In their pioneering study of the microwave oven, Cockburn and Ormrod (1993) showed how the product was designed by male engineers and female input to technological development was limited to the contribution of (female) home economists. The technical skills of these women were undervalued by the engineers and they exerted little influence on product development.

In addition to gender structures, gender symbolism can make a significant contribution to making technologies a male domain (Rommes, Van Osst & Oudshoorn 2001) and technologies may incorporate symbols, metaphors and values that have masculine connotations (Wajcman, 2000). According to Pacey (1983) high-tech areas such as space technologies emphasize hegemonic masculine values such as the power of humankind to control the universe, whereas low-tech areas such as household technologies developed to improve living conditions for the elderly are more likely to stress hegemonic feminine values such as care and user-friendliness. Thus, features can be designed into technologies that reflect and also reinforce gender stereotypes (Faulkner 2001). In other words, the 'symbolic' gendering of the technology can have material effects. For example, the microwave oven was originally designed as a 'brown good' for heating prepared meals and was targeted at young male users who would not wish to spend too much time preparing meals. User instructions suggested that the microwave was complex and high technology and it was sold in brown goods outlets along with video recorders and stereo systems. When the product failed to achieve expected market success, it was redesigned as a 'white good' with more extensive cooking facilities, including roasting and grilling. It was now aimed at the whole family where it was assumed that women would largely engage in meal preparation. Consequently, simpler pictograms suggested use possibilities, and it was sold alongside other white goods such as cookers and refrigerators (Cockburn & Ormrod, 1993; Oudshoorn, Saetnan & Lie 2002).

This example illustrates the problems associated with assuming production-consumption and male-female dichotomies when thinking about gender and technology relationships. The 'gender' of the microwave oven altered in terms of its targeted users, how and where it was sold and in its user instructions. In this instance designers and marketers made assumptions about the users and the meanings they would attach to the product. Similarly, the wireless (radio) crossed gender boundaries. Initially, it was aimed at male hobbyists interested in locating distant stations and advertised as scientific and modern. Whilst the radio audience was largely male, the market for radio advertising was primarily female consumers. As a result, the aesthetics of the product were improved to be more like a piece of furniture and it was promoted as a family product that could enhance domesticity and family life (Carlat 1998). However, users in interacting with the technology can reinterpret the meanings and uses ascribed it by designers and marketers (Silverstone & Hirsch 1992; Berg 1994). The early marketers of the telephone envisioned it as a business tool and, with a domestic connection, businessmen could be contacted at home. Telephone companies did not approve of women using these home telephones for frivolous reasons to chat to friends and family. Women, by contrast, identified the potential of the domestic telephone to build and maintain social networks and relationships. It took a long time for the telephone companies to realize this and charge for the duration of the call rather than the connection made (Martin 1991; Rakow 1992; Fischer 1992).

Clearly, not all technologies are ascribed male or female by producers or consumers. Faulkner (2001) points out that some technologies such as the cassette recorder are not gendered at all or have very weak associations with gender. She goes on to point out that 'plenty of women do jobs that are extremely technical, just as plenty of men are technically incompetent. In short, there are huge mismatches between the image and practice of technology with respect to gender' (86). Despite this, images of technology as male persist and male gender identities continue to be tied up with technology at work and at leisure.

Wajcman (2000: 454) noted that 'men's affinity with technology is now seen as integral to the constitution of male gender identity and the culture of technology'. Studies of professional engineers have revealed the sheer pleasure that these men obtain from working with technologies and is a key element both in their individual identities and professional culture (McIlwee & Robinson 1992; Faulkner 2001). By contrast, female engineers did not share this male obsession with technology (McIlwee & Robinson 1992). Hacker (1989) and Downey and Lucena (1995) have suggested that engineers' pleasure in technology may be compensation when other sources of job satisfaction are limited or where they feel they have relatively less power in the workplace compared with professional managers. Males who have little positional or class power may find a kind of compensatory symbolic power in technology. Referring to various studies on computer hackers, technical hobbyists and computer programmers, Faulkner (2001) quotes Edwards (1996), 'For men, to whom power is an icon of identity and an index of success, a microworld can become a challenging arena for an adult quest for power and control'.

In addition, Cockburn (1985), Wajcman (2000) and Faulkner (2001) have argued that men's absorption with technology may offer sensual and even erotic pleasures. In her study of engineering students, Hacker (1989: 49) identified the erotic possibilities and sensual pleasures that can be gained from working with and exerting control or mastery over technology, 'the discipline in a sense eroticized power relations – glory and status in pain given and taken; or pleasure withheld; the postures of superiority or dominance and submission; a fetishism with special equipment and technique'.

Much feminist writing on gender and technologies strikes a pessimistic note with regard to the difficulties of undermining and reinventing the male-technology association. By contrast, Haraway (1985, 1997) has argued that science and technology in forms such as reproductive technology and virtual reality offer the potential to rewrite gender. In the discussion that follows we focus on the already substantial and increasing body of work on gender and computer-mediated communications.

Gender and Computer-Mediated Communications

It is often assumed that the computer has no inherent gender bias (Turkle 1986). Much research on Internet communications has tended to assume a democratic communication model. In other words, it has often highlighted the potential freedom of access and social anonymity that the Internet provides (Herring 1993; Yates 1993; Landow 1993). It was hoped that this relatively anonymous text-based medium would result in a lessening of communication inequalities based on gender, race, class and other social cues. Similarly postmodern perspectives promote the abstract concept of cyberspace and identity playfulness as escape routes from the physicality of biological sex and from the concomitant social and cultural constrictions of gender. However, there is strong research evidence to demonstrate that, although the computer has no inherent gender bias, computer culture is not equally neutral (Turkle 1986) and that, as with other technologies, its discourses and practices reproduce the same unequal power relations that are embedded in our institutions and cultural processes (Hocks 1999). Online inter-action cannot be separated, therefore, from the offline social and political contexts of participants' everyday lives (Kendall 1999).

Turkle (1986) shows how women's traditional relationship with technology influences their reactions to computer culture, a culture that has been dominated by male-associated images of competition, sports, violence and pornography, aspects that she highlights as keeping women 'fearful and far away from the machine' (41). From an early age boys are socialized into the use of computers through the plethora of computer games that cater for their needs. By contrast, few computer games are designed to appeal to girls and even an innocuous, but highly popular, computer game such as *Tomb Raider* reinforces stereotypical images of women, with its central character portrayed as a sex object complete with bursting bust line (Hocks 1999).

In recent years there has been the development of some girl-orientated soft-ware although this has also received criticism on the grounds that it is based on an essentialist assumption that girls and boys have different preferences and does nothing to challenge the assumptions that underpin traditional gender dichotomies (Yates & Littleton 2001). In their research on children's reactions to computer games, Yates and Littleton (2001) emphasize the importance of social and cultural context and how these influence the reading of software. Different metaphors and representations alter possible readings in the software that children can make and, in turn, affect their performance with the software. They suggest that the preferred readings of most computer games are orientated to male subject positions and cultural competencies.

As regards the Internet, feminists such as Harvey (1997) have highlighted how its origins were in the male worlds of the military, the academy, engineering and industry and how this accounts for the lessened participation of women and other minority groups. The persistence of sexism on the Internet has been well documented (Bruckman 1993; Spender 1995). In her research on social MUDs ('multi-user domains/dimensions/dungeons' where interactive role-playing games take place), Kendall (1996) shows how such online environments may feel particularly foreign to women as they are encountering a social atmosphere with behaviour patterns formed largely by men. The women participants in her study were regularly exposed to sexual harassment in the form of sexist jokes, rude comments and bullying. Although participants in a MUD can choose their gender designation (male, female or gender-neutral), this does not change the expectations that are attached to particular gender identifications. Thus, Kendall (1996) finds that how male and female characters behave depends on wider cultural beliefs about feminine and masculine behaviours so that, even in this new fantasy environment, standard expectations of masculinity and femininity still dominate. Consequently, the attributes of female characters tend to be less valued than their male counterparts, with many fewer people electing to play female characters.

Similarly, in her study of MOOs (multi-user object-oriented worlds), White (2001) argues that MOO commands perpetuate a series of limiting identity constructs. Drawing on feminist theories of the gaze (for example, Mulvey 1986), she shows how, despite other types of character representations, overall there is a stereotypical body construction of characters that supports Mulvey's split of the gaze into active/male and passive/female. According to White (143), these descriptions 'perpetuate the dominant cinema's scripting of male subjects who control and look upon female objects'.

As previously discussed, virtual environments offer ways to go beyond a binary approach to gender. Much has been written about the potential for gender switching on the Internet, particularly in virtual social environments such as chat rooms, discussion groups and MUDS and MOOs (Rheingold 1993; Bruckman 1993; Turkle 1986) and feminists such as Plant (1997) have welcomed the liberating possibilities. For example, LambdaMoo, one of the oldest and largest MOOs, offers a choice of 10 designations: male, female, Spivak, neuter, either, splat, egotistical, plural, second and royal. Yet, in a recent study of 435 MOO users, Roberts and Parks (2001) found that only a minority engaged in gender-switching and more than half of those who did only did so for less that 10 per cent of their time online. Furthermore, 78.7 per cent of participants who switched genders kept within traditional gender binaries and made little use of other, gender-neutral categories. The biggest predictor of gender switching was the type of virtual environment, with participants in role-playing MOOs being twice as likely to gender-switch as those who participated in more socially orientated MOOs. Thus it seems that the tendency to gender-switch is context-dependent and heavily influenced by the fantasy nature of a particular site (Roberts & Parks 2001).

Chen, Davies and Elliott (2002) describe one such fantasy website, 'Raising Men For Fun,' an online dating game that reverses traditional Chinese gender relationships with women playing the role of master and men playing the role of their pet. From an in-depth qualitative study with participants, Chen et al. (2002) find that the website offers only partial liberation from traditional Chinese culture which is often used to authenticate online gender identities. Although participants established relationships in a non-traditional way to engage in types of gender play, this was short-lived and neither men nor women could sustain the reversed gender role of master or pet for long. Moreover, cases of gender deceit (i.e. a women playing a male 'pet' or a man playing a female 'master') resulted in acute anxieties for the deceitful player in terms of their relationship with their online partner which again made this deception unsustainable in the long term.

Gender, Language and Computer-Mediated Communications

Despite the potential afforded by the Internet to gender-switch and to adopt gender-neutral identity, a major reason why Internet communications often fail to mask the gender of their originator is that there are clear differences in the ways that males and females use language. Although there are different schools of thought on the reasons for such language differences (Lakoff 1990; Tannen 1984; Cameron 1997), there is general agreement on what these differences are. From a 'different languages' perspective (Jones 1999), women's speech uses more hedges and fillers (eg 'you know' and 'sort of'), tag questions (eg, 'she's very nice, isn't she?'), qualifiers and so forth (Lakoff 1975; Fishman 1983). In taking this perspective, there is the risk that women's language is seen as deficient and man's language as superior (Spender 1980). For example, it means that women's interactional style is often perceived by others, particularly men, to be uncertain and unassertive. Lakoff (1975) argues that women are socialized to speak in ways that are perceived as weak, thus reproducing the potential for their oppression within a partriarchal system.

In contrast, a 'two cultures' perspective (Jones 1999) seeks to reinstate 'women talk' (Spender 1980) as valid in its own right, seeing men's and women's speech styles as different because they have different conversational goals, the reasons for which are located in the wider sociocultural environment (Tannen 1991; Gilligan 1993). Thus, cultural differences can explain why women use conversation to connect with others (Tannen 1991) and their conversational goals are likely to be relational. They use more narrative in speech, ask more questions, encourage others to speak and give more credit to others' viewpoints. Men's conversational goals, on the other hand, are more likely to be transactional and focused on outcomes. They are likely to get to the point quickly, to interrupt and challenge, to speak more and to make more attempts to control the discussion. By way of illustrating these differences, Tannen (1991: 77) contrasts women's 'rapport-talk' with men's 'report-talk'.

Others, such as Crawford (1995), argue that both these positions polarize men's and women's behaviour and that they fail to take into account other analytical categories of difference such as race, class, age and sexual orientation. Representing male and female language as dichotomous overlooks many of the complexities that exist in everyday speech situations and there are many studies to suggest that interactional context influences the extent to which men's and women's speech can be differentiated (Swann 1989; Bem 1993; Freed 1996). To overcome the limitations of gender polarization, Crawford (1995) suggests a functional rather than a static view of how language is used, emphasizing how difference (and similarities) are continually evolving and changing because they are contextually dependent and created in interaction.

The Internet provides a rich variety of interactive contexts in which to study the relationship between language and gender. In relation to gender and computer-mediated communications environments, much of the research has been informed by the above studies of face-to-face communication. In particular, according to Herring's (1993) study of Web-based discussions the major differences between men and women are:

- Disparity in participation with males contributing more frequently than females;
- Messages from females are shorter than average;
- Females' messages gain fewer replies in mixed-gender interactions;
- Male postings are more likely to be information centered whilst female postings are more personal;
- Males and females conform to different gender-associated language styles and content.

In mixed-sex conversations, even when a discussion topic is closer to women's interests and experience, it has been found that men still tend to monopolize (Herring 1994). Aggressive behaviour such as 'flaming', which is common in electronic communication, favours men (Herring 1994; Spender 1995), allowing them to dominate conversations and often creating a hostile environment for women.

It is also the case that females deliberately engage in 'male strategies' in order to remain in the interaction and make themselves heard. Indeed females deliberately take on 'male' identities in order to gain credibility. These differences have been further supported in the work of Holmes (1992), Pagnucci and Mauriello

(1999), Jaffe, Lee, Huang and Oshagan (1999), Barrett and Lally, (1999) and Yates (2000). A study by Jaffe et al. (1999) that examined the influence of pseudonymous identification indicated that, unlike men, women tended to mask their gender with their pseudonym choice and they also demonstrated more frequent social interdependence than men did.

Drawing on Butler's (1990) conception of gender as a series of performances, a work-in-progress that is constantly under construction, Rodrino (1997) urges us to rethink gender in relation to CMC in a way that overcomes the limitations of traditional gender dichotomizing. She argues that studies on gender differences in CMC styles and the relationship between power and gender in CMC have tended to treat gender as pre-formed, rather than performed. Thus, subtle similarities and differences between men's and women's speaking styles may be overlooked. In her analysis of Internet Relay Chat (IRC), she finds that neither the construction of gender, nor the function of discourse conform neatly to the dichotomous categories implied by past research. Many gender performances that she documents in IRC environments break out of binary gender categories. However, whilst wishing to move beyond a binary approach to gender, she does acknowledge that it is still important to expose the binary system where it is oppressive and that the extent that this has to be done depends on whether research is focused on gender effects or gender creation.

To summarize, then, the extant literature offers strong support for the view that, as in face-to-face situations, communication on the Internet is founded upon the existing social structures that underlie inequalities in interaction, and these lead to particular gendered and gendering effects within specific online contexts. In the next section we will detail a methodology that helps us to explore further the subtleties of gender online by enabling us to analyse online discourse in terms of both its immediate context and its relationship to the wider sociocultural environment.

A Methodology for Studying Gender Online: Netnographic Discourse Analysis

We base our proposed methodology on the use of netnography (Kozinets 1997, 2002) in conjunction with discourse analysis (Potter & Wetherell 1987; Fairclough 1990). Netnography is a term first coined by Kozinets (1997) to cover the use of online ethnography in consumer research. Online ethnography has emerged as a methodology for the Internet only within the past decade and is used by sociologists to understand virtual communities (Fox & Roberts 1999; Ward 1999; Hine 2000). These communities develop around interactive online environments such as: electronic bulletin boards (Usenets/newsgroups); Web Rings that bring together thematically linked web pages; emailing lists united by a common topic or interest; themed virtual locations in which interactions are structured by role-playing rules (MUDs/MOOs); and chat rooms that are organized around common interests. Regardless of structure type, however, virtual communities are characterized by groups of people with common value systems, norms, rules and a sense of identity and association (Fernbank 1999). This means that each virtual community is likely to have its own cultural composition, a unique collective sense that members share.

Kozinets (2002) has demonstrated the importance of these communities for marketers and how many of them deal with consumption-related phenomena. Netnography is defined by Kozinets (1997: 470) as 'a written account resulting from fieldwork studying the cultures and communities that emerge from online, computer-mediated, or Internet-based communications, where both the fieldwork and the textual account are methodologically informed by the traditions and techniques of cultural anthropology'. As suggested by Kozinets (1997), netnographic research requires an immersive combination of participation and observation. The key research procedures and considerations are (see Kozinets 2002):

1 *Cultural Entrée:* The key step in cultural entrée to an online community is a form of non-participant observation, referred to as lurking. Lurking is important to learn the rules or norms of the community because online communities can exhibit an idiosyncratic voice and a community style (Livia 1999).

2. *Fieldnotes and Other Data:* There is a plentiful supply of data that can be downloaded from the online environment and this saves the need for the time-consuming task of tape transcriptions. This data may be in a variety of formats, for example emails, web pages, bulletin board postings (and their archival material) and text capture from chatroom discussions. Throughout the research process more traditionally based fieldnotes (in the form of memos etc.) will still be required to ensure researcher reflexivity and map the process of data collection.

3. *Trust and Rapport:* Building trust and rapport within the community under study is important in any ethnographic research, but it is more difficult for the online researcher to gain the trust of the community. Real life ethnography offers researchers more opportunities to present their credentials and persuade community gatekeepers of the potential (mutual) benefits of research. Online researchers may need to consider establishing a website where these credentials can be displayed along with details of the research project.

4. *Interviews:* Key limitations include the lack of paralinguistic cues and less researcher control over the course of the interview (the interviewer cannot interrupt a response to seek clarification and the informant can easily terminate the interview at any time). Also, in the case of asynchronous CMC such as bulletin boards, there is less spontaneity in participants' responses. Whereas observation and non-verbal cues are important in face-to-face interviews, online interviews can reveal different kinds of paralinguistic cues. These include emoticons (smiling or frowning faces) and the use of capitals and exclamation marks to connote emotions, points of emphasis, and so on.

5. *Ethics:* The term 'harvesting' refers to the collecting of words of others and there have been strong criticisms of researchers who harvest discussion lists without seeking the permission of the individuals concerned (Sharf 1999). Moreover, a researcher's participation may upset the synergy of the community, either by the act of lurking (chatroom facilities signal the presence of lurkers) or by the introduction of particular discussion topics that serve the researcher's interests rather than those of the community.

6. *Member Checks:* Traditionally in ethnographic research, the researcher engages in preparation work before fieldwork, enters the field and then leaves the field for writing up. By contrast, the 'field' is ever present for the online researcher, who may still be participating in the online community during the final stages of the research. This allows for opportunities to check out the researcher's interpretation with online community members and even permit collabourative interpretation.

7. *Research Representation:* From an ethnographic perspective the term 'representation' refers to how the researcher constructs a meaningful account of the phenomena observed. Issues of representation and reproduction in real life ethnographic research are well documented (Hammersley 1992), as is the need to recognize that such interpretation will always be partial, reflecting the theoretical and personal interests of the individual ethnographer (Arnould 1998).

With online ethnography, 'there is no underpinning 'reality' upon which participant's representations might be based: the 'community' exists only in people's heads' (Fox & Roberts 1999: 650). The anonymity of research participants, their greater 'control' over the research situation and the possibilities of a more equitable relationship between researcher and researched means that the online community may, as Ward (1999) suggests, move towards a position of 'speaking for itself'.

Interpretation of Netnographic Data using Discourse Analysis

Given these issues of representation as well as the wealth of text-based data that are generated, online ethnographies lend themselves readily to discourse analysis. Discourse analysis is concerned primarily with the reality that texts construct, a reality that can be evaluated on its own terms (Potter & Wetherell 1987; Fairclough 1990; Potter 1996; Hine 2000). Discourse analysis is a relatively recent development in social psychology and attempts to incorporate aspects of other discursive modes of enquiry, such as semiotics and poststructuralism (see Elliott 1996 for a detailed overview). It focuses on action rather than cognition and does so through language. Specifically, it examines how we use language to make sense of and construct the social world. Discursive social psychology is centrally concerned with talk or discourse (Potter 1996). In experimental social psychology the individual is conceptualized as having a mind rather like a complex computer that struggles to make sense of the world. Discursive psychology, by contrast, shifts the focus from the individual to interaction between people. This makes it particularly relevant for studying virtual communities with their many online interactions that are continuously documented. The central focus becomes the ways in which textual contributions are justified and given authority and on how authors construct and perform their identities through their postings (Hine 2000).

In focusing on how we construct our everyday worlds through the use of language, discourse analysis illustrates how we are also constructed by this use of language. It is sometimes defined as the analysis of language 'beyond the sentence' (Tannen 1991). Like poststructuralism, it recognizes that discourse is not a neutral means of expression, but rather it contains in-built power relations and their concomitant ideological implications. This mode of analysis is therefore particularly suitable for gender researchers who seek to place marketing and consumption phenomenon in the wider socio-economic and cultural structures.

Construction, action and rhetoric are the central concepts of discourse analysis. Rather than only studying the use of grammar, discourse analysts study larger chunks of language in the context of their usage. Construction relates to the ways that people construct versions of the world in the course of their interactions with others, and how these versions are established as solid, real and independent of the speaker. By means of discourse, people perform actions and the nature of these actions can be identified through the analysis of discourse (Potter 1996). Therefore discourse analysis looks at how people produce a version of an account of an issue (i.e. language-in-use). Its aim is to expose the taken for granted and analyse the consequences of underlying assumptions that are made.

Any data that presents itself as text may be subjected to discourse analysis. As previously mentioned, in the online environment, this may include emails, web pages, bulletin board postings and text capture from chatroom discussions. Potter and Wetherell (1987) suggest two main phases in the analytic approach: the first looks for patterns in the data across both the differences and the commonalities that occur; the second examines these patterns for contextual influences. Emphasis is placed on examining and hypothesizing the function and effects that accompany each discursive unit of analysis. Essentially the researcher is concerned with two main components: accounting practices which are how something is warranted or made plausible; and the identification of belief systems which reveal the type of social understanding that is being used. Whereas accounting practices refer to the everyday linguistic strategies that are used to construct an account ('the little d'), the identification of belief systems refers to the wider sociocultural context and power relations ('the big D'). These procedures are accompanied by questions such as:

- What activity are speakers engaged in when they say this?
- What do they think they are *doing* by talking in this way at this time?
- What version of reality is being produced?
- What ways of talking are people drawing on to make their argument?
- What linguistic resources (i.e. symbols, metaphors, etc.) were needed to make this version?
- What is the function, or consequence, of this version and not another?

To begin to answer these questions in the online environment it is crucial for the researcher to have had a sufficient period of observation ('lurking') to learn the 'idiosyncratic voice' and style of the particular community. This learning process also helps to make visible features of interactions that otherwise may be taken for granted. In this way the researcher seeks to understand the 'interpretive repertoires' (Elliott 1996) that exist within a community. In the next section we will illustrate how these principles of netnographic discourse analysis can be applied in specific gender research contexts.

Gendered and Gendering Effects in a Consumption-Related Online Community

The netnography that we use in our illustration was conducted by the authors for a period of six months in a digital camera discussion forum and followed the key procedures outlined above for the collection of netnographic data. We will now look at examples of the application of discourse analysis to data collected from this community and show how it relates to gendered and gendering effects contained therein. In order to do this we consider the accounting practices of the members in conjunction with the underpinning belief systems of the community.

As we will show, both these aspects help us to understand more clearly the 'idio-syncratic voice' of the community and the 'interpretive repertoires' that its members share in relation to gender issues.

The Digital Camera Forum

First, in establishing patterns in the data as Potter and Wetherell (1987) suggest, a pervasive message coming from the nature of the postings within this community is that the digital camera is regarded widely by members as being at the cutting edge of camera technology. Within the context of forum discussions, 'out-dated' is a word that recurs continuously alongside references to the fast changing pace of digital camera development. Members worry that the equipment they have, or are about to buy, will be left behind.

A majority of postings focus on technical aspects as members discuss new products, compare makes and models, and go into lengthy comparisons of equipment and messages relating to such aspects gain the highest number of responses. For example a message entitled 'Grouping primary colour pixels in RAW format', generated 29 responses, 'Digital versus SLR – is price justified' 54 responses and 'Camera Recommendation' 33 responses. The style and nature of the content in the following posting is typical:

> I currently own a Canon Powershot Pro901S and am considering part exchanging it for a new camera with more mega pixels. I'm not wanting a digital slr, just a top of the range prosumer digital camera. I'm looking for 5+ megapixels and also as large as possible optical zoom. Can anyone reccommend any digital cameras that are worth part exchanging for my pro 90?

Overall, these discussions reflect a rational decision-making 'economic man' model of consumer behaviour with the forum facilitating the information search and evaluation of alternative stages of the buyer decision-making process. In identifying belief systems, such discourse is also embedded within wider discourses of high technology with their associations of scientific progress, rationality and the 'male' side of the Cartesian dualisms such as logic, reason, culture and so forth (Plumwood 1993).

Whilst it may be going too far to suggest, following Henwood (1993), McNeill (1987), Edwards (1996) and Faulkner (2001), that these discussions reflect some quest for compensatory symbolic power or erotic pleasure, it is clear that they do reflect a keen interest and pleasure in technical detail. The content and curt nature of the introductions and sign-offs of the postings are also suggestive of a technology orientation and a corresponding absence of people orientation, between masculine instrumentalism and female expressiveness. There is a distinct lack of social engagement between the discussants.

As Turkle (1986) pointed out women are often reticent about computing because they see hobbyist hackers as the only model for intimacy with computers. In a similar vein, an AAWU (American Association of University Women) study (2000) found many female students competent computer users but they were anxious about using them for reasons that included considering computing a solitary activity, disconnected from social relationships. In other words, to work closely with computers is to eschew meaningful social engagement and they may encounter gender inauthenticity in doing so (Cockburn 1985; Keller 1987). Thus, the reasons for the low number of postings from women on the digital camera site may be less to do with disinterest in digital cameras and more to do with the ambience of the site.

The focus on technical talk and the relative absence of people talk, expressiveness and social engagement cannot be viewed as a focus solely constructed by the users of the digital camera technology. As was pointed out in the literature review, technology is constructed by engineers, designers and marketers as well as users. Those involved in the marketing and retailing of digital camera technology are also deeply implicated in its associated symbolism. At this stage in the life cycle or diffusion cycle of the digital camera, the marketing focus is on the superiority of the product over what it is intended to replace, namely 35mm cameras. As such, much of the marketing and retailing of the product will focus on its 'superior' technical capabilities over what was previously considered cutting edge technology. These discussants, as users of the technology, are simply reflecting and reinforcing such technical talk. Over time as the product diffuses to larger market segments, the marketing focus is likely to shift to branding and the discourse linked with the product is likely to alter.

Thus the ambience and character of the site, its 'idiosyncratic voice', is masculine both in its technical orientation and associated talk, and in the dominance of men posting to the site. In contrast, there are very few postings by women and, as the literature suggests (Herring 1993), their postings receive fewer responses. When women are referred to in discussions, the discourse follows traditional patterns of gender roles and their concomitant associations with regard to decision-making over technology. For example, men talk of buying cameras for wives, girlfriends and daughters, usually whilst making the assumption that females will need a less high-tech, and cheaper, version to ensure that the technology is not going to be wasted on them. The following posting about a particular budget model of digital camera, the Canon A40, is illustrative of such underpinning assumptions:

> I bought a Canon A40 for my girlfriend thinking it would be a 'decent' 2 megapixel camera for her. Boy was I wrong, I was jealous at just how damn good the pictures were, almost as good as my $900 camera!

Here the poster clearly identifies himself as the decision-maker for the purchase of his girlfriend's camera. His use of the term 'decent' requires no further explanation by him. It presumes understanding by other members that a 2 megapixel (regarded as 'entry level') camera will be sufficient for her needs with the implicit assumption that she will not have the expertise to appreciate a higher-tech, more expensive version. In another posting of a similar nature, a husband relates how he has bought his wife a digital camera only to find that she wishes to print off 300 photos to show her friends, instead of storing them on a CD or using technology such as email to distribute them. The phrase 'point & shoot' is associated with this social side and is a disparaging term used to denote those photographers (frequently women) who lack technical expertise. This type of discourse is embedded in the wider discourse of the social equals the feminine equals low tech.

Most commonly the style of posting or, in other words, the ways of talking that members draw on to make their arguments, follows a male model of 'big talk' (Alexander, Burt & Collinson: 1995) or 'report talk' (Tannen 1991) and women posting to the site follow this same style. This means that discussions are mainly transactional, containing few relational aspects or narrative devices. This maleness is further emphasized by use of terms such as 'master photographer' and 'pixel-hound' (denoting a digital camera fanatic). Such accounting practices continually reinforce the community's underpinning belief systems as previously identified of high tech being associated with masculinity and, conversely, low tech being equated with femininity.

Women who join in discussions in the forum do so on male terms and most frequently use 'male talk'. As their postings tend to be ignored more frequently, they devise discursive strategies for gaining attention, particularly calling on the 'expertise' of the other (male) members. In the following sequence of postings we see how a couple whose posting has been unanswered for 5 days are helped by a female member who comes to their rescue.

> Hi everyone we are new here and wondering about portrait photography. Does anyone know what is the best kind of camera to use for portrait photography? Another thing is the studio? I know about the backdrops and stuff. But is there anything else? Have a nice day.
>
> (David and Morgan)

> I'm sure there are experienced photographers here who can help you, so I'm bumping this back to the top. (Pam)

It is extremely rare in this discussion forum for a posting to come from more than one person. This posting stands out as markedly different, therefore, clashing with the overall individual and masculine norms of the community. Moreover, the salutations at the beginning and end of the posting, 'hi everyone' and 'have a nice day', contravene the accepted community style of posting, which is to come to a somewhat abrupt end after relevant information is shared with little use of relational devices either at the beginning or the end. These are factors that may explain why the posting goes unheeded for an unusual length of time. By posting as she does in response, Pam ensures that the message is brought to the board's attention again. Her use of the term 'experienced photographers' is strategic and attracts two immediate and helpful responses, one of which we will now use to illustrate a further point:

> You don't need a lot of equipment to take nice portraits. A north facing window and a reflector made from cardboard and aluminium foil (or a silver mylar car window shade) is really all you need to get started. I've got a good basic primer on my web page (http://xxxxx) I learned most of it working as an assistant to Monte Zucker 30 years ago. Monte learned most of what he knew from Joe Zeltsman. You can find tutorials by Monte and Joe at http://www.zuga.net/freelessons/portrait.shtml

Analysis of the discourse used in this response reveals another aspect of the community's gendering effects. Portrait photography together with wedding photography are constructed in community discourse as the softer, more social and feminine side of photography that requires less high-tech equipment. Consequently they are also less esteemed, a fact that is evidenced in the low number of postings that any messages on these topics receives. In the above quote, we can see how the poster sets himself up as an expert by association with other experts and by his long-standing career in photography. This makes him qualified to respond to Pam's call and adds weight to his view that only very basic items are considered to be required initially, such as cardboard and aluminium foil, items that are readily obtainable in most households and that denote the area as low tech.

In a second response to Pam's call, another self-identified 'expert' suggests that portrait photography requires adept social interaction with the subjects of the photograph to put them at their ease. It also requires an intimacy with the subjects – at least for as long as the photographic session lasts. The quality of the photographs will depend more on the interaction between the photographer and his or her subjects (subjects are messy) and perhaps rather less on the technical capabilities of the camera. In a discussion forum that focuses almost exclusively on the technical capabilities of the equipment it is then hardly surprising that the initial posting received such a poor response. Indeed research on those working in technology-focused professions have emphasized the paring down of the social as an irrelevancy. For example, in her study of engineering education

Hacker (1989) found that 'the student must learn to perceive the world of mechanisms and machinery as embodying mathematical and physical principle alone, must in effect learn to see *not* what is there but irrelevant … reductionism is the lesson'. The discussion on digital cameras reflects this paring down of 'social' irrelevancy.

Amid the trading-information type of postings that occur, there are a few that are very noticeably different. For example, two such postings entitled 'Female Logic' and 'Miss America Pageant' generated long threads of 61 and 44 posting respectively. In the former thread stories are shared about experiences of female illogic, while in the latter, the discussion of the photogenic aspects of the contestants leads to a very basic discussion on the merits of their physical attributes:

> I deny anyone to post a link to a photo of a xxxx2 woman with a really nice butt, because all xxxx women have small flat butts. As far as I am concerned, for a woman to be attractive, it is necessary that she have a nice ass, Of course, this disqualifies all Miss America contestants, but at least they aren't 'butt ugly' like xxxx women. Just to make this about digital photography, by 'nice', I mean 'digitally photogenic'.

It is also interesting to note that the webmaster who has censored other controversial threads from the site does nothing to stop this one. The only small note of protest, from one poster who asks if 'ugly' is too strong a word to use in this context, goes unheeded and the discussion continues unabated.

We have characterized this discussion forum in terms of its focus on, almost an obsession with, technical detail and the paring away of any discussion or conversation that might be regarded as social or intimate. This is the overriding 'pattern' or finding to emerge from this research. Therefore, the discussions on 'female logic' and 'Miss America' are the exception and therefore of particular interest to discourse analysts. There are many ways that these exceptions can be accounted for. In hypothesizing the function of such intermittent and very different discussions, it can be argued that they serve to establish the maleness of the site, creating an ambience that is likely to discomfort potential women discussants, the possibility for gender inauthenticity referred to above (Cockburn 1983; Keller 1987). They provide an opportunity for male bonding that excludes women through their objectification as either the target of humorous jibes about their lack of logic and reason, or as objects of the male gaze. Note how in the illustrative quote above from the 'Miss America pageant' thread, the poster employs the term 'digitally photogenic' to validate his highly sexist (and, indeed, racist) comments.

It is also possible that they relate to our previous discussions on the pleasures offered by technology. Florman (1976) talked of the sensual absorption, spiritual connection, emotional comfort and aesthetic pleasures in engineers' intimacy with technology. Balsamo (1996) and Faulkner (2001) referred to the eroticism that surrounds technology. In other words these pleasures that are associated with the digital camera technology discussion have 'spilled over' into the sexist and sexual discussion threads. Furthermore, both the technical and the sexist/sexual discussions offer the discussants a degree of emotional comfort that strengthens their gender power (Henwood 1993). They are in control of the technology and the discussion, and they are 'symbolically' in control of women.

Finally, Balsamo (1996) talked of virtual technologies enabling new forms of social and cultural autism. She reports a woman in the industry as saying, 'I've had men telling me that one of the reasons they got into this business was to escape the social aspects of being a male in America – to escape women in particular' (146). She goes on to say that the anonymity offered by the computer screen empowers antisocial behaviours – in this case the sexist and racist remarks offered by discussants.

To summarize, in a space where gender is not supposed to matter and where we can be as playful with gender as we wish, it is clear from this discussion forum that gender does matter.

Discussion

Our literature review identified firstly how technology was symbolically linked with gender, and particularly with male world views; and secondly how important it is to examine the ways that gender is performed through discourse. In this chapter we have concentrated on a masculine (cyber)space in order to highlight the potential of discourse analysis for gaining insights into the gendered nature of online interactions, and to illustrate how an online community has its own idiosyncratic voice which may also have gendered and gendering effects. Despite the overall masculine bias of the Internet indicated by our literature review, particular online communities may also exhibit a feminine style and, of course, others may not exhibit the characteristics of either gendered style. As we pointed out at the outset, however, online community consumption-related topics tend to skew the discourse towards a masculine or feminine style because production and consumption practices are themselves gendered (Auslander 1996). For example, in another netnography the authors undertook of a cats' behaviour discussion forum (Kozinets, Maclaran, Hogg & Catterall 2003), the idiosyncratic voice of the community was feminine. Men participating in the community did so through the use of feminized discourse, i.e. through the use of language that was often highly emotional and relational.

Discourse analysis enables us to focus on social interaction, including the way that gender is performed and encouraging a functional rather than a static view of how language is used to overcome the limitations of gender polarization

(Crawford 1995). As we can see from the above application of discourse analysis to the digital camera forum, however, there is never going to be a single interpretation of a phenomenon and nor, indeed, can we expect there to be. Given the socially constructed nature of reality that discourse analysis implies, multiple interpretations will always be possible and desirable. Moreover, it should be recognized that this is a highly contested area and that switching from the little 'd' to the big 'D' is not easy to undertake as Alvesson and Karreman (2000) highlight when they say that:

> We think there is a tension between these two levels. Investigations of the local construction of discourse treat discourse as an emergent and locally constructed phenomenon, while the study of Discourse usually starts from well established a priori understandings of the phenomenon in question. It is not easy, we believe, to accurately account for both in the same study. This should not, however, discourage such efforts.

Accordingly, we believe that it is important to continue our efforts in this respect, whilst at the same time recognizing the tensions that are inherent in the elusive nature of gender research. We have tried to illustrate through our own study how the big 'D', (in this case the gendered cultural assumptions woven into the production and consumption of technology) impacts on our interpretation of the little 'd' (the social interactions in the discussion forum). In relation to gender and online consumption-related communities, there are several fruitful areas for future research where we believe our suggested methodology would yield significant insights:

1. Online communities may change over time and most research to date has tended to be fairly short term. More research is needed into longer term changes (i.e. 1–3 year timespans) that may take place in such communities. For example, the product or service may change over time due to the activities of designers and marketers, or through changing patterns of consumer behaviour (see our previous discussions on the microwave oven and the telephone). It is therefore important to study how these changes impact on the discourses that are used within a community and how these reflect shifting gendered positions.

2. The study of communities as they are in the initial set-up phases would also be beneficial to observe how a particular gender script comes to dominate and whether or not various gender styles are contested and negotiated in the early stages of community life.

3. Communities in customer or market turmoil represent a particularly fertile ground for monitoring changes in discourse because it is at such crisis points

that new discourses may emerge. Although these changes may not always be in relation to gender they may have an indirect impact. For example, in the online Mini car brand community there is currently change afoot due to the launch of the new BMW Mini with much hostility being displayed by traditional Mini car owners towards newer BMW owners. This has had the effect of reinforcing existing gender hierarchies that are reproduced in the community through 'big talk' versus 'small talk'. The most respected members are those who can provide detailed technical and historical information about the Mini, and talk knowledgeably about the model of the engines (Broderick, Maclaran & Ma 2003). By contrast those who talk about the aesthetic pleasures of driving around in a Mini are accorded less status and time during the discussions. This technical knowledge is becoming more important as a way to differentiate and distance established Mini members from new BMW Mini owners who lack this knowledge.

4. Comparative research is also required to look at multiple consumption communities devoted to the same product or service and assess how the gendered and gendering effects differ across the respective social settings, for example, whether those communities that are established and mediated by companies differ from those that are consumer-initiated and mediated.

In conclusion, we come back to the fact that gender has no single and universally agreed meaning. Gender theories are informed by different, and often irreconcilable, assumptions. So, whilst it must remain somewhat elusive in that we cannot account for gender and consumption definitively, we can continue, as we have done in this chapter, to better understand its many and varied performances.

Notes

1. Gender is often conflated with sex but the two are not the same. Sex refers to whether a person is biologically male or female. Gender is socially constructed and notions of masculinity and femininity vary across cultures.
2. We do not think it is appropriate to name the particular ethnic group to which this comment referred.

References

Alexander, M., Burt, M. and Collinson, A. (1995), 'Big talk, small talk: BT's strategic use of semiotics in planning its current advertising', *Journal of the Market Research Society*, 37 (2): 91–102.
Alvesson, M. and Karreman, D. (2000), 'Varieties of discourse: on the study

of organizations through discourse analysis', *Human Relations* 53 (9): 1125–50.

American Association of University Women Educational Foundation (2000), *Tech Savvy: Educating Girls in the New Computer Age*, New York: American Association of University Women.

Arnould, E. (1998), 'Daring consumer-oriented ethnography', in B. Stern (ed), *Representing Consumers: Voices, Views and Visions*, London: Routledge, 85–126.

Auslander, L. (1996), 'The gendering of consumer practices in nineteenth-century France,' in V. De Grazia, and E. Furlough (eds), *The Sex of Things: Gender and Consumption in Historical Perspective*, Berkeley: University of California Press, 79–112.

Balsamo, A. (1996), *Technologies of the Gendered Body: Reading Cyborg Women*, Durham and London: Duke University Press.

Barrett, E. and Lally, V. (1999), 'Gender differences in an on-line learning environment', *Journal of Computer Assisted Learning*, 15(1): 48–60.

Bem, S. L. (1993) *The Lenses of Gender*, New Haven and London: Yale University Press.

Berg, A.J. (1994), 'Technological flexibility: Bringing gender into technology (or was it the other way round?)', in C. Cockburn and R. Furst Dilic (eds), *Bringing Technology Home: Gender and technology in a Changing Europe,* Buckingham: Open University Press, 94–110.

Broderick, A., Maclaran, P. and P. Y. Ma (2003), 'Brand meaning negotiation and the role of the online community: A Mini case study,' *Journal of Customer Behaviour*, 2(1): 75–104.

Bruckman, A. S. (1993), 'Gender swapping on the Internet,' *Proceedings of INET93*, San Francisco, CA.

Butler, J. (1990), *Gender Trouble: Feminism and the Subversion of Identity*, New York: Routledge.

Cameron, D. (1997), 'Theoretical debates in feminist linguistics: questions of sex and gender', in R. Wodak (ed), *Gender and Discourse*, London: Sage, 21–35.

Carlat, L (1998), 'A cleanser for the mind: marketing radio receivers for the American home', in R. Horowitz and A. Mohun, (eds), *His and Hers: Gender Consumption and Technology*, Charlottesville: University of Virginia Press, 115–37.

Chen, C. P., Davies, A. and Elliott, R. (2002), 'Limits to ludic gaps: gender and identity in a different cultural context,' in P. Maclaran and E. Tissier-Desbordes (eds), *Proceedings of the Sixth Gender, Marketing and Consumer Behavior Conference*: 69–84.

Cockburn, C. (1983), 'Caught in the wheels: the high cost of being a female cog in the male machinery of engineering', *Marxism Today*, November, 16–20.

— (1985), *Machinery of Dominance: Women, Men and Technical Know-How*, London: Pluto.

— (1992), 'The circuit of technology: gender, identity and power', in R. Silverstone and E. Hirsch (eds), *Consuming Technology: Media and Information in Domestic Spaces*, London: Routledge, 32–47.

— (1997), 'Domestic technologies: Cinderella and the engineers', *Women's Studies International Forum*, 20(3): 361–71.

— and Ormrod, S. (1993), *Gender and Technology in the Making*, London: Sage.

Crawford, M. (1995), *Talking Difference: On Gender and Language*, London: Sage.

Downey, G. L. and Lucena, J. A. (1995), 'Engineering Studies', in S. Jasanoff, G. E. Markle, J. C. Petersen and T. Pinch (eds.), *Handbook of Science and Technology Studies*, Thousand Oaks, CA: Sage, 167–88.

Edwards, P. N. (1996), *The Closed World. Computers and the Politics of Discourse in Cold War America*, Cambridge, MA: MIT Press.

Elliott, R. (1996), 'Discourse analysis: exploring action, function and conflict in social texts', *Marketing Intelligence and Planning*, 14(6): 65–8.

Fairclough, N. (1990), *Discourse Analysis*, Cambridge: Polity Press.

Faulkner, W. (2001), 'The Technology Question in Feminism: A View from Feminist Technology Studies', *Women's Studies International Quarterly*, 24(1): 79–95.

Fernbank, (1999), 'There is a there there: notes toward a definition of cyber-community', in S. Jones (ed): *Doing Internet Research: Critical Issues and methods for Examining the Net*, Thousand Oaks, CA: Sage, 203–20.

Fischer, C. (1992), *America Calling: A Social History of the Telephone to 1940*, Berkeley: University of California Press.

Fishman, P. (1983), ' Interaction: The work women do,' in B. Thorne, C. Kramarae and Henley, N. (eds), *Language, Gender and Society*, Rowley, MA: Newbury House, 89–101.

Florman, S. (1976), *The Existential Pleasures of Engineering*, New York: St Martin's.

Fox, N. and Roberts, C. (1999), 'GPs in cyberspace: the sociology of a virtual community,' *The Sociological Review*, 47(4): 643–71.

Freed, A. F. (1996) 'Language and gender in an experimental setting ' in V. L. Bergvall, J. M Bing and A. F. Freed (eds), *Rethinking Language and Gender Research: Theory and Practice*, Harlow: Addison Wesley Longman, 54–76.

Gilligan, C. (1993), *In A Different Voice*, Cambridge, MA: Harvard University Press.

Hacker, S. (1989), *Pleasure, Power and Technology: Some Tales of Gender, Engineering and the Cooperative Workplace*, Boston: Unwin Hyman.

Hammersley, M. (1992), *What's Wrong With Ethnography*, London: Routledge.

Haraway, D. (1985), 'A manifesto for cyborgs: science, technology and socialist feminism in the 1980s', *Socialist Review*, 15(2): 65–108.

— (1997),   *Modest_Witness@Second_Millenium_FemaleMan@Meets_ OncoMouse™: Feminism and Technoscience*, New York: Routledge.

Harvey, L. (1997), 'A genealogical exploration of gendered genres in IT cultures,' *Information Systems Journal*, 7: 153–72.

Henwood, F. (1993), 'Establishing gender perspectives on information technology: problems issues and opportunities', in E. Green, J. Owen and Den Pain (eds), *Gendered by Design? Information Technology and Office Systems*, London: Taylor and Francis, 31–52.

Herring, S. (1993), 'Gender and democracy in computer mediated communication', *Electronic Journal of Communication*, 3(2).

— (1994), 'Politeness in computer culture: why women thank and men flame,' in Bucholtz et al. (eds), *Cultural Performances: Proceedings of the Third Berkeley Women and Language Conference*: 278–94.

Hine, C. (2000), *Virtual Ethnography*, London: Sage.

Hocks, M. E. (1999), 'Feminist interventions in electronic environments', *Computers and Composition*, 16: 107–19.

Holmes, J. (1992), 'Women's talk in public contexts', *Discourse and Society*, 3(2): 131–50.

Jaffe, J. M., Lee, Y-E., Huang, L-N. and Oshagan, H. (1999), 'Gender identification, interdependence, and pseudonyms in CMC: Language patterns in and electronic conference', *The Information Society*, 15: 221–34.

Jones, C. M. (1999), 'Shifting sands: Women, men, and communication,' *Journal of Communication*, 49(1): 148–55.

Keller, E. F. (1987), 'Learning about women, gender, politics and power', *Daedalus, Journal of the American Academy of Arts and Sciences*, 116(4): 77–91.

Kendall L. (1999), 'Recontextualizing 'Cyberspace' Methodological Considerations for On-Line Research' in Jones, S. (ed), *Doing Internet Research: Critical Issues and methods for Examining the Net*, Thousand Oaks, CA: Sage, 57–74.

— (1996), 'MUDer? I hardly know 'er!,' in L. Cherny and E.Weise (eds), *Wired Women: Gender and New Realities in Cyberspace*, Seattle: Seal Press.

Kozinets, R. V. (1997), '"I want to believe': a netnography of the X-philes' subculture of consumption', *Advances in Consumer Research*, 25: 470–5.

— (2002), 'The field behind the screen: using the method of netnography to research market-oriented virtual communities', *Journal of Marketing Research,* 39 (1): 61–73.

— Maclaran, P., Hogg, M.K. and Catterall, M. (2003), 'Boys talk facts, girls talk feelings? Questioning gendered consumption discourse in online communities of consumption,' *Advances in Consumer Research*, 30, Punam Anand Keller and Dennis W. Rook (eds) Valdosta, GA: Association for Consumer, 92.

Lakoff, R. T. (1975), *Language and Woman's Place*, New York: Harper and Row.

— (1990), *Talking Power*, New York: Basic Books.

Landow, G. (1993), 'Electronic conferences and Samiszdat textuality: The example of technoculture' in G. Landow and P. Delany (eds), *The Digital Word: Text-based Computing*, Cambridge, MA: MIT, 350–66.

Livia, A. (1999), 'Doing sociolinguistic research on the French Minitel', *American Behavioral Scientist*, 43 (3): 422–35.

Lorber, J. (1999) 'Embattled Terrain: Gender and Sexuality', in M.M.Ferree, J. Lorber and B. B. Hess (eds), *Revisioning Gender*, Thousand Oaks, CA: Sage, 417–48.

Lubar, S. (1998), 'Men/women/production/consumption', in R. Horowitz and A. Mohun (eds), *His and Hers: Gender Consumption and Technology*, Charlottesville: University of Virginia Press, 7–37.

Martin, M. (1991), *'Hello Central?': Gender Technology and Culture in the Formation of Telephone Systems*, Montreal: McGill-Queens University Press.

McIlwee, J. S. and Robinson, G. J. (1992), *Women in Engineering: Gender, Power and Workplace Culture*, Albany, NY: SUNY Press.

McNeill, M. (1987), 'Being reasonable feminists', in M. McNeill (ed), *Gender and Expertise*, London, Free Association Books, 13–61.

Mulvey, L. (1986), 'Visual pleasure and narrative cinema,' in P. Rosen (ed), *Narrative, Apparatus, Ideology: A Film Theory Reader*, New York: Columbia University Press.

Oudshoorn, N., Saetnan, R. and Lie, M. (2002), 'On gender and things: reflections on an exhibition on gendered artefacts', *Women's Studies International Forum*, 25 (4): 471–83.

Pacey, A. (1983), *The Culture of Technology*, Cambridge, MA: MIT Press.

Pagnucci, G. S. and Mauriello, N. (1999), 'The masquerade: gender, identity and writing for the web', *Computers and Composition*, 16: 141–51.

Plant, S. (1995), 'The future looms: weaving women and cybernetics,' *Body and Society*, 1(3–4): 45–64.

Plumwood, V. (1993), *Feminism and the Mastery of Nature*, London: Routledge.

Potter, J. (1996), *Representing Reality: Discourse, Rhetoric and Social Construction*, London: Sage.

— and Wetherell, M. (1987), *Discourse and Social Psychology: Beyond Attitudes and Behaviour*, London: Sage.

Rakow, L. F. (1992), *Gender on the Line: Women, the Telephone and Community Life*, Urbana and Chicago: University of Illinois Press.

Rheingold, H. (1993), *Virtual Community: Homesteading on the Electronic*

Frontier, New York: Addison-Wesley.

Roberts, L. D. and Parks, M. R. (2001), 'The social geography of gender-switching in virtual environments on the Internet,' in E. Green and A. Adam (eds), *Virtual Gender: Technologies, Consumption and Gender*, London: Routledge, 265–85.

Rodrino, M. (1997), 'Breaking out of binaries: Reconceptualizing gender and its relationship to language in computer-mediated communication,' *JCMC*, 3 (3).

Rommes, E., Van Osst, E. and Oudshoorn, N. (2001), 'Gender in the design of the digital city of Amsterdam,' in E. Green and A. Adam (eds), *Virtual Gender: Technologies, Consumption and Gender*, London: Routledge, 241–62.

Sharf, B. (1999) 'Beyond Netiquette: The ethics of doing naturalistic discourse research on the Internet' in Jones, S. (ed) *Doing Internet Research: Critical Issues and Methods for Examining the Net*, Thousand Oaks, CA: Sage, 243–56.

Silverstone, R. and Hirsch, E. (eds) (1992), *Consuming Technologies: Media and Information in Domestic Spaces*, London: Routledge.

Spender, D. (1995), *Nattering on the Net: Women, Power and Cyberspace*, North Melbourne: Spinifex.

— (1980), *Man Made Language*, London and New York: Pandora.

Swann, J. (1989), 'Talk control: An illustration from the classroom of problems in analysing male dominance of conversation,' in J. Coates and D. Cameron (eds), *Women in their Speech Communities*, New York: Longman, 123–40.

Tannen, D. (1984), Conversational Style: *Analyzing Talk Among Friends, Norwood: Ablex*.

— (1991), *You Just Don't Understand: Women and Men in Conversation*, New York: Ballantine Books.

Turkle, S. (1986), 'Computational reticence: Why women fear the intimate machine', in C. Kramarae (ed), *Technology and Women's Voice: Keeping in Touch*, New York: Routledge, 41–61.

Wajcman, J. (2000), 'Reflections on gender and technology studies: in what state is the art?', *Social Studies of Sciences*, 30(3): 447–64.

Ward, K. J. (1999), 'The cyber-ethnographic (re)construction of two feminist online communities', *Sociological Research Online*, 4(1), http://www.socioresonline.org.uk/socioresonline/4/1ward.html

White, M. (2001), 'Visual pleasure in textual places: gazing in multi-user object-oriented worlds,' in E. Green and A. Adam (eds), *Virtual Gender: Technologies, Consumption and Gender*, London: Routledge, 124–49.

Yates, S. J. (1993), 'Vender, computers and communication: The use of computer-mediated communication on an adult distance learning course', *International Journal of Computers in Adult Education and Training*, 3(2): 21–40.

Yates, S. J. (2000), 'Gender, language and CMC for education', *Learning and Instruction*, 11(1): 21–34.

— and Littleton, K. (2001), 'Understanding computer game cultures: A situated approach,' in E. Green and A. Adam (eds*), Virtual Gender: Technologies, Consumption and Gender*, London: Routledge, 103–23.

Part IV
Visual Visuality

9

Dreams of Eden: A Critical Reader-Response Analysis of the Mytho-Ideologies Encoded in Natural Health Advertisements

Craig J. Thompson

What is an advertisement? For many consumer researchers, an advertisement is a form of marketing communication designed to provide information and generate favourable consumer attitudes. For a large cadre of critical theorists, an advertisement is a significant mode of ideological indoctrination serving the interests of the capitalist marketplace (Belk & Pollay 1985; Ewen 1976, 1988; Frith 1997; Lears 1994; Leiss, Kline, & Jhally 1990; Williamson 1978). As Goldman and Papson (1996: 216) write, 'the power of advertising lies in its ability to photographically frame and redefine our meanings and our experiences and then turn them into meanings that are consonant with corporate interests.'

Critical theorists often assume that the meanings and evocative imagery conveyed through advertising constitute a unified hegemony, inducing material-istic desires, infatuations with status symbols (Ewen and Ewen 1992; Leiss, Kline & Jhally 1990; Richins 1995, 2001; Schor 2000) and, per de Graaf, Wann, and Naylor (2001), the societal ill of affluenza. However, this assumption is increasingly anachronistic. The postmodern marketplace encourages consider-able differentiation among consumer lifestyles and it promulgates innumerable goods, services, themed environments and specialist media serving goals of experience seeking and self-enrichment (Brown 1995; Cova 1996; Holt 2000; Pine & Gilmore 1999; Sherry 1998; Thompson & Tambyah 1999). Furthermore, censures of materialism and status emulation are now part of the lingua franca of consumer culture (Holt 2002; Thompson 2000a, 2000b). The increasing usage of self-reflexive advertising campaigns that lampoon image-oriented marketing pitches is a case in point.

Accordingly, critical studies of advertising ideologies need to become more attuned to the heterogeneous, fragmented and self-reflexive nature of the post-modern marketplace and the concomitant prospect that its ideological messages are similarly diversified. While the capitalist economy is structurally dependent upon continuously rising levels of consumption, its ideological representations must be far more varied than suggested by conceptualizations of advertising as a hegemonic force. The age of mass marketing has given way to competition within nuanced niche markets (Brown 1995; Cova 1996; Firat & Schultz 1997). This strategic shift is a function of post-industrial production capabilities and the increasing prominence of consumption as a locus of social identification and affiliation.

The postmodern marketplace is fragmented across consumer groups sharing distinctive clusters of avocational interests, aesthetic tastes and value systems (Firat & Venkatesh 1995; Holt 1997, 2002; Kozinets 2001; Thompson & Troester 2002). Many of these consumer groups also function as interpretative communities: that is, they share common beliefs, background knowledge and interpretative strategies for making sense of media and advertisements (e.g., Jenkins 1992; Ritson & Elliott 1999; Scott 1994). Accordingly, ideological appeals need to be tailored to the collective outlooks and values of the myriad interpretative communities who are targeted across the postmodern mediascape.

I posit that much of this ideological tailoring occurs by leveraging cultural myths that are resonant to an interpretative community of consumers. My argument is a reader-response adaptation of Roland Barthes's (1972) sociosemiotic classic *Mythologies*. According to Barthes, an expansive network of everyday myths structures popular culture. These second-order semiological systems represent cultural signifiers that are already meaning laden and they simultaneously portray and assuage salient sociocultural tensions in ways that serve specific ideological agendas. For example, Barthes (1972) theorizes that a *Paris-Match* cover showing a black soldier reverently saluting the French flag encodes the cultural contradiction between France's imperialist legacy and its historical commitment to an ideal of liberty. According to Barthes (1972: 116) the magazine image signifies 'that France is a great Empire, that all her sons, without any colour discrimination, faithfully serve under her flag.' Hence, the historical conditions that led to black soldiers' inscription in the French army are tacitly rendered as a benevolent natural order while the troubling spectre of colonial subjugation is masked.

Drawing from Barthes, I refer to representations that recruit mythic appeals into an ideological agenda as *mytho-ideologies*. My critical analysis concerns the mytho-ideologies encoded in a set of natural health advertisements. Rather than just effecting an associative transfer of meanings to a brand (McCracken 1986, 1989), mytho-ideologies depict cultural tensions, concerns and contradictions salient to an interpretative community of consumers and further connote that the promoted goods directly or indirectly provide a satisfying resolution. They convey symbolic benefits that are ignored by the top-down, hegemonic view of advertising ideologies that predominates among critical theorizations.

The Interpretative Community of Hardcore Natural Health Users

In the consumer research literature, reader-response analysis has largely been discussed and implemented as a research method in which consumers are first ask to interpret selected advertisements. These consumer readings of the ads then become the textual data for further analysis (e.g., Mick & Buhl 1992). However, this methodological protocol is more accurately classified as a phenomenology of the ad approach. Reader-response research focuses on the collectively shared reading strategies and underlying cultural models that a specific audience (i.e., interpretative community) uses to make sense of texts (see Radway 1991). For reader-response theorists, individuals' specific interpretations of a text and their idiosyncratic motivations per se have little theoretical interest. Rather, the goal is to explicate the collectively shared frameworks-of-meaning that enable a text to be read in a certain sociocultural light and for certain kinds of meanings to be derived from it.

As discussed by Scott (1994: 463), a major genre of reader-response research aims to 'show how a text works with the probable knowledge, expectations, and motives of the reader'. In this case, the reader of interest is not a particular individual but an ideal reader who is constructed from an analysis of the cultural perspectives and reading conventions (i.e., strategies for interpreting a text) relevant to a given interpretative community. Rather than focusing on personal life themes or idiosyncratic connotations, a reader-response analysis is concerned with how an advertisement would be read by individuals sharing a common interpretative frame-of-reference (Scott 1994; Stern and Holbrook 1994).

Reader-response research often begins by empirically documenting how a specific group of consumers read a literary genre or other types of cultural texts (Gamson 1994; Radway 1991). My methodological approach is similar in spirit but I am primarily focused on the collective outlooks that underlie specific interpretative strategies. Rather than having consumers interpret an advertisement and then identifying their reading strategies, my approach first elicits the worldview of ardent natural health consumers. Drawing from this elicited world-view, I then critically analyse the mytho-ideologies encoded in a set of natural health advertisements, with an emphasis on the sociocultural tensions and myths most relevant to this interpretative community of consumers.

The characteristics of ardent natural health consumers (in the American context) support the claim that these women are members of a discernible interpretative community. The most devoted consumers of natural health alternatives tend to be women, between the ages of 30 to 50 years old, college educated, and middle-class (Goldstein 1999). Many of these consumers are also battling some kind of chronic autoimmune disorder (Showalter 1997). Interpretative predispositions exist among these women owing to cultural commonalities in their class and gender socialization, age cohort (such as the influence of feminist thought on this generation of women) and, more specifically, common experiences of living with chronic illness and negotiating medical bureaucracies. The latter set of experiences can often precipitate feelings of dehumanization and alienation (see Frank 1995). This negative experiential outcome is quite focal to the four women in this study, each of whom turned to alternative medicine in hopes of finding a more responsive, humane and optimistic therapeutic paradigm.

In the following sections, I first explicate the cultural models these women use to understand their bodies, illnesses, and relationships to conventional and alternative medicine. Next, I apply the cultural models at work in their collective viewpoints to illuminate meanings encoded in a set of natural health advertisements. In so doing, a critical assessment of the structural features of the advertisements (Schroeder 2002) can be situated within the viewpoints relevant to a group of consumers who are likely targets for the advertisements. This approach transcends the theoretical antinomy between critical-semiotic readings of ad structures that ignore collectively shared reading strategies (see Scott 1994 for further discussion) and the phenomenology of the ad approach (e.g., Mick and Buhl 1992) that reduces ad meanings to idiosyncratic constructions – reflecting individual life themes – and thereby, elides advertising's ideological function as the lingua franca of capitalism. Furthermore, I will show how the interpretative movement between interpretative community narratives and advertisements offers an additional emergent benefit: highlighting (through another iterative round of analysis) paradoxes and ideological meanings implicit in the consumer viewpoints.

Space limitations make it impossible to present all four cases. Due to their textual similarities, however, the collective meanings, concerns and ideals manifest in their reflections can be profiled through a single case study. For purposes of representing the collective outlook relevant to members of an interpretative community, a case study format has two major advantages over a thematic approach that samples vignettes from across different participants. A case study allows for a more contextualized understanding of how a given individual interprets different facets of his/her experience and, second, it offers a more holistic account of the narratives and cultural models that underlie these interpretations (Shore 1996; Thompson 1997).

Jane's Story
Jane is a Caucasian woman in her late thirties who is using natural health approaches to manage Juvenile Rheumatoid Arthritis (JRA). She is a divorcee raising two teenage sons. She has a bachelor degree in liberal arts. Her family background is middle-class. She is the oldest of five children and describes herself as a having been a little jock before the onset of JRA at age ten. Her

primary holistic health practices are rolfing (a deep massage technique that claims to release stress points and energy blockages that accumulate in the connective tissue); acupuncture; cranial-sacral therapy (a subspecialization within chiropractic); routine practices of detoxification; vegetarianism; and herbal, vitamin and nutritional supplementation.

Crisis. Jane began her interview by describing the sudden onset of her illness: a traumatic experience that she now understands as forever changing her life and her outlook toward the medical profession:

J: Well about three to five percent of the kids who get JRA [i.e., Juvenile Rheumatoid Arthritis] get it over night. Boom. I showed the symptoms boom. All over my entire body, over night, at once. It felt like I was on fire. It felt like a fever, a raging fever and all my joints were swollen and tender.

       We lived right across the street from the hospital. My mom was a nurse there and so they took a blood test to see if they could find out what was going on and my white count was like off the charts. So it was showing I was fighting off some infection. And that's where the paths diverge. In western medicine they just hit you with antibiotics and try to squash down what-ever's going on and in Eastern medicine, they would have said, 'she's fighting off something, let's help her purge.' They would have had me do a fast or an intestinal cleanse.

I: At that time, did you know anything about eastern medicine?

J: Not a thing. I was in a really tiny town, only about 8000 people. Not an acupuncturist to be seen, not a colonic therapist to be seen. Nothing. So, I just took one pill after another. I took one pretty colored medicine after another. So, I was 'look at the pretty colors!' And I'd swallow the stuff and 20 minutes later I'd vomit. So my body was definitely saying, 'get every-thing out of the gut. Empty the stomach. Clean out the intestinal tract.' I was throwing up, I had diarrhea and I was sweating like crazy. So my body was saying 'immediately we need to purge.' But what they were doing was trying to squish the symptoms. Stop the nausea. Stop the vomiting. Stop the diar-rhea. So it's like having a train that wants to barrel down the track while everyone else is putting the brakes on it. Well, I went into a coma, and they came in and gave me the last rites. I was in the hospital for three months. I weighed like 65 pounds when I came out. I hardly ate at all for three months. My body was saying 'fast, fast, we have to clean your entire gut out' and I couldn't keep anything down.

Jane's retrospection expresses a tension between science and nature and she clearly privileges the latter term. She attributes an innate healing wisdom to her body. Jane also reframes the conventional meanings of emergency room medical practices. Rather than heroic, life-saving interventions, she interprets them as ineffectual disruptions of her body's natural healing process that nearly caused her death. This nexus of meanings is a key facet of Jane's holistic theory of wellness/healing and her concomitant rationales for eschewing conventional medical treatment protocols.

As Jane recounts, she experienced a revelatory insight soon after returning from the hospital that motivated her first concerted effort to take control of her health:

> I became vegetarian. I had an epiphany related to our family dog. It was a Yorkshire terrier. It was a pedigree dog and he had to have this special diet. You're supposed to take this hamburger, roll it up into little balls and boil it in water so it will pull all the fat out. So being the oldest of five kids, I was given the job. So I'm standing there boiling hamburger for this dog and watching all this scuz come out of the meat and float on the top of the water. Then I had to take a spoon and scrape the scuz off and remove the precious little hamburger balls and set them on a plate for this dog. I thought wait a second. The dog is eating the hamburger without the scuz and I'm eating hamburger with the scuz! So that was the epiphany. So I went off the red meat, the hamburgers, the brats, the hot dogs, the pork chops, the barbecues. I started trying to figure out what's healing for the stomach lining. I started studying foods that were acidic versus foods that are alkaline. I learned that arthritis is an acidic constitution. I started incorporating alkaline foods or neutral foods into my diet and staying away from the acidic ones. I was learning about potatoes, eggplant, tomatoes, all the nightshade vegetables, citrus fruits that are highly acidic versus neutral fruits that aren't.
>
> So in terms of choosing to be a vegetarian, I perceived it as a choice for my life. I was no longer trying to eat to flatter the cook, or my parents or anybody, you know the lunch line at school. I was eating to keep my body alive. So it wasn't like a lot of those decisions you normally make in your teen years where you're rebellious and you're doing something to tick someone off. I was doing unusual things and it certainly was confusing a lot of the adults around me but it wasn't in reaction to anyone, it wasn't a reactive choice, it was an active choice.

In this reflection, many conventional foods are portrayed as a source of pollution or disharmony that undermines her health. Defying the foodways of her family and community, she adopts an entirely new dietary programme (and as she later notes, in a time and place where vegetarianism was considered strange). Her new found belief in the healing powers of vegetarianism led to further investigations of food properties and the germination of a personal theory concerning the linkages between her diet and illness. As exemplified by her distinction to normal (reactive) teen rebellion, Jane understands these dietary decisions as signifying the cultivation of her own voice and ability to make self-directed choices.

*Following A Holistic Path.*For Jane, illness-inducing imbalances are precipitated not only by improper dietary patterns but also by a lack of knowledge about holistic dynamics, such as the biochemical interactions precipitated by otherwise healthy foods. She locates the deep sources of health (and illness) in the micro-details of diet, complex food-body chemistry interactions, and other seemingly picayune aspects of her everyday consumption patterns. In this way, she lays claim to a specialized knowledge (derived from the natural health community) that exists outside the conventional medical model and its theories of the body:

> Our [Western] medicine system, it's really compartmentalized thinking where we just attack one aspect of the problem and don't see it as a whole, the whole system. If we have an achy knee, we go in and have the achy knee treated. We don't look at the whole body, you know. In eastern medicine, the kidneys are connected with the knees. So when the knees are all swollen, which happens to a lot of adults, it means the kidneys are screaming for water. The kidneys, the liver and the gall bladder, all those organs are detoxing organs. They filter all the crap out, after the stomach has gotten done and the glands have gotten done doing their job. So by the time you have an immense amount of toxins trying to make the last voyage out of our body, the kidneys will let you know: 'we are not getting enough liquid to do the job we need to do.' So when you have grownups in their mid 20s or older saying well 'I don't want to kneel on the floor' or 'I don't want to sit squatting on the floor sewing', or all of those things we used to do as little kids on the floor, it's the kidneys are screaming for good liquid. Not soda pop, not coffee. They're screaming for water or juice that will pull stuff out. You can juice an orange or a carrot and get two different effects. Oranges are acidic and give the kidneys more work to do. Carrots are alkaline and will pull things out. It depends on what kind of liquid you're putting in your body.

Her holistic theory of wellness (and the causes of illness) further supports her willingness to diverge from the recommendations of her physicians. Importantly, this counter knowledge is not understood as an abstract system of propositions. Rather, it is something that she has acquired over time through social networks, formal information gathering, intuitive insights and, most significantly, personal experience:

> I set my brain on alert. I'm always looking and listening for another piece of the puzzle. And invariably, when you have that mindset or attitude, that's what happens. If you have someone really negative, going 'oh, my life is over, this is never going to change', it's pretty much a self-fulfilling prophecy. So I was looking and listening and staying alert for information and lo and behold, I found right in my own community, I found acupuncturists, I found rolfers. I found massage therapists, I found cranial-sacral therapists, I found physical therapists and I found out about a lot of things – just stuff in your kitchen, what you can eat, apple cider vinegar baths, castor oil packs.
> So I was pulling information from different sources and the books that I'd read, some

of which seemed really way out in left field (e.g., folk remedies found in a book by the mystical healer Edgar Cayce). Well I would just try stuff and see what would work. I started learning about internal and external. You know, there are things that you can do externally in terms of poultices, hot packs, and massage oils. And then there are things you can do internally to clean out the body. So it started to be a combination of internal and external tools. I started accumulating basically a bunch of tools to use, depending on how much time I had and what the situation was.

By cultivating an open and optimistic outlook, Jane feels that she is receptive to a positive karmic energy that guides her toward new health enhancing discoveries. These discoveries are seen as a nexus of time-proven, folk remedies whose tangible biochemical effects have been disregarded by conventional medical practitioners.

These passages also illustrate a postmodern erasure of conventional cultural boundaries (and hierarchies) between scientific medicine and folk traditions of healing. For Jane, the legitimacy and authority of scientific medical diagnoses and recommendations are no longer accepted as a taken-for-granted social reality. She interprets her medical diagnoses and prognoses as contestable readings of her body that are needlessly Draconian and parochial.

Jane's sceptical stance toward conventional medicine is rationally justified through a relativizing comparison to the long history of Eastern medicine. Rather than viewing Western/scientific medicine as a progressive acquisition of knowledge and technological advances, Jane frames it as a cultural forgetting of ancient Eastern wisdom and, from her standpoint, an unfathomable reliance on highly invasive techniques and drugs. Her brutally blunt descriptions of recommended surgical procedures serves to reinforce her belief that gentle, non-invasive natural health options are far more reasonable and far less risky than the conventional medical treatments for her condition:

I call it more traditional medicine. In western medicine, taking a pain pill is considered traditional and that acupuncture is considered alternative. But in my mind, acupuncture has been around for 3000 years. You know, castor oil packs have been around for hundreds of years. That stuff had been around longer than cortisone shots. So, I'm going to err on the side of caution. I'm going to try something that's been around for hundreds of years or thousands of years. Because things don't last that long if they don't work, people quit doing it. I also didn't like the idea of surgery. I didn't want to do something so dramatic. I'm not a gambler. So, it's real ironic, if I tell the average person what I do for healing, they think it's really wacky and strange. In my mind, it's very cautious. It's very traditional. It's very tried and true and it's very moderate. I think of swallowing a pain pill that glues me to the sofa because I'm so drugged out as shocking. And I really consider having my joints sawed away with a large buzz saw and having a steel rod rammed down my bone marrow to be incomprehensible. That is a tremendous gamble, because once you do that kind of surgery and it's a coin toss. You might as well go to Las Vegas and take the mortgage money and gamble it away. Half the people who go in for joint replacement surgery come out in agony. And their lives are miserable. And they have side effects. And they have reactions. And they have swelling. And they have drainage. Not to mention you can't lift anything over 12 pounds, you can't cross your legs, you can't carry things while walking up stairs, you can't lift your grandchildren. Those restrictions are unbelievable to me. I can't even comprehend how people think that is a better solution than taking an apple cider vinegar bath or wrapping a castor oil pack on your achy knees. You know what I mean? So to me, I'm completely confused as to why people think it's strange to do something that's moderate and cost less that certainly gets results. I have a classic case of juvenile rheumatoid arthritis. So, I'm not supposed to be able to walk, I'm not supposed to be able to stand, and I'm supposed to be in blinding, eye-crossing pain.

Throughout her narrative, Jane interprets natural health approaches as a time-tested array of techniques that are open, flexible and adaptable. Moreover, she transfers these meanings onto her body, which is similarly understood as having the potential to be an open, flexible and regenerative system. For Jane, maintaining her physical mobility is an act of defying the degenerative course of her illness. Conversely, conventional medicine signifies a domain of degeneration, immobilization and finality that would permanently inscribe the current ravages of her illness upon her body via artificial joints and the limitations they impose. Experimentation with the plethora of natural health remedies is seen as a hopeful practice while acquiescence to conventional medical interventions is seen as precluding any hope of becoming fully whole.

Summary. Jane interprets the natural health marketplace as a liberating hetero-doxy of diverse holistic perspectives (or healing vernaculars) that can and should be blended into a personalized whole. In contrast, conventional medicine is understood as a confining orthodoxy. Jane chafes against having her treatment options limited to those endorsed by conventional medical practitioners, whom she regards as emotionally detached, parochial and doctrinaire. Implicit and explicit claims for the superiority of a holistic perspective over the piecemeal approach of mainstream medicine abound in her reflections and they provide the rational justifications for not following the recommendations of her medical doctors.

More generally, Jane expresses an interpretative outlook that is organized by key cultural tensions that have long provided the semiotic raw material for mythic constructions (Barthes 1972): mysticism versus rationality, nature versus technology, Eastern versus Western views of health and wellness, degeneration versus regeneration, heterodoxy versus orthodoxy, holistic versus piecemeal, open-minded versus parochial, empowering versus disempowering and, finally, spiritual transcendence versus the materiality of the body. These consumer narratives further suggest that the mytho-ideological appeals conveyed in natural health advertisements should leverage the idea that these salient binaries can be syncretically blended into a munificent whole. The question now becomes what critical insights can be gleaned from reading natural health's advertisements in relation to these mythic tensions and desires for synthetic resolution.

Illuminating the Mytho-Ideology of Natural Health Advertisements

The Intertextuality of Natural Health Media and Advertising

For the purposes of this paper, I focus on natural health advertisements that are disseminated through a media form known as *magazine medicine*. As defined by Bunton (1997: 232), magazine medicine diffuses 'popular health knowledge that lies beyond the epicenter of medical authority, yet it reports on and comments upon medical findings, extrapolates and interprets these findings for the general reader, and makes judgments about the quality of knowledge.'

Leading natural health publications – such as *Natural Health*, *Alternative Medicine*, *Prevention*, *Herbs for Health*, *Energy Times* and *Vegetarian Times* – exemplify a postmodern form of magazine medicine. These glossy format publications report holistic health information that ostensibly lies outside the institutional bounds of mainstream medicine. Moreover, they continuously highlight risks associated with conventional medical options and raise questions about their overall efficacy, particularly in regard to prescription drugs. These reports and exposés set the stage for paid promotions of natural health alternatives.

The advertisements that financially support these magazines are situated in a constellation of articles, expert advice columns, reader forums, editorials and invited commentaries that endorse and reinforce natural health ideas and ideals. Natural health media also provide extensive background knowledge regarding the preferred holistic remedies for different health problems and relevant details such as recommended dosages. Reciprocally, these advertisements draw from this same constellation of meanings, ideas, recommendations, wellness philosophies and lifestyle outlooks when promoting their products and treatments.

The regulatory environment practically demands that natural health media exude an infomercial quality. In the United States, federal regulations on natural health treatments are relatively lenient (see Goldstein 1999). As a case in point, the FDA classifies herbal products as food supplements. The main benefit to manufacturers is that their products are exempted from the long and expensive process of safety and efficacy testing required for pharmaceuticals.

To avoid more stringent regulatory requirements, advertisements for natural health remedies must also refrain from making drug-type claims concerning their efficacy for treating specific medical conditions (see Mason 1998).

Accordingly, their ad copy advances nebulous claims, such as supporting general well-being or maintaining the balance of the immune system. In their magazine medicine context, natural health advertisements can signal all sorts of information about the palliative benefits of their products while taking the art of euphemistic expression and evocative imagery to new heights. In sum, natural health's advertising rhetoric stands in a symbiotic relationship to its magazine medicine.

For example, the herbal remedy St. John's Wort is widely discussed by natural health writers as an effective treatment for mild to moderate depression that is free of the major side effects associated with prescription antidepressants. Very specific instructions for its self-administration can easily be found in the texts of natural health's magazine medicine:

> I often recommend St. John's Wort for mild to moderate depression. Begin by taking 300 mg of 0.3 percent Hypericum (i.e., St. John's Wort primary active ingredient) three times a day. It may take four to six weeks to notice results. (Gordon 2000: 87)

These magazine medicine narratives provide the requisite background knowledge for readers to readily infer the medicinal claims implicit to advertisements for this product. As a case in point, the ad in Exhibit 1 carefully skirts the clinical word depression through several euphemisms: emotional upset, unhappiness of daily life, seeking more 'sunshine in your life', and the selling point that this herbal product 'can help you naturally maintain a healthy emotional outlook'. The ad also offers technical details, such as references to a standardized dosage of Hypericum, without any additional explanation. All these textual features play off a presumed understanding regarding the medicinal uses of St. John's Wort and the constituent components believed to be most important to its antidepressive effects.

To begin interrogating the mytho-ideological structures encoded in these intertextual texts, let us consider the advertisement presented in Exhibit 2. The image of the product emerging from pristine, blue water sets the mythic context for this ad's rhetorical claim: this natural supplement brings the sea's deep healing properties to the surface of everyday life. The image of a pristine natural setting associates the product with the healing powers of nature and invokes the Romantic view of nature as a sacred place for calm reflection and the attainment of inner peace. These appeals to nature and purity are juxtaposed with technocratic references to labouratory research, standardization to precise percentages and the identification of a technical sounding active ingredient – alkylglycerols. The repeated emphasis on strengthening the immune system, the purity of the product and the package epithet 'prevention is the first step toward defense' all connote that the immune system is being overloaded by pandemic environmental

threats and impurities: a threatening condition which can be magically ameliorated by consuming this gift from nature. This gift framing also elides problematic connotations associated with the primary ingredient, shark liver oil: the
ethical dilemma of killing living animals, driving species to extinction, and the
ecological degradation posed by humanity's harvesting of nature.

Exhibit 3 illustrates natural health advertising's fusion of mysticism, ancient
folk traditions and science. Noni is promoted as 'a miracle fruit' used for 'thousands of years for its many health benefits'. The island imagery that blankets the
ad forges a semiotic link between Noni and a pristine state of nature. Scientific
credibility is signified by the endorsement of an MD/PhD who proclaims Noni
to be a 'medical miracle.' With bullet point efficiency, the ad delivers technocratic rhetoric such as 'patent pending process using whole fruit' and 'rich in
peroxine.' This juxtaposition encompasses the mystical idea that healing derives
from the irreducible properties of a perfectly balanced whole and the technocratic claim that the product's efficacy has been enhanced by isolating a key
active ingredient. The ad's coda aptly summarizes the mythic resolution to these
structural tensions: *'Earth's Bounty* Noni – The Best of Ancient Wisdom and
Modern Science™'.

The ideal of holistic balance is also quite prominent in Exhibit 4. This ad
exhibits the familiar array of naturalistic imagery: a pristine natural setting and
a woman dressed in hiking gear balancing on a wooden fence while watching a
sunrise. The other key marker of the natural is the ad copy's emphasis on Chinese
traditional medicine. These natural significations are punctuated by one of the
more technocratic brand names in the natural health marketplace – Spectrum –
and the reference to a series of trademark formulations of essential fatty acids
and herbs. As with the previous ads, the ultimate promise is that Western science
and Eastern medicine have been optimally synthesized and, by implication, that
these products can sustain a state of healthful balance in the face of the 'unnat-
ural stresses of life'. This ad also implies scientific precision through the idea
that these respective trademarked EFA and herbal combinations promote
different states of balance respectively needed for women experiencing stress,
PMS or menopause.

Last but not least, the ad in Exhibit 5 profiles the recurrent natural health idea
that the body is a regenerative system, though environmental toxins and stresses
compromise its potential for self-healing. Magical, deistic hands strike a
supportive pose against the backdrop of a glowing sky. The product's pyramid-
shaped packaging is semiotically resonant (McQuarrie & Mick 1992) with the
advertisement's references to a 'powerful three tier revitalizing pyramid.' The
pyramid is itself a polysemic image, invoking the familiar idea of the healthful
food pyramid – a cultural metaphor for balance – and the New Age belief that
this geometric shape possesses mystical properties (Heelas 1996). Moreover, the

pyramid also conveys the idea of a scientifically developed, multilayered system. Accompanying the ad's mystical imagery and holistic references to balance and natural support is the familiar litany of technocratic jargon. We are told that the product is fortified with CHROMEMATE®, which is defined in a technical notation as 'a patented chromium formulation delivering increased bioavailability for maximum absorption'. The ad copy is replete with other technocratic references to standardized botanical extracts and an antioxidant formulation, all connoting that this technologically enhanced but still natural product can unleash the body's miraculous regenerative capacities.

Representing the Encoded Mytho-Ideological Structure

Figure 1 presents a semiotic model of this mytho-ideological structure. My semiotic mapping is an adaptation of Greimas's (1983) theory that the meanings of cultural terms are constituted by a series of structural relations: (1) *contrarity* (or contrast) where terms are opposites on a continuum; (2) *negation* where the meaning of the one term is defined by the absence of a quintessential quality possessed by a contrasting term; and (3) *mutual implications* where a subordinate term logically follows from a dominant one (see Floch 1988; Mick 1991).

According to Jameson (1981: 62), Greimas's semiotic square demonstrates that 'any initial binary opposition can, by the operation of negations and the appropriate syntheses, generate a much larger field of terms'. The square is

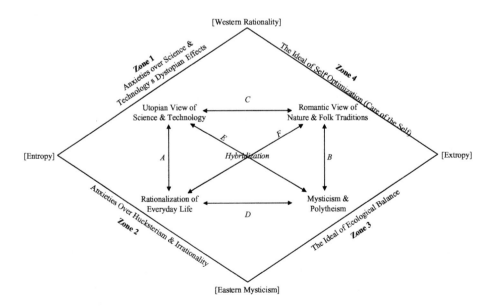

Figure 9.1 The mytho-ideological structure of natural health advertisements

particularly suited for analysing the tensions and contradictions that exist (at a given time) within an ideological system (see Jameson 1981; Haraway 1992). James Clifford (1993) further contends that the semiotic square can be used to illuminate higher order semantic relationships – which he calls semantic zones – that contextualize a cultural system of contradictions, negations and mutualities. Clifford's extension offers a very useful approach for representing the mytho-ideological tensions and resolutions encoded in this set of natural health advertisements.

Turning to the specifics of the semiotic model, the A axis is a mutually implicative relationship. The utopian view of science and technology supports (and is reciprocally supported by) the rationalization of everyday life. This latter term refers to a normative pronouncement that individuals' lives (and bodies) should be governed by principles of rationality (Foucault 1984). The rationalization of everyday life is also historically associated with the cultural dream of transcending the material limits of the body through the assiduous applications of scientific principles and technological interventions (see Davis 1998; Noble 1997).

This semiotic relation highlights the most venerated meanings of scientific progress and the technocratic ideals of effectiveness and efficiency. However, these natural health advertisements eschew the quintessential modernist-rationalist metaphor of the body as a machine. Instead, they deploy the ecological trope of a biological system. This alternative metaphor still coheres with the idea that the system can be scientifically optimized and that its function (or dysfunction) can be fully explained within the grid of scientific knowledge.

Modernism's celebration of science and technology has always been tempered by the specter of spiritual disenchantment and anxieties over the contamination and destruction of nature (see Arnould, Price, & Otnes 1999; Haraway 1992, 1997). These countervailing meanings are brought to the fore in the B axis. This second semiotic relationship is also mutually implicative. A Romanticized view of nature and rediscovered folk traditions of healing supports the idea that natural health ultimately flows from an ineffable, mystical source. Through association with these healing powers, natural health products are represented as elixirs for the ecological and social ills wrought by technology and the pandemic stresses of contemporary life.

The C and D axes are both relations of contrasts (in the sense of a semantic continuum). Modern science and technology stand in direct contrast to folk wisdom and nature, in its pure, uncontaminated state. Similarly, the rational and the mystical pose another pivotal contrast. The diagonal axes (E & F) represent relations of negation; that is, the respective meanings of each term on the diagonal are defined by the *absence* of properties associated with its counterpart term. Hence, the progress of science and technology is devoid of mystical connotations whereas mysticism is devoid of the technology-over-nature dualism that characterizes the modernist ideal of scientific progress. In a parallel fashion, folk traditions and nature are portrayed as the absence of rationalizing and disenchanting forces and conversely, the rationalization of everyday life is not marked by the pejorative connotations of superstition and irrationality.

The mytho-ideology encoded in these advertisements transforms these structural negations into comforting and compelling hybrids that promise the proverbial best of both worlds. These holistic hybrids are portrayed as propitiously expanding the horizons of wellness and metaphysical self-understanding by transcending conventional oppositions between science and nature, the rational and the mystical, and Western and Eastern cosmologies.

The negations located on the E axis are resolved by the mythic claim that the Eastern-infused approaches being advertised have been validated and even enhanced through procedures of scientific testing, calibration and standardization. Hence, the technocratic and mystical come into symbolic alignment. Similarly, the negations on the F axis are resolved through a hybrid formulation. The dystopian aspects of the rationalization of everyday life – emotional stress, hectic fast-paced living, and manifold competing demands – are represented as near inevitabilities. Conversely, the rationalization of everyday life is implicitly sold through these very convenient to use material embodiments of nature and folk traditions. In this mytho-ideological formulation, individuals can healthfully manage these demands and, thereby, accomplish more by consuming these technologically enhanced natural remedies.

The paradox of these advertisements is that they do not encourage individuals to slow down, in the manner of the voluntary simplicity (e.g., Elgin 2000). Rather, they offer ideological instructions for sustaining one's health and vitality while fully engaging the hustle-bustle, work-hard-to-get-ahead ethos of contemporary, career-oriented life. The operative idea is that the hectic, multiphrenia of everyday life affords innumerable opportunities for achievement and self-fulfilment if individuals have the capability to sustain this invigorating pace. Given that these ads are primarily targeted to women, it makes sense that their mytho-ideological promise – you can do it all healthfully – would try to tap desires relevant to a juggling lifestyle (e.g., Thompson 1996).

This system of semiotic relationships gives rise to four semantic zones that are organized around the two dominant cultural tensions: Western Science versus Eastern Mysticism, and Entropy versus Extropy. This first tension manifests a version of Orientalism (see Said 1978) whereby the cultural identity of the West is defined through a contrast to an Eastern other. Orientalism construes the East as a homogenous, timeless and exotic world that stands in distinction to the heterogeneity, dynamism and rationalism of the West. More than just a symbolic contrast, the Eastern other also functions as a projection of valued meanings (i.e., tradition, mystical wisdom) deemed lacking in the rationalized West. Orientalism is often incorporated into a paradisiacal discourse that locates Westerners' lost Eden in the East or Eastern symbolism (see Costa 1998). However, natural health's encoded mytho-ideology does not present the East as an ineffable and fundamentally alien other that can only be pleasurably gazed upon or dominated (i.e. the modernist form of Orientalism). Rather, the East is portrayed as a family of self-care practices for revitalizing and re-enchanting Western lifestyles and, reciprocally, which can be enhanced (but not fundamentally altered) by the West's scientific procedures and technologies.

The second tension expresses the metaphysical opposition between the brute material reality of physical degeneration and the dream that these entropic forces can be magically transcended. Entropy of course refers to the inherent tendency of organized systems to eventually lose energy and fall into disorder or death in the case of biological systems. The less familiar term extropy refers to a creative force or *élan vital* which, as Davis (1998) notes, is regarded by New Age and techno-utopian communities as generating novelty, breeding complexity, producing insights and countering forces of entropy. This set of natural health advertisements represents many facets of everyday life as an entropic threat to holistic well-being and, conversely, it associates these promoted products with the forces of extropy. The tacit competitive positioning is that conventional medicine's technological interventions can only (temporarily) suppress the symptoms of entropy. In contrast, natural health approaches are represented as tools for mining extropic resources and, hence, attaining a deep state of holistic wellness. Though the metaphors are mixed, the terms whole and deep serve a nearly interchangeable rhetorical function in this mytho-ideological system by signifying meanings of regeneration.

Zone 1 represents the Frankenstein-ish fear that science and technology are out-of-control forces precipitating illness and ecological devastation. Also associated with this semantic zone are anxieties that the pervasiveness of science and technology in contemporary life has alienated individuals from the healing and edifying powers of nature. The incorporation of folk and mystical meanings into natural health's claims for scientific credibility and technological enhancement helps to assuage these concerns. Zone 2 represents anxieties over irrationality, hucksterism, or less malevolently, misunderstandings of Eastern approaches that could lead malproductive outcomes. In a semiotic reversal of the preceding semantic zone, the idea that these holistic claims have been rigorously researched, scientifically validated and rationally explained distinguishes natural health remedies from the many superstitions, unfounded beliefs and frauds (such as patent medicine) that have historically plagued popular medicine. Natural health's advertising mytho-ideologies exploit this symbolic distinction, even though the conventional medical establishment routinely challenges the scientific credibility of many holistic treatments.

Zone 3 represents the ideal of ecological balance. The balanced ecological system is construed as a magical and sacred entity that can endlessly regenerate itself. This regenerative power is the deep source of holistic health and it provides the healing energy that natural health remedies presumably possess. Another facet of this semantic zone is that natural health remedies are symbolically aligned with a mystical knowledge for living in harmony with nature. An Orientalist construction of the East adumbrates a distinction between the dystopian view of Western science and a timeless, beatific wisdom.

Zone 4 represents the ideal of self-optimization. In the postmodern medias-cape, this ideal is often represented as a cybernetic, techno-utopia whereby human capacities are maximized through technological fusions (Davis 1998). In natural health's mytho-ideology, this ideal is less overtly cybernetic – though it does imply a synthesis of nature and technology. It is closer in spirit to what Foucault (1986) characterizes as the care of the self.

These self-care practices are directed toward the goal of attaining self-mastery and discovering one's true self. They also involve an ethical component – to care for the self one must lead an ethical life that aims for 'the good of others' (Foucault 1994: 7). The knowledge embodied in these self-care practices must also be understood as offering incontrovertible ethical directives and insights. Historically, these practices of self-discovery have been undertaken with the ascetic assumption that purifying the body will bring clarity to one's thoughts and enable self-enlightenment (Foucault 1986). The moral subtext of natural health's mytho-ideology and its implications for this interpretative community are further elabourated upon in the following section.

Illuminating Elusive Edenic Meanings

An origin story in the Western humanist sense depends on the myth of original unity, fullness, bliss, and terror, represented by the phallic mother from whom all humans must separate, the task of individual development and of history, the twin potent myths inscribed most powerfully for us in psychoanalysis and Marxism (Donna Haraway 1994: 84).

This critical tacking between the viewpoints expressed by these ardent natural health consumers and the mytho-ideologies encoded in this set of advertisements provides an emergent benefit. These advertisements function as an interpretative mirror from which to discern meanings and ideologically driven paradoxes in the consumer interviews that had not been previously noticed. The case study high-lighted the juxtaposition of rational and mystical meanings. However, there is another paradoxical aspect of Jane's narrative that I had overlooked and that suggests potential relationships between natural health consumption and a broader consumer phenomenon – the so-called New Spiritualism (e.g. Harrison 1997).

Jane embraces the idea of becoming attuned to a beneficent, karmic (and ener-gistic) force that connects all living things. This mystical power is seen as guiding her intuitions and orchestrating the seemingly serendipitous discoveries that she has incorporated into her programme of holistic healing. This fatalistic, though optimistic, construction of her natural health experiences and choices is paradoxically juxtaposed against her feminist commitment to thinking for herself and taking control of her life.

This benevolent fatalism enables Jane, and the other participants as well, to imbue some sense of purpose and meaning to a serious health condition. These participants all state that their illnesses provided a needed impetus not only to explore different healing philosophies but also to embark upon their transforma-tive journeys of self-discovery. This purposeful and comforting view is buttressed by the belief that their natural health choices and practices are anchored in a greater metaphysical knowledge and principles of ecological/spir-itual balance that transcend their personal circumstances.

Beyond an existential need to ascribe meaning to a serious illnesses, these reflections may also be indicative of a broader postmodern cultural condition. Contemporary consumer culture saturates individuals in a proliferating plenitude of lifestyle options and consumer choices (Gergen 1991; Holt 2002; McCracken 1997). Moreover, mass media and advertising celebrates and encourages identity experimentation. However, the postmodern ethos that nearly all facets of one's life are contingent and malleable can give rise to an accentuated form of exis-tential anxiety over just who one really is (see Giddens 1991). When identity is a matter of choice, rather than something handed down by tradition or duty, the life paths taken as well as those not taken can become the subject of profound doubt and uncertainty.

This cultural condition can help to explain the prevalence of the anti-choice discourse across many different strains of New Spiritualism and their correspon-ding niche markets for media, self-help seminars and spiritual services (Heelas 1996). The New Age (Sutcliffe 2000) and voluntary simplicity movements (Elgin 2000) are two well-known and predominantly middle-class expressions of New Spiritualism. In both cases, individuals understand themselves as choosing to make fewer choices on the assumption that a simpler life is more joyful, rewarding, ecological sustainable and, in some sense, morally justifiable. Though more subtly manifested, arguments for middle-class downshifting also invoke similar moralistic discourses (see de Graaf et al. 2001; Schor 2000).

Advocates of voluntary simplicity adamantly distinguish the choice to follow an anti-materialistic lifestyle from other kinds of consumer choices. According to Elgin (2000), this meta-choice (to choose less) is said to reflect inviolate principles of ecological balance and moral responsibility, fundamental human needs, and the elemental association between material asceticism and spiritual enlightenment found in many of the world's religious traditions. Not incidentally, Elgin (2000) identifies prevention-oriented holistic health practices as one pragmatic means for enacting the virtuous, simple life.

Social conservatives take the discourse of anti-choice in a different direction. They too lament the moral ambivalence, the paucity of communal solidarity and the variegated superficialities that supposedly pervade contemporary culture (see McAllister 1996). They attribute the demise of organic communities and spiritual enchantment to the ascent of modernist individuality. Their proposed solution is an ethos of limited horizons and foundational morality based upon traditional ideals of character and virtue (Bennett 1994; Kilpatrick 1992; Leo 2000).

Gertrude Himmelfarb (1996) decries the cultural shift from Victorian age virtues – which connote inexorable moral duties and obligations – to modern values which are more relativistic, volitional and individualistic in nature. Virtues bind citizens together through a nexus of irrevocable and reciprocal moral commitments and obligations. In sharp contrast, values encourage self-involved, materialistic lifestyle shopping. For Himmelfarb, this cultural shift has produced moral chaos, wanton individualism and a selfish, status-conscious society that can only be ameliorated by returning to a virtuous society. Christian fundamentalist movements (see Harding 2000; O'Guinn & Belk 1989) also invoke an anti-choice discourse that advocates unerring commitment to a foundational morality and they express a similar antipathy for consumer culture's grand bacchanalia.

Of course, committed natural health consumers, New Age seekers, adherents to voluntary simplicity maxims, downshifters, social conservatives and Christian fundamentalists are not actually liberated from the demands of making consumer choices. Yet, these differing social articulations of the anti-choice discourse enable individuals to interpret their lifestyles and personal orientations as being based upon something far more secure and foundational than a contingent set of values or preferences, thereby mitigating existential anxieties. The specific choices they do make within this social construction are interpreted as virtuous ones evincing binding moral principles. All bear similarities to Foucault's (1986, 1994) proposals regarding the care of the self as an ethical orientation but they arise in a considerably different sociocultural context and may serve unique compensatory identity functions.

Rather than voluntary (read volitional) simplicity, natural health's mytho-ideology appeals to the simplicity (and clarity) of leading a life that is attuned to a greater cosmological balance. This mytho-ideology is an anti-choice discourse because it suggests that individuals can follow an optimal life course that, in some sense, is predestined, although the stresses and distractions of everyday life hinder its recognition. The mytho-ideological emphasis is on the epiphanic discovery of one's inherent place in the grand cosmic scheme, rather than the construction of one's identity. In many quarters of the natural health community, this meta-choice not to choose – in the conventional consumerist sense – is deemed a necessary prelude to self-discovery and spiritual transformation (see Schneirov & Geczik 1996). The driving rationale is that individuals must first become disentangled from consumer culture's many distractions to open the mindspace needed for ethical self-discovery. This mytho-ideological mandate is supported every step of the way by products, services, specialitist media and a plethora of culturally specific advertisements.

At work in this paradoxical anti-choice discourse is a cultural denial that is intrinsic to a Romantic conception of nature. This denial is structurally similar to that found in contemporary (Romanticizing) discourses of ecotourist travel (MacCannell 1992). The touristic promise is that these intrepid (and generally affluent) travellers will be magically transported to majestic, pristine, natural (and native) worlds, unspoiled by the encroachments of modernity. Although the very presence of tourists and a tourist infrastructure renders such purity as a de facto impossibility, the Romantic view of nature and the native as a timeless, unchanging realm of otherness enables this ideological conceit to be maintained. Similarly, natural health ideology promotes the idea of a timeless, pure nature – which is the Goddess-like healing force – and it also suggests that these holistic approaches to wellness are a means to live in perfect harmony with nature. To harmonize is neither to disrupt nor to corrupt the purity and sanctity of nature.

This ideological framing returns us to the myth of the fall and the prelapsarian ideal. As Haraway (1992, 1994, 1997) has cogently argued, nature in its Romanticized, pure form has never existed in the course of human history. Human actions have fundamentally shaped and transformed ecological habitats. Much of what we venerate as natural ecological diversity (such as the Amazon rainforest) has resulted from many generations of agrarian interventions by indigenous people (Hecht & Cockburn 1989). Cultural definitions of nature have been constantly reworked to accommodate human interests, whether the overt aim is to preserve or exploit natural resources. Rapid advances in genetic engi-neering bring into stark relief that demarcations between the human, the natural and the technological are culturally constructed ones whose boundaries are increasingly malleable. The Romantic dream of living (or taking refuge) in an unspoiled Edenic paradise masks awareness of these ecological-technological interdependencies and the distressing prospect that there is no timeless realm of natural purity – a maternal force who can balance and rectify patriarchy's exploitive excesses – into which we can retreat. To paraphrase Nietzsche by way of Charles Revson, the marketplace ideology of holistic well-being sells hope that the Goddess is not dead.

Exhibit 9.1 'With Perika St John's Wort life can feel good again' (Perika St John's)

Craig J. Thompson

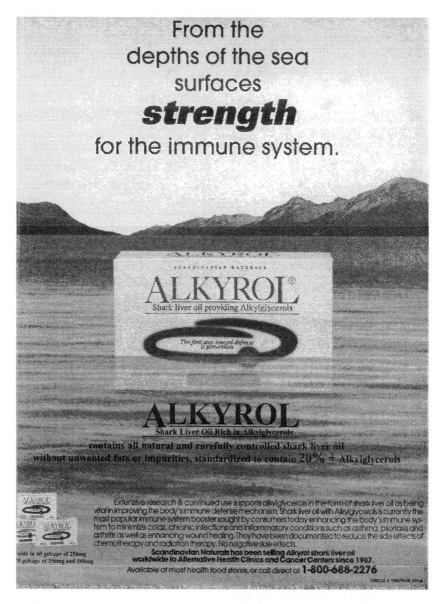

Exhibit 9.2 'From the depth of the sea comes strength for the immune system (Alkyrol)

Exhibit 9.3 The miracle fruit (Noni)

Exhibit 9.4 'Living well requires balance' (Spectrum Essentials)

Regeneration, the most miraculous process in nature.

Millions of your cells die each day. Millions more are created. Cellular regeneration is essential to life.

Until now there was no formula on the market created specifically to assist in your body's natural regenerative process.

Nature's Plus is proud to introduce **Regeneration**, an innovative supplement nutritionally designed to support the process of regeneration.

Each softgel capsule contains a powerful three tier revitalizing pyramid:

Tier I replenishes the body's nutrients with a high energy profile of twenty-seven vitamins and minerals fortified with CHROMEMATE.

Tier II helps support the natural detoxification process with botanical extracts such as standardized milk thistle, celery seed and parsley leaf concentrate.

Tier III helps protect the body from the harmful effects of free radical damage with support from antioxidant botanicals such as standardized ginkgo biloba, wild grape seed extract and Chinese green tea.

CHROMEMATE is a Patented chromium formulation delivering increased bioavailability for maximum absorption. Trademark of InterHealth N.I.

REGENERATION. Replenish, Detoxify, Protect, Energize.

REGENERATION. The three tiered nutritional support to health and well-being.

REGENERATION. Designed to nutritionally support bodily functions and structures essential to life.

For discount coupons call 1-800-937-0500, ext. 2756 today.

I want to replenish, detoxify, protect and energize. Please send me FREE discount coupons plus a FREE copy of *All Vitamins Are Not Created Equal* booklet. Please mail to: Nature's Plus. P.O. Box 91719, Long Beach. CA 90809-1719

Name _____

Address _____

City _____ State _____ Zip _____

Offer expires 4/30/01.   2756

Visit us at our Web Site www.naturesplus.com

Nature's Plus.
The Energy Supplements.

Exhibit 9.5 'Regeneration, the most miraculous process in nature' (Regeneration Vitamins)

Craig J. Thompson

References

Craig J. Thompson

References

Arnould, E., L. Price, and C. Otnes (1999), 'Making Magic Consumption: A Study of White Water River Rafting', *Journal of Contemporary Ethnography*, 28: 33–68.

Barthes, R. (1972), *Mythologies*, trans. A. Lavers, New York: Hill and Wang.

Belk, R.W. and R.W. Pollay (1985), 'Images of Ourselves: The Good Life in Twentieth Century Advertising', *Journal of Consumer Research*, 11: 887–997.

Bennett, W. (1994), *The De-Valuing of America: The Fight for Our Culture and Our Children*, New York: Touchstone Books.

Brown, S. (1995), *Postmodern Marketing*, London: Routledge. Bunton, R. (1997), 'Popular Health, Advanced Liberalism, and *Good Housekeeping Magazine*', in A. Petersen and R. Bunton (eds), *Foucault, Health, and Medicine*, New York: Routledge, 223–48.

Clifford, J. (1993), 'Collecting Art and Culture', in S. During (ed), *The Cultural Studies Reader* New York: Routledge, 49–73.

Costa, J.A. (1998), 'Paradisiacal Discourse: A Critical Analysis of Marketing and Consuming Hawaii', *Consumption, Markets, & Culture*, 1: 303–46.

Cova, B. (1996), 'What Postmodernism Means to Marketing Managers', *European Management Journal*, 14: 494–99.

Davis, E. (1998), *TechGnosis: Myth, Magic, & Mysticism in the Age of Information*, New York: Three Rivers Press.

De Graaf, J., D. Wann, and T. Naylor (2001), *Affluenza: The All-Consuming Epidemic*, San Francisco, CA: Berrett-Koehler Publishers.

Elgin, D. (2000), 'Voluntary Simplicity and The New Global Challenge', in J.B. Schor and D.B. Holt (eds), *The Consumer Society Reader*, New York: The Free Press, 397–413.

Ewen, S. (1976), *Captains of Consciousness*, New York: McGraw-Hill.

— (1988) *All Consuming Images*, New York: Basic Books.

— and E. Ewen (1992), *Channels of Desire*, 2nd Edition, Minneapolis, MN: University of Minnesota Press.

Firat, A.F. and C. Schultz (1997), 'From Segmentation to Fragmentation: Markets and Marketing Strategy in the Postmodern Era', *European Journal of Management*, 31: 83–207.

— and A. Venkatesh (1995), 'Liberatory Postmodernism and the Reenchantment of Consumption', *Journal of Consumer Research*, 22: 239–67.

Floch, J. (1988), 'The Contribution of Structural Semiotics to the Design of the Hypermarket', *International Journal of Research in Marketing*, 4: 233–52.

Foucault, M. (1984), *Power/Knowledge: Selected Interviews and Other Writings: 1972–1977*, ed. C. Gordon, New York: Pantheon.

– 200 –

— (1986), *The Care of the Self: The History of Sexuality, Vol. 3*, New York: Random House.

— (1994), The Ethic of the Care of the Self as a Practice of Freedom, in J. Bernauer and D. Rasmussen (eds), *The Final Foucault*, Cambridge, MA: MIT Press, 1–20.

Frank, A. (1995), *The Wounded Storyteller: Body, Illness, and Ethics*, Chicago: University of Chicago Press.

Frith, K.T. (1997), 'Undressing the Ad: Reading Culture in Advertising', in K.T. Frith (ed), *Undressing the Ad*, New York: Peter Lang, 1–17.

Gamson, J. (1994), *Claims to Fame: Celebrity in Contemporary America*, Berkeley, CA: University of California Press.

Gergen, K.J. (1991), *The Saturated Self: Dilemmas of Identity in Contemporary Life*, New York: Basic Books.

Giddens, A. (1991), *Modernity and Self-Identity: Self and Society in the Late Modern Age*,

Stanford, CA: Stanford University Press,

Goldman, R. and S. Papson (1996) *Sign Wars: The Clutter Landscape of Advertising*, New York: Guilford Press.

Goldstein, M.S. (1999), *Alternative Health Care: Medicine, Miracle or Mirage?* Philadelphia, PA: Temple University Press.

Gordon, J. (2000), 'Advice & Common Problems', *Natural Health*, 30 (May), 87–8.

Greimas, A.J. (1983), *Structural Semantics: An Attempt at a Method*, trans. by D. McDowell, R. Schleifer, and A. Velie, Lincoln, NE: University of Nebraska Press.

Haraway, D. (1992) 'The Promises of Monsters: A Regenerative Politics for Inappropriate/d Others', in L. Grossberg, C. Nelson, and P. Treichler (eds), *Cultural Studies*, New York: Routledge, 295–337.

— (1994), 'A Manifesto for Cyborgs, Science, Technology, and Socialist Feminism in the 1980s', reprinted in S. Seidman (ed), *The Postmodern Turn*, New York, Cambridge University Press, 82–118.

— (1997) *Modest_Witness@Second_Millenium.FemaleMan©_Meets_Onco Mouse™: Feminism and Technoscience*, New York: Routledge.

Harding, S.F. (2000), *The Book of Jerry Falwell: Fundamentalist Language and Politics*, Princeton, NJ: Princeton University Press.

Harrison, J. (1997), 'Advertising Joins the Journey of the Soul', *American Demographics*, 19: 22–8.

Hecht, S. and A. Cockburn (1989), *The Fate of the Forest: Developers, Destroyers, and Defenders of the Amazon*, New York: Verso.

Heelas, P. (1996), *The New Age Movement*, Malden, MA: Blackwell.

Himmelfarb, G. (1996), *The De-Moralization of Society: From Victorian Virtues to Modern Values*, New York: Vintage Books.

Holt, D.B. (1997), 'Poststructuralist Lifestyle Analysis: Conceptualizing the Social Patterning of Consumption', *Journal of Consumer Research*, 23: 326–50.

— (2000), 'Postmodern Markets', in *Do Americans Shop Too Much?*, eds. J. Cohen and J. Rogers, Boston, MA: Beacon University Press, 63–8.

— (2002), 'Why Do Brands Cause Trouble: A Dialectical Theory of Consumer Culture and Branding', *Journal of Consumer Research*, 29: 70–90.

Jameson, F. (1981), *The Political Unconscious: Narrative as Socially Symbolic Act*, Ithaca, NY: Cornell University Press.

Jenkins, H. (1992), *Textual Poachers*, New York: Routledge.

Kilpatrick, W.K. (1992), *Why Johnny Can't Tell Right from Wrong*, New York: Simon & Schuster.

Kozinets, R.V. (2001), 'Utopian Enterprise: Articulating the Meaning of Star Trek's Culture of Consumption', *Journal of Consumer Research*, 28: 67–89.

Leo, J. (2000), *Incorrect Thoughts: Notes on Our Wayward Culture*, Transaction Press.

Lears, Jackson T.J. (1994) *Fables of Abundance: A Cultural History of Advertising in America*, New York: Basic Books.

Leiss, W., S. Klein, and S. Jhally (1990), *Social Communication in Advertising: Persons, Products, and Images of Well-Being,* New York: Routledge.

MacCannell, D. (1992), *Empty Meeting Grounds: The Tourist Papers*, New York: Routledge

Mason, M. (1998), 'Drugs or Dietary Supplements: The FDA's Enforcement of the DSHEA', *Journal of Public Policy & Marketing*, 17: 296–302.

McAllister T.V. (1996) *Revolt Against Modernity: Leo Strauss, Eric Voegelin, and the Search for a Postliberal Order*, Lawrence, KS: University of Kansas Press.

McCracken, G. (1986), 'Culture and Consumption: A Theoretical Account of the Structure and Movement of the Meanings of Consumer Goods', *Journal of Consumer Research*, 13: 71–84.

— (1989), 'Who is the Celebrity Endorser: Cultural Foundations of the Endorsement Process', *Journal of Consumer Research*, 16: 310–21.

— (1997), *Plenitude: Culture By Commotion*, Toronto, Canada: WWW. cultureby.

McQuarrie, E.F. and D.G. Mick (1992), 'On Resonance: A Critical Pluralistic Inquiry into Advertising Rhetoric', *Journal of Consumer Research*, 19: 180–97.

Mick, D. (1991) 'Giving Gifts to Ourselves: A Greimassian Analysis Leading to Testable Propositions', in H.H. Larsen, D.G. Mick, and C. Alsted (eds), *Marketing and Semiotics*, Copenhagen: Handelshjskolens Forlag, 142–59.

Mick, D.G. and C. Buhl (1992), 'A Meaning Based Model of Advertising Experiences', *Journal of Consumer Research*, 19: 317–37.

Noble, D.F. (1997), *The Religion of Technology*, New York: Alfred A. Knopf.

O'Guinn, T.C. and R.W. Belk (1989), 'Heaven on Earth: Consumption at Heritage Village', *Journal of Consumer Research*, 16: 227–38.

Pine, J.B. and J.H. Gilmore (1999), *The Experience Economy: Work is Theatre and Every Business is a Stage*, Boston, MA: Harvard Business School Press.

Radway, J. (1991), *Reading the Romance: Women, Patriarchy, and Popular Literature*, 2nd edition, Chapel Hill, NC: University of North Carolina Press.

Richins, M. (1995), 'Social Comparison, Advertising, and Consumer Discontent' *American Behavioral Scientist*, 38: 593–607.

— (2001) 'Presidential Address: Consumer Behavior as a Social Science', in M.C. Gill and J. Meyers-Levy (eds), *Advances in Consumer Research*, Vol. 28, Provo, UT: Association for Consumer Research, 1–5.

Ritson, M. and R. Elliott (1999), 'The Social Uses of Advertising: An Ethnographic Study of Adolescent Advertising Audiences', *Journal of Consumer Research*, 26: 260–77.

Said, E. (1978), *Orientalism*, London: Routledge.

Schneirov, M. and J.D. Geczik (1996), 'A Diagnosis for Our Times: Alternative Health's Submerged Networks and the Transformation of Identities', *Sociological Quarterly*, 37: 627–44.

Schor, J. (2000), 'The New Politics of Consumption: Why Americans Want So Much More Than They Need', in J. Cohen and J. Rogers (eds), *Do Americans Shop Too Much?*, Boston, MA: Beacon University Press, 3–36.

Schroeder, J.E. (2002), *Visual Consumption*, New York: Routledge.

Scott, L.M. (1994), 'The Bridge From Text to Mind: Adopting Reader-Response Theory to Consumer Research', *Journal of Consumer Research*, 21: 461–80.

Sherry, J.F. (1998), 'The Soul of the Company Store: Nike Town Chicago and the Emplaced Brandscape', in J.F. Sherry (ed), *Servicescapes: The Concept of Place in Contemporary Markets*, Lincolnwood, Ill: NTC Business Books, 109–46.

Shore, B. (1996*), Culture in Mind: Cognition, Culture, and the Problem of Meaning*, New York: Oxford University Press.

Showalter, E. (1997), *Hystories: Hysterical Epidemics and Modern Media*, New York: University of Columbia Press.

Stern, B.B. and M.B. Holbrook (1994), 'Gender and Genre in the Interpretation of Advertising Text', in J.A. Costa (ed), *Gender Issues and Consumer Behavior*, Thousand Oaks, CA: Sage, 1–41.

Sutcliffe, S. (2000), 'Wandering Stars: Seekers and Gurus in the Modern World', in S. Suttcliffe and M. Bowman (eds), *Beyond New Age: Exploring New Age Spirituality*, Edinburgh: Edinburgh University Press.

Thompson, C.J. (1996), 'Caring Consumers: Gendered Consumption Meanings and the Juggling Lifestyle', *Journal of Consumer Research*, 22: 388–407.

— (1997), 'Interpreting Consumers: A Hermeneutical Framework for Deriving Marketing Insights from the Texts of Consumers' Consumption Stories', *Journal of Marketing Research*, 34 (November): 438–55.

— (2000a), 'A New Puritanism', in J. Cohen and J. Rogers (eds), *Do Americans Shop Too Much?*, Cambridge, MA; Beacon Press, 69–74.

— (2000b), 'Postmodern Consumer Goals Made Easy', in S. Ratneshwar, C. Huffman, and D.G. Mick (eds), *The Why of Consumption*, New York: Routledge, 120–39.

— and S.K. Tambyah (1999), 'Trying to be Cosmopolitan', *Journal of Consumer Research*, 26: 214–41.

— and M. Troester (2002), 'Consumer Value Systems in the Age of Postmodern Fragmentation: The Case of the Natural Health Microculture', *Journal of Consumer Research*, 28: 550–71.

Williamson, J. (1978), *Decoding Advertisements: Ideology and Meaning in Advertisements*, London: Marion Boyars.

–10–

Is the Modern Consumer a Buridan's Donkey?
Product Packaging and Consumer Choice

Franck Cochoy

In order to overcome the 'elusiveness' of consumption, wouldn't it be possible, and maybe useful, to ask one question only: isn't there another way to deal with consumption choices? Mainly, would it be possible to study consumption without first studying the consumer? Asking such a question amounts firstly to proposing an armistice: it provisionally implies that the competing consumer theories of economics, sociology and consumer research are right altogether. Michel Callon (1998a) recently showed all the advantages that demonstrate that calculative agencies of economists really exist in contemporary markets. Such a recognition does not lead us to adopt naively the economic conception; on the contrary, it leads us to discover and study all the 'cognitive devices' that render computing possible: software, management sciences, checklists, written procedures, etc.[1] But we should not stop after such a good start. We have to admit the existence of socially conditioned agents beside calculative agencies, and we also have to acknowledge the reality of all other consumer types that consumer research discovers everyday.[2] Moreover, we must wonder what makes the existence of each of these consumers possible, and what renders them present, active or even compatible.

At first glance, this triple recognition may seem contradictory, if we think that the issues at stake are on the consumer's side. But the perspective I'd like to put forward is rather to leave the consumer in peace in order to look elsewhere, and to bet that such a detour will enable us to understand why the consumer's driving forces may be numerous and distributed between the consumer and his environment. More precisely, I suggest considering what the consumer looks at, who looks at him, and how the people looking at the consumer make him look at things.[3] Proposing to look at what the consumer looks at may seem irrelevant, considering how useless such a proposition appears: the consumer looks at the products, of course! But are we really sure of this? The consumer looks at the products, but the products he looks at are not really products, they are *packaged* products. Thus, I would like to show that packaging is probably one of the most important and powerful mediators in the building of consumer choices.

In other words, my programme is to subordinate the study of consumers and producers to a sociology of packaging (Cochoy 2002a). In order to investigate the resources and power of packaging, I will start from very simple and concrete examples. I propose to study the packaging of four products that are inseparable in French bars: alcohol, tobacco, coffee and politics.[4] The alcoholic beverage Ricard sets up the consumer choice problem, and it also underlines the packaging contribution in this choice. We will also see how the Gauloises cigarettes help to 'unfold' all the hidden preferences and motives that are built into packaging, and finally, we will see how packagings are implied in politics and the other way around (in the coffee case). Discovering to what extent packaging participates in the building of consumer drives and preferences will enable us to acknowledge the possible coexistence of calculation and routine. Ultimately, we may even discover new dynamics that bet on their possible combination.

A Ricard? Or the donkey's thirst?

A famous French proverb says that 'one cannot make a donkey drink if the donkey is not thirsty.' But what happens if the donkey at stake is a Buridan's donkey? In contrast to his proverbial cousin, Buridan's donkey is a very, very thirsty, donkey! Buridan's donkey is an animal as thirsty as it is rational. When placed between two identical water buckets, this thirsty but rational animal lets himself die of thirst because it doesn't know how to choose. So, Buridan's donkey fable teaches us that it is always very difficult to make a donkey drink, be it thirsty or not. Bear in mind that the problem of Buridan's donkey balancing between two similar goods is not only an old philosophical case aimed at proving the existence of free will by reducing it to the absurd. This problem is also the quandary market professionals have to deal with on a daily basis. Indeed, the market professionals' job is to help consumers choose between competing products that they often find difficult to distinguish (Coke versus Pepsi, Fuji versus Kodak, Canon versus Nikon, etc.). In order to understand this point, let's look at an advertisement of the French alcohol company Ricard (Fig. 10.1).

The advertisement clearly stages the Buridan's donkey's classical dilemma: we are facing two bottles of equal size, of the same colour, both placed at an equal distance from the central axis we are facing. In short, the problem at stake is clearly that of the donkey, the problem of the hesitation between the same and the same. But the problem is also topped by its exposition and immediate solution. On the left, a question: 'A Ricard?'; on the right, the answer: 'Yes.'

A polysemic question
The evidence of the answer – the choice of Ricard – is matched by the extraor-

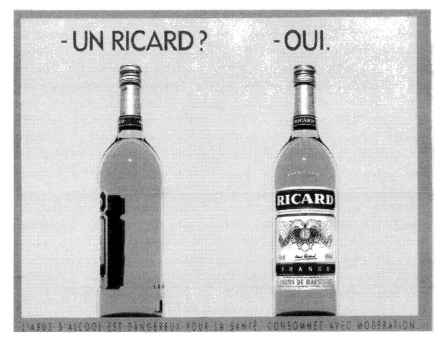

Figure 10.1 Ricard advertisement, 'Un Ricard? Oui.' (4×3 billboard)

dinary polysemy of the question. Asking in two words 'A Ricard?' can indeed have not less than three different meanings:

1. The first meaning is 'Would you like to drink this Ricard I am offering you?' In this case the choice is: does one agree to play the consumption game or not, and it is independent of the nature of the product. Rather, the problem is to make a donkey that is not thirsty purchase the drink because he has been placed in front of an anticipatory image of the convivial aperitif ritual.
2. The second meaning stems from the first one: 'Would you like a Ricard or a whisky ... or, of course, a Martini, a Gin and tonic, or even an orange juice or any other beverage?' In this case, the purpose is to make a thirsty donkey choose between a variety of products that it perceives as distinct, thanks to its subjective preferences. Here too, the commercial strategy consists in tempting the consumer. The purpose is to link the consumer's present evaluation with a future consumption scene, but also to bias this choice a little: the question 'what would you like to drink' is skilfully replaced by 'would you like a Ricard or something else,' the 'something else' being neither named nor shown.
3. Finally, the third meaning of the question is the most crucial one: 'Is the bottle I am looking at really a Ricard brand bottle, or is it one of its clones?' As soon as it is exposed, the Buridan's donkey problem is here denounced as a fool's

game. There is no more choice between the left bottle and the right bottle because these two bottles are one and the same! In this advertisement, we discover that the spatial hesitation problem between two identical and equidistant water buckets has been astutely replaced with the sequential presentation of a single alcohol bottle. After reflection and a quarter of a turn later, the puzzle is solved, the good choice is obvious: yes, it is a Ricard! I recognized it even before it was turned; it is this 'pastis' that I want and that I will drink.

All this advertising rhetoric is aimed at reminding us of what we are supposed to know (or rather, of what the company wants us to know), that is: the Ricard beverage is a quasi-generic product, whose name is (or should be) a synonym for aniseed alcohol, in the same way that Xerox means a photocopying machine. Implicitly, this advertisement targets all the possible substitutes of Ricard, and primarily its main competitor, Pastis 51. Obviously, the advertising iconography tries to pose the Buridan's donkey problem: it tries to have everyone experience the feeling of choosing between the same and the same – Ricard and Pastis 51. But it does so by immediately indicating how to get out the dilemma: Ricard should not be confused with any other product.

A monosemic answer

But how is this problem solved, and who solves it? Firstly, the problem is solved by taking into account its temporal dimension. Market professionals know well that consumer hesitation is a rare and fleeting moment. Consequently, they know that this moment must be seized and fixed with care, speed and dexterity. The very task of market professionals is to provoke a hesitation in order to solve it as soon as it is introduced. They have to subordinate the act of choosing to the use of cognitive equipments so that consumers do not decide on their own. The advertiser replaces the possible hesitation between a left and a right glance with a narrative move following the reading direction (– A RICARD? – YES) and with the rotation of the same bottle. In so doing, the advertiser succeeds in gaining all the advantages of the situation, in imposing the evidence of *his* solution. Secondly, the problem is solved spatially. Indeed, the proposed solution is not only the answer to the riddle (YES), it is also the instrument of this answer: the solution comes from the packaging itself; the bottle label is the only way to go beyond appearances, and to make a difference between two similar products. Indeed, how could the consumer choose alone between two visually indiscernible drinks that he cannot taste immediately?

Thus, from the donkey's water to the pastis, we discover that packaging is both the condition and the solution of choice: the packaging device intervenes in the exposition of the problem as well as in its elucidation. This point is important, since it shows to what extent mimicry is the necessary complement of differentiation: in order to differentiate products, one is better to present them first as similar along a series of lines (Pointet 1997). Now, the combined use of mimicry and differentiation teaches us that the economic calculation of the consumer is not a pure economist's fantasy but rather something that may cautiously be prepared by supply side actors. Indeed, the latter work hard to make 'everything else equals' calculations possible by giving their products all the attributes of their competitors (flavour, colour, composition ...) in order to better underline *the* difference they want to favour: a brand name in the Ricard case, technical characteristics in the automobile industry, etc.

A Gauloise? Or the double smokescreen

Of course, the example I have just used is quite elementary; packaging involves much more than mimicry through appearances and brand differentiation. In order to go further in our exploration of the packaging economy, I now propose to shift the products, to puff at a cigarette after the drink; in short, I propose to move from Ricard to its indispensable companion: the Gauloises pack.[5]

Figure 10.2 Gauloises Light packaging, 1999

How Criticism Clears Up the Smokescreen of Commercial Symbols
What can we think and say about a cigarette pack? What is the contribution of such a device to the consumer's cognition? For a connoisseur, Gauloises is a code-name, that masks, or rather used to mask, the name of the company making and marketing the cigarettes: SEITA in the past, ALTADIS today (a name we find

on the pack but in very small characters). This discrepancy between the brand name and the manufacturer's name prompts me to be on my guard. Firstly, I ponder over the meaning of the word itself: Gauloises establishes a questionable link between the cigarettes and the ancestral way to name the French people. This feeling of national identification is confirmed by the writing of the words 'liberty, always': these words take up one of the three words of the French national motto: 'liberty, equality, fraternity.' Secondly, I am all the more led to suspicion as my first feeling is confirmed by the use of a symbol, the Gallic helmet, and many other connotations.

The Gallic man and his helmet inevitably remind me of the famous comics hero Asterix, whose portrait amazingly resembles my cigarette pack's logo, colour and graphics included! Encouraged by such a profusion of symbolic meanings, I pursue this line by focusing this time on gender games. On the one hand, the helmet figures a male and virile warrior, who obviously is the French equivalent of Marlboro's cowboy. On the other hand, the feminine gender 'Gauloises' undoubtedly introduces an erotic meaning. Indeed, we have to open the pack to meet the product – to undress the 'Gauloises' in order to embrace them. The desire of my manly warrior is probably all the more excited as these 'Gauloises' are described as 'blonde' and 'light.' These two adjectives are disturbing in French: a 'light blonde' means a blonde woman of easy virtue. Moreover, the French language uses almost the same word for a vamp and a match: a vamp is called an *allumeuse* and a match an *allumette*. Now, isn't a match the necessary companion of a smoker and his cigarette? Of course! Matches and cigarette makers have long played on words and images, they have forced the analogy between the *allumette* and the *allumeuse*, they have played with sexual symbolism as is evidenced on these three old matchboxes:

Figure 10.3 Old matchboxes and erotic symbolism © Association Vitolphilique et Philuménique

In short, when considering the symbolic side of packaging, we are led from one interpretation to another, as if we are trapped in the intoxicating whirl of criticism: we slip from pictures to symbols, from connotations to manipulations; we revisit the lessons of Sidney Levy, Ernest Dichter, Herbert Marcuse, Jean Baudrillard and today Naomi Campbell: we are soon convinced that products are bought not for what they are but for what they mean (Levy 1959), we are persuaded that we are influenced by market professionals (Dichter 1960), alienated by commercial narratives (Marcuse 1964; Baudrillard 1970), blinded by the advertising smokescreen which makes us take the logos for the products themselves (Klein 2001), until we believe that a mortal poison is a source of fantasy and pleasure!

How Criticism Screens the Perception of Commercial Information

Now, if we should be careful with advertising mirages, should we not also beware of the sirens of criticism? A smokescreen could hide either the symbolic or the critical views of advertising from one another. So, we have to be vigilant in examining both sides clearly and we can not allow ourselves to be swayed too heavily by only one side or view of these questions. There is another side to packaging that we must be careful to consider. This other side of packaging deals with all that criticism doesn't look at, all the dimensions built into packaging that criticism fails to see. In order to take this other side of packaging into account, we must proceed by subtraction and make a systematic list of what criticism does not list. At the end of such an operation, we easily obtain the double list (Fig. 10.4) of what criticism does and does not look at.

Thanks to such an inventory we discover a stunning paradox: there are almost three times as many things on the side of what criticism doesn't see or refuses to see as on the side that it sees and only wants to see! If we now consider not only the number – 13 vs. 5 – but also the nature of these elements, we discover a contrast just as astonishing. On the one hand, we have the symbolic dimension which is supposed to move us away from the materiality of the product; on the other hand we have the informational dimension. This dimension points to the product's substantial and material components: the '20 filter cigarettes' clearly indicates the pack's content, the rubrics 'tobacco,' 'cigarette paper,' 'flavour and texture agents,' 'nicotine' and 'wood tar' precisely detail the cigarettes' composition, the phrases 'very dangerous to your health' and 'smoking causes cancer' signal tobacco's long-term effects, the expressions 'Altadis,' 'made in France' and 'sold in France' give precise details not only about the product's name, but also about its origin and destination.

Consequently, the certainties I mentioned before are now turned upside down. By taking into account the evident content of the pack – cigarettes and cigarettes only – I realize that the adjectives *blond* and *légères* may point out a type of

What Criticism Sees	What It Neglects
Gauloises	label éco-emballage [eco-packaging label]
Blondes [Light]	
Casque [Helmet]	
Légères/Light	
Liberté, Toujours [Liberty, Always]	Nuit gravement à la santé [Very dangerous to your health]
	Fumer provoque le cancer [Smoking causes cancer]
	20 Cigarettes filtre [20 Filter cigarettes]
	Tabac [Tobacco]: 86,5%
	Papier à cigarette [Cigarette paper]: 5,5%
	Agents de saveur et de texture [Flavour and texture agents]: 8%
	Nicotine: 0,60 mg
	Goudrons [Wood tar]: 8,0 mg
	Altadis
	Fabriqué en France [Made in France]
	01 Vente en France [Sold in France]

Figure 10.4 What criticism sees, and what it neglects

tobacco rather than a hair colour (*blond* is the French word for *mild*); they indicate a manufacturing method rather than a behaviour of easy virtue (*légères*). Finally, I am now wondering if I have not used the wrong column, or at least if I should not have written some information twice, on the left on the symbolic side and on the right on the information side. A short while ago I was facing polysemous images that bet on the possible manipulation of the consumer through his unconscious drives. I am now facing very factual and denotative references that bet, on the contrary, on the consumer's computing abilities. Thanks to what I read, I know what I am buying, in what quantity, and with what effects; I am 'equipped' to exercise my rationality, my preferences, and to make a choice between competing products.

In fact, for more than a century now, the packaged description of products has completely transformed our relationship to market matters. The transformation is threefold: firstly, packaging led us to discover some product dimensions that where completely invisible before; secondly, packaging taught us a legal way to look at things; thirdly, packaging helped us to reach not only the market of products, but also a market of evaluative methods of goods and services.

Packaging: How to make One see the Invisible Before cigarette packs were invented, tobacco was sold in bulk like many other products, or it was packaged by the local dealer in anonymous packets. The packaging innovation was mostly an answer to the risks associated with this first way of product presentation. Indeed, with bulk sales it was possible to market very different things under the same generic product name. The frauds that often happened as a result of this alarmed some producers who reckoned they were harmed by the unfair competition of lower quality products that were indiscernible to the individual consumer's eye. In order to signal the difference, some producers packaged their products and put their brand name on it (Strasser 1989); others took court action that led to pure food and competition laws (Cochoy 2002b). These two types of action finally forced the marking of product content and origin and, by the way, the packaged presentation of products.

Now, this packaged presentation completely changed the relationship between consumers and products. With bulk sale, the Buridan's donkey problem did not exist – there was only one choice – and the only way to evaluate the products was to taste them. With packaging however, it became possible not only to hesitate between two occurrences of the same product, but the same product could also receive two different presentations. With packaging, differences could be named, invented, underlined. Moreover, tasting the products became impossible, and the consumer was thus forced to refer to an indirect and scriptural evaluation of goods. Consequently, the consumer learned new methods of product examination. Physical feelings were complemented by or replaced with the consideration of chemical, scientific or even cultural dimensions. Packaging made it possible to reach some product aspects that were inaccessible before, such as the nicotine percentage we already dwelt on. Here comes the main paradox of packaging: packaging is a screen that, while hiding what it shows, also shows what it hides, but shows it differently, and thus ends up teaching us more about the product itself than what we could learn on our own.

Packaging: How to put the Law into Practice The second transformation stemming from the packaging mediation was the learning by each consumer of the legal way to look at products. We all know that the law as a whole relies, curiously enough, on a completely unrealistic maxim: 'no one should ignore the law.'

Now, thanks to packaging, this maxim lost part of its unrealistic character in order to progressively come into the realm of reality. When today we read on our cigarette pack 'very dangerous to your health' or 'smoking causes cancer,' we guess that there is little chance that the producer is the actual author of these messages! But the health warnings are the latest and most obvious traces of law on packaging. Indications such as content, weight, product's composition, far from being the natural expression of products are, on the contrary, the result of a patient work of codification that was largely enforced by the law.

The chronological account of packaging inscriptions reveals both the importance and the contingence of this type of market mediation. For instance, in the French tobacco case, it was only with the Veil law of 9 July, 1976, that packs were branded with the complete composition of cigarettes. Before this law, the evaluation of the product relied only on the tobacco type and the cigarettes' name, limiting consumer evaluation to taste and symbols. On the contrary, with the indication of composition, the consumer learnt how to judge according to a new possible preference, like the preference for health he was previously unable, if not to know, at least to exercise. As a consequence and through the continuous display of compulsory information, packaging progressively succeeded firstly in presenting the letter of the law on a daily basis, and secondly in relaying new ways to evaluate the products. These ways were more analytic and rational; they were as much oriented towards origin and production matters as focused on the product and its consumption. All things considered, by showing the law directly on the product, packaging succeeded in changing the identity of the consumer himself. Thanks to packaging, the consumer became able to take into account new choice criteria, to question the quality of products, to express his point of view and to defend his interest.

Packaging: How to build a Market of Product Qualifications The branding of the law on the product's body highlights the third transformation of the market relationship that occurred thanks to packaging. Indeed, packaging transforms the old bilateral relationship between the vendor and the consumer into a multilateral exchange. The packaging appears as a place of expression, a genuine platform, a forum where a plurality of entities can simultaneously argue to gain the consumer's attention. Thanks to packaging indeed, the vendor is no longer the only actor talking to the client: the vendor must now share his right to speak with the producer, who praises his product and brand in his own way, but also with the health authorities that propose an alternative vision of the product, with the 'eco-packaging' logo, that wants to signal the importance of an ecological management of waste! Thanks to packaging, we are not even certain that the consumer is alone in front of the product. The bar code for instance, that we forgot to mention hitherto, is unreadable for the consumer but very significant for the scanner it is talking to. This code can delegate the consideration of prices to back-office automatisms; it thus concentrates consumer attention on the evaluation of the qualitative dimensions of products.

Of course, the comparison between packaging and a platform leads us to consider the management of speaking time or rather, in this particular case, to check the writing space allowed to each one. From this point of view, the critics' interpretation wins through its graphical evidence: on my cigarette pack, the brand name, the helmet, the adjectives 'blonde' and 'light' obviously occupy the front of the scene; the symbols play the first roles and consequently relegate factual information to the periphery of the central face, or even to the other sides of the pack. Is public health losing the game? We can wonder. The counter-attack has already occured: since September 2003 a new European regulation has been imposed, requiring health warnings to occupy between 30 and 50 per cent of the packaging surface. Moreover, these warnings are becoming more shocking ('Smoking kills/may kill').[6] So, while one side tries to divert the other's speech, the others are elbowing their way back onto the pack: this unceasing struggle around the packaging battlefield highlights the existence of a true market of product qualifications; this market offers to the consumer many ways to take, taste and test the products.

The proposed qualifications go from product to brand, from taste to symbolic references, from product composition to public health issues. This last issue of public health is particularly interesting, since it reinjects political matters into the product itself. Here many questions arise: where is the border between market and politics? In my French bar, alcohol and tobacco effects are combined and people get very heated: the dispute around the advantages and drawbacks of products is drifting away towards a political debate, where the choice of a French President ends up replacing that of pastis and cigarettes.

A President? 'Marketization' of Politics and 'Politicization' of the market

Marketization of Politics

Up to now, I have essentially dwelt on the role of packaging, on the way this apparently trivial envelope succeeds in deeply transforming the consumer's cognition on the one hand, the supply side strategies on the other hand. But the particular resources of packaging action may also set its limits. Even if very powerful in the art of concealment and display, does not packaging lose all its talents when things – or men, such as politicians – are impossible to cover with a material wrapping? In order to answer such a question, let's start from the cover of a well-known consumerist magazine published a few days before the French presidential election (Fig. 10.5).

Figure 10.5 *Que choisir*, Jalons, April 2002

Obviously enough, this cover easily destroys my hypothesis according to which some 'products' such as politicians may escape the packaging game. On the cover, we see two dolls, one with the face of the former President Jacques Chirac, the other with the face of the ex-Prime Minister Lionel Jospin. Now these dolls are duly packaged, as ordinary Barbie dolls. Moreover the boxes are packaged according to the rule book. Nothing is missing: neither the colors and logos of their respective brands – I beg your pardon: of their parties! – nor the eco-packaging label and the bar code, neither the certificate of product conformity to European standards nor the pictogram indicating that these toys are not suitable for children under 18! Thanks to packaging, each one of the two dolls receives a nickname, 'Inaction man' for Chirac, 'Moralisator' for Jospin, and each one is flanked with a flashy sticker highlighting their respective advantages. Backed with photographs, *Chirac-Inaction-man* is 'certified: 3000 handshakes an hour!', *Jospin-Moralisator* receives his 'New feature 2002: built-in smile!' The journal presents the perfect political Buridan's donkey scene. This structure is reinforced with the name of the magazine *Qui choisir* (who can we choose?), and confirmed with the title of the comparative test itself: 'Presidential election. Defective programmes, hidden flaws, lack of guarantees: a real draw!'

But I suddenly fall on a little detail and I pull a face. I almost confused an 'i' and an 'e,' I almost mixed the copy with the original, I almost mistook a parodic *Qui choisir* (the equivalent of *Who?*) for the very serious *Que choisir* (the equivalent of *Which?*)! If it weren't for this little vowel, the sacrilege would have been perfect: a major French consumer magazine has dared to package politics; it has dared to apply a consumer test to politicians as if they were ordinary goods (Mallard 2000). Finally, the top heading of the parodied magazine sets my mind at rest: 'One more ordinary forgery signed Jalons.' I am in front of a pastiche, of a diversion full of irony, whose humour and impertinence finally reinforces the autonomy of politics. If we smile, it is of course because the situation seems ill-placed, it is of course because we consider that politicians may not be chosen as toys, that persons (*Qui*: who) cannot be treated like objects (*Que*: which). In brief we think that politics and market matters cannot be mixed.

However, before concluding that politics and market cannot mix, I have to check if the truc *Que choisir* journal has not committed the same crime, if one of the main press outlets of French consumerism has not yielded to the temptation of confusing the vote and the purchase, to put the candidates to a test like home appliances (Fig. 10.6). And here comes the surprise! I fall on the second degree Buridan's donkey, I discover that *Que choisir* made quietly and seriously what its clone *Qui choisir* only dared with much ado and humour (see the heading: 'Presidential election: 17 candidates tested')

However, the genuine journal *Que choisir* does not dramatize the issue of the 'voter test.' It adopts a cautious method on at least four points. Firstly, the doll's

Figure 10.6 *Qui choisir* vs. *Que choisir*

box is replaced with a ballot box. Secondly the proposed test on the cover is much more circumspect: the duel between Chirac and Jospin is enlarged to the 17 candidates running for President.[7] Thirdly, the journal examines the candidates only according to the criteria it favours and is competent to deal with. This restriction is perceptible on the ballot envelopes: 'not free checks,' 'GMOs'; it is also confirmed when one looks at the pages in the magazine: *Que choisir* clearly conducts a comparative test, but this test is restricted to the issues that are more likely to interest consumers and their representatives (food, money, environment, justice, health, public services). Fourthly, politicians are not 'tested' without their consent, but according to the answers they formerly gave themselves to a questionnaire that was sent to them by the journal editorial staff. (*Que choisir* thus concedes the possibility of a self-test method for this particular type of product!) *Que choisir*'s procedure appears to be ponderous, respectful, dispensatory and restricted, as if politicians could not be tested like ordinary products, as if market and politics were not really compatible. In short, a careful examination of *Que choisir* practices tends to show that the marketization of politics does not go as far as we might suppose when looking at the magazine's cover (Fig. 10.7).

However, two important questions remain.

The first question is that of *Que choisir*, when the journal questions all the candidates on the consumption issues they usually neglect. By antiphrasis this

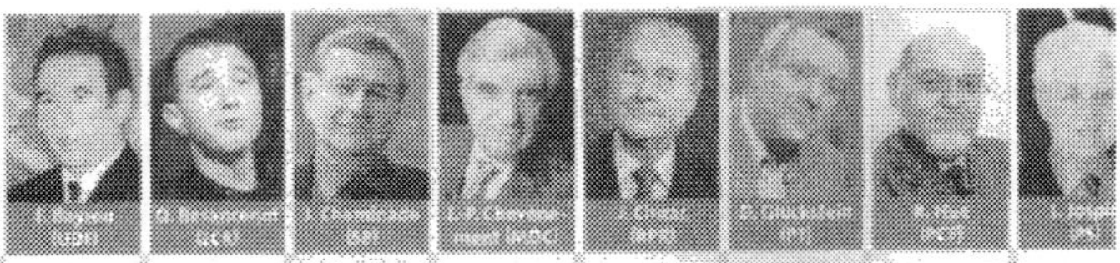

Figure 10.7 *Que choisir*, no. 392, April 2002, p.18

question points at the implicit packaging of all political discourses. Indeed, in the same way as each packaging proposes a limited, exclusive series of evaluation criteria to the consumer, the political discourse arbitrarily selects the debate dimensions and sometimes leaves themes in the dark that may be crucial. For instance, if the French presidential election largely focused the French voters on security issues, it completely forgot the themes of consumption, European construction or foreign policy. The unexpected intrusion of *Que choisir* makes us discover the considerable extension of the packaging economy which often takes immaterial forms, and secondly the importance of the upstream selection of the criteria along which we build our preferences and choices.

Finally the second question arises from the caricatural battle between *Chirac-Inaction-man* and *Jospin-Moralisator*. This dramatization of the political choice only furthers the polls' and commentators' anticipation: the media were all forecasting a duel between these two candidates for the second run of the election, while presenting this duel as a Buridan's choice between the same and the same. We thus learn that, upstream of the framing of choice criteria through packaging, there occurs a less perceptible framing which sets choice scenes, selects alternatives, and favours some products over others. But the history of the French presidential election also teaches us that excessive framing may cause some overflowing (Callon 1998b), it shows that the voters-consumers can be 'recalcitrant'

(Latour, 1997) and that pernicious effects may appear: thanks to the Buridan's donkey rhetoric of the media and of the candidates themselves, French electors were convinced that the first round was already played, they were persuaded that the second round would oppose two similar candidates. Thus voters took advantage of it to express some little preferences … little preferences whose accumulation ended up with a ridiculous score for the former president, the elimination of his prime minister, and the surprising promotion of the abominable Le Pen. The unusual perspective of the consumerist magazine as the tragic fancies of French electors make us discover the importance of the hidden packaging of political choices: democracy implies not only the vote computation for a given political supply, but also the building up of new preferences and the setting of new possible choices.

But what is true for politics is also true for the market. The setting of choices, be they political or commercial, is a political matter for at least two reasons. Firstly, the importance of the framing of choice scenes and criteria determines a power struggle between supply and demand representatives that deserves to be revealed and studied. Secondly, the possible use of packaging as a public debate arena makes it accessible to many expression forms, including political ones. For these two reasons packaging becomes a privileged means for market politization.

The Politicization of the Market

Talking in terms of politization of the market may be surprising if we consider the traditional separation between market and political issues. Since Adam Smith's *Wealth of Nations*, we know that the market institution has been presented as an alternative to politics, as a means to obtain social order without the help of public authority, thanks to the virtuous combination of private interests (Hirschman 2002). Since Polanyi's *Great Transformation*, we also know that the Smithian market has been politically founded and ruled: the free market utopia came into facts only when it became a true political project supported by public authorities; then, if the market economy has endured, it is only thanks to the assistance of public institutions aimed at protecting and controlling its functioning (Polanyi 2001). Now, a new development emerges as an extension or a by-product of these two forms of evolution: economic actors are more and more bent on including political issues into the market itself.

In order to understand how the material inscription of politics into the market works, we would do better to shift products. I propose to look at commodities that are a priori more independent from public policy issues than cigarettes and alcohol: I suggest looking at their table companion: coffee. Indeed, after drinking, smoking and talking a lot, a little cup of coffee is quite welcome to regain (political) consciousness. The only problem here is that before drinking we must as usual choose the beverage we are going to drink. The donkey sleeping in us then makes a dramatic comeback; once again, the choice between similar packagings precedes and determines the beverage consumption (Fig. 10.8).

As usual we are facing two strangely similar packets. On each side, we have the same type of coffee: '100 % arabica,' with the same brown 'colour code' attached to this variety; we also have the same exotic and colourful tones with Gringo and Kalinda, the same far-away origins (Latin America and Africa, Haiti). However, and as usual, similarities are present to underline differences. While a packaging bets everything on images, and calls for seduction, the other one prefers literacy and calls for reflection. The packaging on the left focuses on giant coffee beans placed on an exotic geographic background. Moreover, these coffee beans astutely refer to the brand logo: the coffee bean replaces the circular shape of the 'Q' letter in 'JACQUES VABRE.' By contrast, the packaging on the right contents itself with typed words aimed at qualifying both the coffee ('fine and flavoured') and its production mode ('traditional and craft roasting'). Here the product and its production are inseparable. This is what the only iconic element of the packaging suggests: the drawing of a moustached peasant carrying a coffee bag on his back and the binary motto 'a great coffee, a great cause.'

Drawing a parallel between a 'coffee' and a 'cause' aims at establishing a relationship between a personal and material pleasure on the one hand and a collec-

Figure 10.8 Jacques Vabre vs. Max Havelaar

Franck Cochoy

tive and ethical goal on the other hand. The key of this relationship is given to us on the back of the packaging, where we can read the following explanation:

> What is the Max Havelaar guarantee?
> The assurance of drinking a high quality coffee that was handled with care from its culture to its roasting.
> The assurance of helping small coffee producers to live decently from their work.
> Indeed, the coffee you are about to drink was bought directly from small producers at prices above the world rates, after a partial financing of their harvests.
> By purchasing this coffee:
> • You help the preservation of a high coffee quality level.
> • You contribute to improving fair trade between the North and the South.
> • You favour the betterment of the living conditions of the families of small Southern producers.

The purpose here is to refer choices to a new preference: the preference for 'fair trade,' that is: for the ethical and political content of products. The institution is the 'Max Havelaar' NGO, that works in favour of more justice in international trade, and that comes to give its 'guarantee,' to certify the exchange conditions, thanks to a 'third party' auditing system.

In order to legitimize the politicization of products, in order to link consumer preferences with the producers' fate, Max Havelaar wavers between two logics: the brand logic, which is always suspected of behaving as judge and judged, and the regulation or certification logic, which both rely on a much larger and clearer basis. The Max Havelaar label makes us understand the potential strength of the politicization movement which is gathering a growing number of actors and institutions: 'buycott' actions aimed at granting virtuous companies (Friedman 1999), the 'clean clothes campaign' (Lalanne 2003), the voluntary codes of conduct (Daugareilh 2002), the SA 8000 standard for social certification (Cochoy 2003), the ethical investment funds (Giamporcaro 2002), the movement for business social responsibility (Salmon 2000; Minvielle 2001), the group for 'ethics on labels' in France (Grenouillet 2001), and more generally all the other forms of contemporary 'political consumption' (Micheletti 2003; Micheletti Föllesdal & Stoll 2003).

This undertaking has at least four main characteristics. Firstly, it favours a voluntary and substantial politicization of the products. As a consequence, it can be confused neither with the old method consisting in introducing politics into the markets from the outside and by force like law on cigarette packs, nor with old strategies like 'cause-related marketing' proposing to give some money to a charity organization for the sale of each Big Mac (Varadarajan & Menon 1988). The aim of the politicization of products is neither to do politics at products' expense, nor to do marketing at causes' expense, but to sell the political content

Franck Cochoy

tive and ethical goal on the other hand. The key of this relationship is given to us on the back of the packaging, where we can read the following explanation:

> What is the Max Havelaar guarantee?
> The assurance of drinking a high quality coffee that was handled with care from its culture to its roasting.
> The assurance of helping small coffee producers to live decently from their work.
> Indeed, the coffee you are about to drink was bought directly from small producers at prices above the world rates, after a partial financing of their harvests.
> By purchasing this coffee:
> • You help the preservation of a high coffee quality level.
> • You contribute to improving fair trade between the North and the South.
> • You favour the betterment of the living conditions of the families of small Southern producers.

The purpose here is to refer choices to a new preference: the preference for 'fair trade,' that is: for the ethical and political content of products. The institution is the 'Max Havelaar' NGO, that works in favour of more justice in international trade, and that comes to give its 'guarantee,' to certify the exchange conditions, thanks to a 'third party' auditing system.

In order to legitimize the politicization of products, in order to link consumer preferences with the producers' fate, Max Havelaar wavers between two logics: the brand logic, which is always suspected of behaving as judge and judged, and the regulation or certification logic, which both rely on a much larger and clearer basis. The Max Havelaar label makes us understand the potential strength of the politicization movement which is gathering a growing number of actors and institutions: 'buycott' actions aimed at granting virtuous companies (Friedman 1999), the 'clean clothes campaign' (Lalanne 2003), the voluntary codes of conduct (Daugareilh 2002), the SA 8000 standard for social certification (Cochoy 2003), the ethical investment funds (Giamporcaro 2002), the movement for business social responsibility (Salmon 2000; Minvielle 2001), the group for 'ethics on labels' in France (Grenouillet 2001), and more generally all the other forms of contemporary 'political consumption' (Micheletti 2003; Micheletti Föllesdal & Stoll 2003).

This undertaking has at least four main characteristics. Firstly, it favours a voluntary and substantial politicization of the products. As a consequence, it can be confused neither with the old method consisting in introducing politics into the markets from the outside and by force like law on cigarette packs, nor with old strategies like 'cause-related marketing' proposing to give some money to a charity organization for the sale of each Big Mac (Varadarajan & Menon 1988). The aim of the politicization of products is neither to do politics at products' expense, nor to do marketing at causes' expense, but to sell the political content

Franck Cochoy

tive and ethical goal on the other hand. The key of this relationship is given to us on the back of the packaging, where we can read the following explanation:

> What is the Max Havelaar guarantee?
> The assurance of drinking a high quality coffee that was handled with care from its culture to its roasting.
> The assurance of helping small coffee producers to live decently from their work.
> Indeed, the coffee you are about to drink was bought directly from small producers at prices above the world rates, after a partial financing of their harvests.
> By purchasing this coffee:
> • You help the preservation of a high coffee quality level.
> • You contribute to improving fair trade between the North and the South.
> • You favour the betterment of the living conditions of the families of small Southern producers.

The purpose here is to refer choices to a new preference: the preference for 'fair trade,' that is: for the ethical and political content of products. The institution is the 'Max Havelaar' NGO, that works in favour of more justice in international trade, and that comes to give its 'guarantee,' to certify the exchange conditions, thanks to a 'third party' auditing system.

In order to legitimize the politicization of products, in order to link consumer preferences with the producers' fate, Max Havelaar wavers between two logics: the brand logic, which is always suspected of behaving as judge and judged, and the regulation or certification logic, which both rely on a much larger and clearer basis. The Max Havelaar label makes us understand the potential strength of the politicization movement which is gathering a growing number of actors and institutions: 'buycott' actions aimed at granting virtuous companies (Friedman 1999), the 'clean clothes campaign' (Lalanne 2003), the voluntary codes of conduct (Daugareilh 2002), the SA 8000 standard for social certification (Cochoy 2003), the ethical investment funds (Giamporcaro 2002), the movement for business social responsibility (Salmon 2000; Minvielle 2001), the group for 'ethics on labels' in France (Grenouillet 2001), and more generally all the other forms of contemporary 'political consumption' (Micheletti 2003; Micheletti Föllesdal & Stoll 2003).

This undertaking has at least four main characteristics. Firstly, it favours a voluntary and substantial politicization of the products. As a consequence, it can be confused neither with the old method consisting in introducing politics into the markets from the outside and by force like law on cigarette packs, nor with old strategies like 'cause-related marketing' proposing to give some money to a charity organization for the sale of each Big Mac (Varadarajan & Menon 1988). The aim of the politicization of products is neither to do politics at products' expense, nor to do marketing at causes' expense, but to sell the political content of products. The second point sets very intimate links between the politicization of products and the economics of quality (or qualities) (Karpik 1989; Callon, Méadel & Rabeharisoa 2000). Indeed, the politicization of products extends classical product differentiation through material characteristics or services with a differentiation through the ethical and social content of the products. Thirdly, market politicization reverses Marx's commodity fetishism. Marx denounced market goods as idols hiding the scandal of the production relationships they came from. On the contrary, with political consumption it is the production relationship itself which becomes a fetish and works as a commercial argument! (Cochoy 2002b). The fourth characteristic of this type of undertaking is its close relationship with the market mechanism, since it paradoxically uses the market power as the only means to fight against its abuses and to relay the criticism against globalization. In the absence of an efficient international law, a competition grounded on ethical and political preferences appears as the only way to sustain and preserve human and citizenship values. Bruno Latour (forthcoming) shows very well how the new ecological issues urgently call for the construction of new democratic procedures aimed at bringing things into politics. Symmetrically, it seems as if the growing politicization of the market asks for the setting of new and more transparent rules aimed at welcoming politics into things.

Conclusion: What Packaging Makes us Do

We left the consumer in order to look at these packagings the consumer looks at. Where did this detour lead us? From bottles to cigarette packs, from dolly-politicians to coffee, we understood to what extent the packaging device equips and transforms our choices: packaging teaches us to consider the product under a new light, they deceive and inform us, they are symbolically seductive but they also reveal the hidden properties of products, they bind us to the egoist and material pleasure of consumption, but they also uncover the political side of things. Finally our packagings have four interrelated dimensions: an emotional dimension that bets on symbolic appeals and seduction, a sociological dimension that plays on routine and attachments, a logical dimension that calls for our reflexive and calculative abilities, an axiological dimension that looks towards values, collective consciousness and the consumer's political commitment. We thus find again on packagings themselves the four action patterns we thought were reserved to human actors: the calculation of economists and the routine of sociologists, but also the seduction and politics of ordinary people. Sometimes, one of these action schemes prevails; sometimes, they all are present and fight each other to gain the consumer's attention. Each one of these dimensions distributed on the product's face tries to activate a particular action pattern, to drag the consumer from the routine to the calculative scheme, to break up the consumer's calculation in order to provoke a political commitment, etc. Then, where do our preferences come from? From within ourselves or from the packaging's surface? Where do we have to look for the consumer's theory? Inside the consumer or on the objects held out to him?

In order to answer these tricky questions we should not stay as before in bars reserved to adults to protect children, but rather listen to children when they care about adults, when they worry about their tendency to talk, drink and smoke too much. Bruno Latour (1999) quotes a touching comic where a father says to his little daughter that he is smoking, and the little girl answers to her father that she thought he was rather smoked by his cigarette. Bruno Latour rejects the alternative between the active and passive voices by suggesting the following solution: neither do we smoke our cigarettes nor are we smoked by them. Simply, cigarettes make us smoke. What is true for cigarettes is even truer for the packagings that precede and direct the choice: we no more choose cigarettes packs than we are chosen by them. Simply, packagings make us choose. For Bruno Latour, the particular contribution of objects to action precisely lies in this 'make do,' in the ability that objects have to lead people beyond themselves, without however denying their initiative and action. When taking into account these packagings that make us choose, we finally understand that consumer theories are distributed between persons and things and exchanged through action. We also understand why the consumer finally escapes the Buridan's donkey identity: his hesitation lasts only a split second, it lasts the time for supply to suspend the consumers' action scheme and to propose him other references as preferences, in order to help him to *make his choice*, to choose in the right way.

Notes

1. This perspective proposes to trace people's cognitive resources out of themselves, in the material devices that equip and help them to make decisions; it is directly inspired by the study of situated cognition of Norman (1988), Hutchins (1994) and Suchman (1987).
2. For a social history of marketing and consumer research, see Cochoy, 1998; Cochoy 1999.
3. The purpose is to take seriously an old proposal of Morris Holbrook (1984): In my view, [the business system] differs from other types of systems by virtue of the fact that a business always involves inter-relations between managers and customers or consumers. So, if we want to understand business, we had better study *both* managers *and* customers' (177).
4. All that walking [in New York] had made the appetite grow, so ... we made a variety of stops ... finally on to Pastis on Ninth Avenue, which is hip and

currently very hot. ... The white tiles on the pillars came from a Parisian Metro and the furniture gives the impression of a fin-de-siecle brasserie. Enamelled advertisements for Ricard and Gauloises complete the effect." (Tullio, 2001)

5. This cigarette pack was photographed in 2001, and thus complies with the legal rules of that time. The appearance of Gauloises' packagings has recently been changed according to the requirements of the new EU directive which came into force on 30 September, 2003.

6. Directive 2001–37, *Journal Officiel des Communautés européennes*, 18 juillet 2001.

7. A few days later Charles Pasqua was put 'out of sale' for a lack of signatures (according to the French constitution, each candidate needs to obtain 500 signatures from elected representatives in order to run for President).

References

Baudrillard, J. (1998) *The consumption society, myth and structures (theory, culture and society)*, London: Sage.

Callon, M. (1998a), 'Introduction: The Embeddedness of Economic Markets in Economics,' in Callon, M. (ed.), *The Laws of the Markets*, Oxford: Blackwell, 2–57.

— (1998b),'An Essay on Framing and Overflowing: economic externalities revisited by sociology,' in Callon, M. (ed.), *The Laws of the Markets*, Oxford: Blackwell, 244–69.

— Méadel, C. & Rabeharisoa, V. (2000),'L'économie des qualités,' *Politix* 13 (52): 211–39.

Cochoy, F. (1998), 'Another Discipline for the Market Economy: Marketing as a Performative Knowledge and Know-how for Capitalism,' in *The Laws of the Markets*, Callon, M. (ed.), Sociological Review Monographs Series, Oxford: Blackwell, 1998, 194–221.

— (1999), *Une histoire du marketing, Discipliner l'économie de marché*, Paris: La Découverte.

— (2002a), *Une sociologie du packaging, ou l'âne de Buridan face au marché*, Paris: Presses Universitaires de France.

— (2002b), 'Une petite histoire du client, ou la progressive normalisation du marché et de l'organisation,' *Sociologie du travail*, 44, (3): 357–80.

— (2003), 'The Industrial Roots of Contemporary Political Consumption. The Case of the French Standardization Movement,' in Micheletti et al. (eds.), *Politics, Products and Markets: Exploring Political Consumerism Past and Present*, New Bruswick, NJ: Transaction Press.

Daugareilh, I. (2002), 'Globalisation and Labour Law,' in Barbier, J.-C. & Van

Zyl, E. (eds.), *Globalisation and the world of work,* Paris: L'Harmattan, 97–111.

Dichter, E. (1960), *The Strategy of Desire*, Garden City, NY: Doubleday.

Friedman, M. (1999), *Consumer Boycotts. Effecting Change Through the* * *Marketplace and the Media*, New York: Routledge.

Giamporcaro, S. (2002), *Le système d'action concret de l'investissement sociale-ment responsable: entre stratégies de pouvoir et forums hybrides*, mémoire pour le DEA de sociologie, Université René Descartes-Paris V, Paris.

Grenouillet, F. (1999), *Fair trade and free trade: état des lieux*, mémoire de DEA Économie Industrielle et de l'Emploi, LIRHE/Universtité Toulouse I.

Hirschman, A.O. (2002), *Passions and Interests: Political Party Concepts of American Democracy*, Princeton, NJ: Princeton University Press.

Holbrook, M.B. (1984), 'Belk, Granzin, Bristor, and the Three Bears,' in *1984 AMA Winter Educators' Conference: Scientific Method in Marketing*, Anderson, P.F. & Ryan, M.J. (eds.), Chicago: American Marketing Association, 177–8.

Hutchins, E. (1994), *Cognition in the Wild*, Cambridge, MA: MIT Press.

Karpik, L. (1989), 'L'économie de la qualité,' *Revue Française de Sociologie*, 30, (2): 187–210.

Klein, N. (2000), *No logo, Taking Aim at the Brand Bullies*, London: Picador.

Lalanne, M. (2003), 'L'ét(h)iquette, ou comment capter l'attention. Des fibres textiles au tissu social,' in Cochoy, F. (ed.), *La captation des publics*, Toulouse, Presses Universitaires du Mirail (forthcoming).

Latour, B. (1997), 'Des sujets récalcitrants. Comment les sciences humaines peuvent-elles devenir enfin 'dures'?' *La Recherche*, n° 301, septembre, p. 88.

— (1999), 'Factures/fractures: from the concept of network to the concept of attachment' *RES*, 36, Fall.

— (forthcoming), *Politics of Nature: How to Bring the Sciences into Democracy*, Cambridge, MA: Harvard University Press.

Levy, S.J. (1959), 'Symbols for Sale,' *Harvard Business Review*, 37, (4): 117–24.

Mallard, A., (2000), 'La presse de consommation et le marché. Enquête sur le tiers consumériste', *Sociologie du travail*, 42, (3): 391–409.

Marcuse, H. (1964), *One Dimensional Man*, Boston, MA: Beacon Press.

Micheletti, M. (2003), *Political Virtue and Shopping: Individuals, Consumerism, and Collective Action*, Basingstoke: Palgrave Macmillan.

— Föllesdal, A. and Stolle, D. (eds.) (2003), *Politics, Products, and Markets: Exploring Political Consumerism Past and Future*, New Brunswick, NJ: Transaction Press.

Minvielle, A. (2001), *Responsabilité sociale de l'entreprise, ou comment rendre l'entreprise descriptible*, mémoire de DEA, Centre de Sociologie de l'Innovation, Ecole Nationale Supérieure des Mines de Paris, Paris.

Norman, D. A. (1988), *The Psychology of Everyday Things*, New York: Basic Books.

Packard, V. (1957), *The Hidden Persuaders*, New York: Pocket Books.

Pointet, J.-M. (1997), 'Le produit automobile entre différenciation et mimétisme,' *Les cahiers de recherche GIP Mutations Industrielles*, n° 72, 30 mai.

Polanyi, K. (2001), *The Great Transformation, The Political and Economic Origins of Our Time*, Boston, MA: Beacon Press.

Salmon, A. (2000), 'Le réveil du souci éthique dans les entreprises. Un nouvel esprit du capitalisme?' *Revue du MAUSS, Éthique et économie, l'impossible (re)mariage?* n° 15 (premier semestre) 296–319.

Strasser, S. (1989), *Satisfaction Guaranteed, The Making of the American Mass Market*, New York: Pantheon Books.

Suchman, L. (1987), *Plans and Situated Actions: the problem of human-machine interaction*, Cambridge, MA: Cambridge University Press.

Tallio, P. (2001), 'The food and wine net', http://www.foodandwine.net/food/food023.htm.

Varadarajan, R.P. & Menon, A. (1988), 'Cause-Related Marketing: A Coalignment of Marketing Strategy and Corporate Philanthropy,' *Journal of Marketing*, 52: 58–74.

–11–

Visual Consumption in the Image Economy

Jonathan E. Schroeder

This chapter presents a visual approach to consumer research, dislocating the consumption domain away from the attitude researcher's laboratory, beyond the behavioural decision theorist's rational model, and off the marketing strategist's brand map, toward concerns about what consumers look at, what they see, and how they make sense of the visual world. Following the interpretative turn in consumer research, my perspective on the production and consumption of images draws from art history, photography and visual studies to develop an interdisciplinary, visual approach to understanding consumer behaviour. I focus on the image and its interpretation as foundational elements of elusive consumption, bringing together theoretical concerns about image and representation to build a multidisciplinary approach to consumption in what I call 'the image economy' (Schroeder 2002).

An image serves as a stimulus, a text or a representation that drives cognition, interpretation and preference (cf. Zaltman 1997). As psychologist and art historian Rudolf Arnheim argues, 'one must establish what people are looking at before one can hope to understand why, under the conditions peculiar to them, they see what they see' (Arnheim 1977: 4). Thus, I pay a great deal of attention to identifying what consumers look at, how this is informed by the *visual genealogy* of contemporary images, and how those images signify. I draw upon several image theorists to develop a way of understanding images for consumer researchers, and make visible particular possibilities of meanings relative to certain images. Images function within culture, and their interpretative meanings shift over time, across cultures and between consumers. My aims are interpretative rather than positive – to show how images *can* mean, rather than demonstrate *what* they mean. Image interpretation remains elusive – never complete, closed, or contained, meant to be contested and debated.

To discuss the prominence and proliferation of images, I developed a theoretical approach to *visual consumption*. By visual consumption, I mean not just visually oriented consumer behaviour such as watching videos, tourism or window-shopping, but also a methodological framework to investigate the interstices of consumption, vision and culture, including how visual images are handled by consumer research (Schroeder 1998, 2002, 2003). Visual consumption constitutes a key attribute of an experience economy organized around attention. We live in a digital electronic world, built with images designed to capture eyeballs, build brand names, create mindshare and produce attractive products and services.

In a market based on images – brand images, corporate images, national images and images of identity – vision is central to management in the information society. Today's organizations are faced with the 'frantic production of images which are circulated; a frantic translation of incoming images into collages of "ideal companies"; less frantic but steady attempts to translate those images into the local practices and vice-versa; and once again a production of self-images to be sent around' (Czarniawska 2000: 216). Global consumers enthusiastically consume images; brand images, corporate images and self-images are critical economic and consumer values; global market culture is constructed of symbolic environments; visual consumption emerges as critically important for understanding contemporary consumers.

Visual consumption begins with images. Visual consumption of images is an important, but by no means comprehensive approach to understanding consumers. Rather, by focusing on visual issues in consumer behaviour, we gain an appreciation of the prominence of the image in brand-building campaigns, consumer self-construction, and visual consumption processes that dominate contemporary culture.

My work has focused on how visual representation works within a semiotic system of meaning influenced by cultural processes including marketing, the Internet and mass media. If we agree that products, services, brands and concepts are marketed via images, then we need to think carefully about what this implies economically, managerially, psychologically and politically. One logical conclusion is that this implies rethinking competition. From a consumer point of view, competition need not be constrained by standard industrial classifications, product categories, or corporate discourse such as the McDonald vs. Burger King wars. However, current discussion about competition often reflects a modernist, rational, physical product based view of the market that is at odds with the way the consumption really works (see Holt 2002; Schroeder 2002). In this essay, I focus on advertising, photography and the World Wide Web's interconnected roles in visual consumption.

The Visual Imperative

Toyota Motor Corporation's Website, Gazoo.com, is named after the two Japanese language characters for 'visual' (Strom 2000). The Toyota Website, so dubbed to celebrate its ability to bring the showroom to the consumer, visually represents the company – its brand, products, dealer showrooms and customer service. In a recent publicity photo, Akio Toyada, the force behind the site, writes the *ga zoo* characters with the phonetic translations below – without PowerPoint slides, fancy graphics or sophisticated visual equipment. Rather, he uses a felt-tip marker on a rather nondescript whiteboard, relying on an ancient tradition of writing characters to communicate his message about the latest in information technology – the World Wide Web. Gazoo.com signifies the centrality of vision in today's market, as well as the problems of translating corporate strategy into computer screens.

The World Wide Web mandates visualizing almost every aspect of corporate strategy, operations and communication. Moreover, the requirements and potentials of the Web have profoundly influenced the dissemination of financial analysis, corporate reports and consumer information. The Web produced a visual revolution in marketing in which 'everything from the structure of the book to the layout of pages, distribution of images such as photographs, illustrations or digital backgrounds, and use of typography are brought to bear on conveying the company's image' (Murray 2000: 5). To a large extent, competitive advantage depends on effectively presenting visual information.

From the consumer perspective, visual experiences dominates the Web (cf. Venkatesh 2003). The *navigational aesthetics* of the Web depend upon clear pages that involve viewers, blending coherence and interest in an easily navigable site; consumers prefer environments in which they can make sense of what they see and in which they can gain new knowledge (Kaplan & Kaplan 1982). However, the Web's rapid growth, combined with a still emerging understanding of how to design sites, has made Web navigation often difficult, messy, and frustrating. One commentator contends that Web designing 'comes down to a simple problem: how to make navigating the Web a more visual experience' (Wagstaff 2001: 25). Web design has brought visual issues into the mainstream of strategic thinking, and spurred research about perception and preference of visual displays.

The Web, among its many influences, has put a premium on understanding visual consumption. Internet economics consolidates corporate activity into visual displays. Clearly, the look of Web pages is fundamentally related to strategy – visual design has become foregrounded as a key e-commerce tool. The World Wide Web presents sites in which consumers navigate through an artificial environment almost entirely dependent upon their sense of sight. Web designers try to 'capture eyeballs' with visually interesting, coherent and easily navigable sites. Although the Web is a contemporary, sophisticated image delivery system, it relies on the visual past to generate meaning. Moreover, the digital electronic architecture of the Web draws from the classical laws of architecture laid down centuries ago (Schroeder 2003).

Photography provides a large component of Web graphics – and the logic of photographic reproduction informs Internet economics. The Internet's economies of scale rely on reproducibility – the ability to digitize and copy information without loss of quality (Shapiro & Varian 1999). The computer screen driven Web limits input from the other senses – it makes visual information primary, and it attenuates other navigational clues such as body position, touch and sound. On the Web, visual consumption clearly assumes centre stage.

Understanding Visual Communication

Despite its ubiquity, the visual context of consumption remains under explored within consumer research. Too often, information processing models dominate research on visual issues, to the neglect of those scholars who deal specifically in the visual realm – art historians. Most existing visual consumer research has focused on images as stimulus material within experimental research, or used photography as a data-gathering tool (see chapters by Cochoy and O'Guinn in this volume). In contrast, my approach places the image at the centre of consumer behaviour. I pay particular attention to photography – which encompasses still photography, film, and video – as a key communication and information technology (cf. Crawshaw & Urry 1997).

Today's visual information technologies of television, film, and the Internet are directly connected to the visual past (e.g., Borgerson & Schroeder 2003; Schroeder & Borgerson 2002). Research on information technology (IT) or information and communication technology (ICT) usually focuses on complex, sophisticated systems such as mass media, , the Internet, telecommunications, or digital satellite transmission arrays. These constitute the basic building blocks of the information society – where information is a crucial corporate competitive advantage as well as a fundamental cultural force. Photography remains a key component of many information technologies – digital incorporation of scanned photographic images helped transform the Internet into what it is today. Photography, in turn, was heavily influenced by the older traditions of painting in its commercial and artistic production, reception, and recognition (e.g., Kress & van Leeuwen 1996; Schroeder 1997; Schroeder & Borgerson 1998; Scott 1994; Stern & Schroeder 1994).

Despite photography's dominance of information technology and communication, most consumers receive little photographic training, and few consumer research studies place photography at the centre (see Belk 1998). Photography just is, apparently, its transparency falsely lulls us into believing no special tools are needed to comprehend its communicative power. We have become so used to photographic representation that it seems inevitable, a natural record of what exists or what has happened. Further, advances in photographic technology –

including cameras, lenses, digital technology, film and printing – push a realist vision that photography is becoming progressively more accurate, more realistic and more able to capture almost any subject digitally or on film. Partially due to this invisibility 'we pay little attention to this technology – to its workings and its effects on our lives – even as we ingest massive amounts of its outputs on a daily basis, produced for our consumption by ourselves and others' (Coleman 1998: 114). I consider photography a cornerstone of visual consumption.

Associating visual consumption with the art historical world helps to position and understand photography as a global representational system. This approach to consumption affords new perspectives to investigate specific art historical references in contemporary images, such as the gaze, display and representing identity (see Schroeder & Borgerson 1998). In addition, consumer research can take advantage of useful tools developed in art history and cultural studies to investigate the poetics and politics of advertising as a representational system. Finally, art-centred analyses often generate novel concepts and theories for research on issues such as patronage, visual attention, information technology and advertising.

Advertising acts as a representational system that produces meaning beyond the realm of the advertised product, service or brand. Considering ads as cultural artefacts helps connect images to broader cultural codes that help create semiotic meaning; indeed, ads themselves perform identity within cultural discourses. As consumer researchers increasingly acknowledge cultural codes, consumer response and deconstruction as essential in understanding how advertising produces meaning, the multidisciplinary approach presented here aims toward integrating knowledge from social science and humanities to situate advertising within perception and culture. Advertising images contradict Roland Barthes's influential notion that photography shows 'what has been' (1981). As consumers we should know that what is shown in ads hasn't really been, it is usually a staged construction designed to sell something. Yet, largely due to photography's realism, combined with technological and artistic expertise, advertising images produce realistic, pervasive simulations with persuasive power.

Constructing a visual genealogy of contemporary images helps illuminate how advertising works as the 'face of capitalism', harnessing the global flow of images, fuelling the image economy. For example, I have applied basic issues of art criticism to an iconic CK One image (shot by Steven Meisel for Calvin Klein) that profoundly influenced advertising photography. I argued that CK One ads drew on several distinctive visual genres, including group portraiture and fashion photography (Schroeder 2000). Group portraits, genealogically linked to the golden era of Dutch art, are a masculine genre – historically, men inhabited most portraits of groups such as guilds, corporate boards and sports teams. Fashion photography is a feminine genre, more closely associated with images of women than men (although men dominate the scene behind the lens). I argued that by juxtaposing and superimposing these two gendered genres, the CK One image creates an androgynous atmosphere – subtlty supporting its brand identity of a genderless cologne. Thus, the art historical technique of genre delineation provides a powerful theoretical insight into how CK One works as an image, an ad and a visual icon, and helps illuminate key tensions within the politics of representation, identity and consumption.

Propositions about Visual Consumption in the Image Economy

1. *Advertising is the dominant global communication force.* Advertising – and the mass media which it supports – has emerged as a primary societal institution. For advertising is no longer a means of merely communicating information about products, it is the engine of the economy, and a primary player in the political sphere. The major technological medium of advertising is photography, which, of course, includes still photography, film and video.

2. *The world's photographability has become the condition under which it is constituted and perceived.* No single instant of our life is not touched by the technological reproduction of images. (Cadava 1999). Politics and history are now to be understood as secondary, derivative forms of telecommunications. No significant events of the past century have not been captured by the camera; indeed, photography and film make things significant.

3. *Identity is now inconceivable without photography.* The world has taken on a photographic face. Personal as well as product identity (already inextricably linked via the market) are constructed largely via information technologies of photography and mass media. The visual aspects of culture have come to dominant our understanding of identity, as well as the institutionalization of identity by societal institutions.

4. *The image is primary for branding products and services.* Products no longer merely reflect images – the image often is created prior to the product, which is then developed to fit the image. Many informational, or content, products share this production cycle. For example, films are pitched as ideas – images – first, before they are produced. If they seem worthwhile, then they may attract captial and a production budget. Many products are designed to fit a specific target market; they conform to an image of consumer demand (cf. Firat, Dholakia & Venkatesh 1994; Reynolds and Gutman 1984; Schroeder 2002). This represents a seismic economic shift towards experience, towards images, towards attention.

These four propositions create an interdisciplinary matrix for analysing the roles visual consumption play in the economy. Specifically, they call attention to photography as an overlooked process within the cultural marketplace of ideas and images. This set of propositions directs our gaze to the cultural and historical framework of images, even as it questions the information that feed those discourses.

Visual Consumption and its Critics

One might think that the ascendancy of visual images would lead to unprecedented visual literacy; that consumers immersed in an image-based world might emerge picture savvy, accomplished semioticians able to decode and decipher images easily. Some researchers argue that 'postmodern' consumers are not fooled by images – they know how ads work and resist, embrace, deconstruct or ignore them at will. Moreover, goes this line of thought, consumers see most ads from an ironic, detached or playful perspective that dampens their effectiveness as persuasive messages. Others claim that consumers know what advertising is all about, that they 'see through' its techniques, and understand its influence upon them. Others have suggested that the visual environment is so heavily saturated with images that advertisements have lost their rhetorical power, thus leading the advertising industry to develop shock ad campaigns in a desperate measure to gain consumer attention.

These pronouncements might seem like obstacles for a visually oriented approach to consumption, so I turn my attention to clarifying the role of visual consumption in contemporary culture. Currently, there seem to be four distinct and often contradictory propositions that concern visual consumption. The first proposition suggests that consumers pay little attention to images, including ads. Cognitive capacity, heuristic processing, interest and motivation limit human attention. I dub this the zapping hypothesis. Consumers 'zap' through ads with their handy remote control units, rarely resting their eyes on commercial images. The second proposition holds that today's consumers enjoy high levels of visual literacy – they are successful semioticians of the image economy who understand how images work. This is the savvy consumer, for whom marketing is transparent. In other words, everyone knows ads are designed to sell things. Third, some commentators contend that most consumers are unaware – and thus unaffected by deep meaning in advertising imagery. Whereas close scrutiny of images often reveals semiotic signification, advertising is only skin deep – an ephemeral, playful part of visual culture. This proposition – seemingly the antithesis of the previous claim – revolves around what I call the clueless consumer. Fourth, advertising is doomed by emerging economic phenomena – pricing information on the Web, alternative marketing strategies, and changing media use are combining to alter advertising's role in corporate strategy. Advertising is dead, in other words; the visual landscape will be irrevocably transformed via revolutionary developments in marketing communication technology and market information.

Zapping

In many ways, doubts about how much consumers pay attention to ads – and how effective advertising images are – constitute an empirical question. However, several strands of evidence can be gathered to refute the claim that consumers pay little attention to advertising. First, advertising appears in more forms than ever – on the Web, product placements, on buildings, on bus shelters, in sponsored events – the logic of advertising underlies much of visual culture. These advertising images present zapping challenges – designed to subtly occupy consumer attention within the visual environment, they are difficult to ignore. Certainly, the entire corporate world would be reluctant to continue such practices if they did not find them fairly effective. Second, consumers clearly pay attention to some marketing campaigns – certain print ads in particular have become collector's items, and hundreds of Websites post popular images from CK One, Absolut, Nike and other celebrated campaigns (e.g., Schroeder and Borgerson 2003). Ads provide many teenager's bedroom with colourful pictures; companies like Bare Walls sell poster-sized advertising specifically for home decor. There is little distinction between many celebrity images and advertising – pictures have long been part of the publicity machine. Third, most ads work through repeated exposure – one need not pay much attention to advertising imagery to recognize the dominant figures and images of the ad world. Fourth, images often function without awareness or attention, in automatic ways that consumers have relatively little conscious control over (cf. Bargh 2002).

The Savvy Consumer

Once when lecturing on the interconnections of art and advertising, I began to describe a particular painting and its signification system. As the students looked at the image – it was a minor eighteenth century portrait of a nobleman – I discussed some formal features of portrait painting: what appears in the background, pose, clothing, personal effects, and studio props. I pointed out that by including things like globes or maps near the model, painters signified worldliness, scientific knowledge, and possession; and that – like an advertisement – each part of a painting is put there for a reason. For example, one need only consult a dictionary of art for a paragraph or two about the globe's symbolic significance in art history. Globes are an attribute of truth, fame, and abundance, and commonly appear as an allegorical attribute of still life paintings and portraits (Hall 1979). With a bit of knowledge about cartography, intellectual history, and exploration, objects like a globe's presence in the pantheon of painted objects becomes clearer. The painting we were looking at, for example, showed the subject's hand resting on some books. I suggested that this is a traditional symbol of education, literacy, and higher learning. I pointed out that few people of the time could read, and that the painter may have added the books on his own – they needn't have been there during the portrait sitting. Thus, the man's hand gently resting on an open book signified certain things about his character, in a way that was perhaps more clear to viewers when it was painted, but still resonant today.

After this point, one of my students became upset. 'You mean that those things in the painting mean something?', he said, his voice rising. 'That the painter put those books in there for a reason – they aren't just there in the room?' He was angry. No one had ever taught him about the visual language of images – that painted objects often signify, that things are not always just as they appear, and that seeing is only one part of knowing. 'How come no one ever told me this?' he asked. A wealth of knowledge has passed him by, and once he began to understand this, he realized how much he had been missing – a world had been hidden away from him.

For most consumers, the growing volume of images mitigates against understanding how they function. We rarely take the time to thoroughly reflect on advertising imagery, its position as something that apparently comes between programs, articles, or Websites make it seem ephemeral or at least peripheral to serious consideration. However, despite the reductionist research paradigm that distorts our view, advertising does not exist in a vacuum, it is vitally connected to the cultural worlds of high art, fashion, and photography on one hand, and media realms of journalism, mass media, and celebrity on the other (see e.g., Antick 2002). Part of a long line of visual expression, advertising is embodied and embedded within a myriad of historical, cultural, and social situations, contexts and discourses.

The Clueless Consumer

I draw on clinical experience – introducing scores of students to visual consumption processes – to discuss the notion that consumers don't see signification in ads, that interpreters 'read in' meanings that are lost in the marketplace. This proposition – which runs counter to the savvy consumer claim – is fairly easily refuted by the literature. When asked, consumers produce detailed inferences about imagery and meaning in ads (e.g., Hirschman and Thompson 1997; McQuarrie and Mick 1999; Mick and Buhl 1992; O'Donohoe 2001; Ritson and Elliott 1999; Zaltman and Coulter 1995). However, this could be a demand artifact – when prompted by the interested interviewer people may be creating meanings on the spot. In my experience, however, most people readily make associations and symbolic connections from ads, using metaphors, images, and semiotics, often without awareness of their surreptitious semiotic abilities.

For example, one of my students wanted to write about a Salem cigarette ad. The image showed a young woman with greenish skin, black pointed fingernails, wearing a choker of round beads that reflected several images of a man who appeared to be knocking on a door, attempting to get the woman's attention. To me, the image immediately called to mind a witch – and connecting this with the Salem brand completed the semiotic link. Salem, Massachusetts was the site of the notorious seventeenth century witch trials – recalled by Arthur Miller's play *The Crucible.* My student said that her roommate thought the image was offensive, but she herself thought it was cool. Resisting the urge to impose my views upon her, I told her that perhaps the image could be both cool and offensive, and that it would make an exemplary image for her term project. I recommended that she consult a book called *The Painted Witch: How Western Artists have Viewed the Sexuality of Women* (Mullins 1985). She turned in an exceptional paper that examined the image from the historical, social, and semiotic perspective that I have written about here, persuasively connecting the Salem cigarette ad to the larger domains of history, oppression, and target marketing. I think that her strong interest in the image – as built in by the ad's art director – was predicated on these deeper connections that she was vaguely aware of, but lacked the vocabulary to describe. Further, by encouraging her to delve into the image's signifying power – without giving her my interpretation – I enabled her to make more sense of the witch's status as a visual icon. I think that considering consumers clueless vastly underestimates their semiotic ability, interpretive power, and critical thinking potential.

Can images mean anything? Some approaches suggest that images float in the 'postmodern' world – signs disconnected from signifiers – allowing consumers free to generate novel, resistant, and idiosyncratic meaning. Although I agree that consumers generate their own meaning, and that they bring their own cognitive, social, and cultural lenses to whatever they see, this does not mean that the historical and political processes that also generate meaning are eliminated. Some colleagues maintain that images are open to interpretation, with little to anchor or fix them to a particular meaning. However, as I have argued, there are systems of meaning and representational practice that do indeed anchor and fix images, a claim supported by more recent work in cultural studies and art history that is critically opposed to the poststructural notion that signs float free of historical situatedness. This is not to imply that meanings are fixed historically, and that once an image is decoded, interpretive work ceases. Rather, within a theoretical understanding of visual consumption, images exist within cultural and historical frameworks that inform their production, consumption, circulation, and interpretation.

Is Advertising Dead?

In 1991, marketing guru Regis McKenna predicted the demise of advertising. He argued that marketing relationships and technology will come to replace advertising, which 'serves no useful purpose' (McKenna 1991: 8). The 'monologue of advertising' cannot accommodate feedback for emerging paradigms such as relationship marketing, McKenna claimed, and most advertising promised more than products could deliver. Many others have predicted the downfall of the one-to-many model of traditional media communication, citing the interactivity of the Net as more effective and efficient. So far, however, Websites often resemble mass media outlets, advertising imagery dominates many Websites and portals, and the Web creates its own brands, largely via traditional marketing efforts.

A recent article in *the New Yorker* goes further with the claim that one of the most famous ad campaigns in history – for Marlboro cigarettes – was largely ineffective: 'People smoked before those ads, and they'll continue to smoke after they're gone. I don't think they sold a single cigarette' (photographer Richard Prince, quoted in Surowiecki 1999: 38). This spectacular assertion seems diametrically opposed to recent court decisions about tobacco advertising that dramatically curtailed cigarette advertising in the USA Remarkably, this puzzling pronouncement appeared without critical commentary in an influential intellectual forum.

Another attack on advertising's continued significance comes from pricing enthusiasts. The Web, some claim, will make price transparent, and consumers will be less willing to pay higher premiums for well-known brands. In the information economy, substitutes abound – who needs books when you can download the 'information'? (I have always found that people who predict the end of the book don't really like books.) The brand, then, will become less important, hence advertising will come to focus (again) on product utilities. Although the Web does make comparison shopping easier for many products, it is unlikely to uproot consumption behaviour developed over the past hundred years. Consumers lack technical know-how to evaluate most products, they lack information about quality, and they often have low motivation to make utilitarian decisions. Consumers use products to meet expressive needs, they want to minimize cognitive effort. In general, consumers do not shop around – most consumer behaviour is routinized, and despite market fragmentation, many consumers remain brand loyal (Sirgy & Su 2000). The promise of the Web for perfect information and efficient markets may be realized, but consumer behaviour will not completely change.

Jonathan E. Schroeder

The Continuing Prominence of the Image

I propose visual consumption as an alternative approach for consumer research, one that relies on interdisciplinary methods, based on the semiotics of contemporary images. Approaching visual representation within consumer research via the interpretative stances presented offers researchers a grounded method for understanding and contextualizing images. As art historian Keith Moxey argues:

> semiotics makes us aware that the cultural values with which we make sense of the world are a tissue of conventions that have been handed down from generation to generation by the members of the culture of which we are a part. It reminds us that there is nothing 'natural' about our values; they are social constructs that not only vary enormously in the course of time but differ radically from culture to culture (1994: 61).

In connecting images to the external context of consumption, we gain a more thorough – yet never complete – understanding of how images function.

As visual spectacles, advertising encourages '*audience participation within a small set of approved responses*' (Peñaloza 1999: 348, emphasis in original). This set of responses rarely includes broader political, social and historical contexts that might interfere with preferred image decoding. Furthermore, perception depends largely on expectations – what we expect to see we often see. Advertising conventions encourage use of a narrow set of expectations to decode and decipher imagery – positive expectations, generally, which lead to promising conclusions about the advertised item. Contrary to museum going, for instance, looking at ads seems to require checking one's cultural knowledge at the door, so that ads become spectacles of visual consumption. I find studying visual communication, photography and art history develops my students' critical thinking. The mass media provide a multitude of sites that students are engaged in and familiar with to work on critical thinking skills. Advertising and photography in particular are of vital interest to students, and mine have enjoyed learning more about a way of apprehending and critiquing visual imagery.

Advertising remains 'the privileged discourse for the circulation of messages and social cues about the interplay between persons and objects' (Leiss, Kline & Jhally 1990: 50). Certainly, some consumers are savvy, others may indeed be clueless, many people zap commercials when they can, and advertising is changing from its role on the Web. However, the very prominence of images makes it difficult to understand them; marketing appeals work best if 'consumers cannot hold their attention, or focus their desire on any object for long; if they are impatient, impetuous, and restive, and above all easily excitable and equally losing interest' (Bauman 1998: 81–2). Given time to unpack and understand advertising imagery, my students often react critically to the messages they began to see in ads. Upon serious reflection, many promises of advertising seem unfulfilled and unfulfillable. Just as the perfect vacation remains an elusive goal, the world of advertising imagery remains always in the future, beyond the reach of today, a wonderful world of whimsy that bears little resemblance to lived experience. Advertising, like travel, carries with it a promise of bliss, of consumer nirvana around the next corner, at the next itinerary stop or the newest software update.

Information technology makes looking at many things possible, but it does not necessarily improve our capacity to *see* – to engage our senses actively in reflective analysis. Photography now dominates how we conceive of people, places and things. Yet photography is not the truth, it is not a simple record of some reality. I find it useful to think of photography as a consumer behaviour as well as a central information technology. Photography's technical ability to reproduce images makes it a central feature of visual consumption. Furthermore, photographs tell us where we have been, who we are, and what we value.

Visual consumption characterizes life in the information age – the computer, the Web, and television structure twenty-first century lives, commanding time and attention, providing a steady stream of images that appear to bring the world within. Whether images are approached from psychophysiological, semiotic or art historical perspectives, it is clear that they are critically important for understanding elusive consumption. Visual consumption places the image within a multidisciplinary matrix, underscoring their complexity, their connections to ethics and values, and their psychological nature. The image, now as in the past, provides a key to understanding how we make sense of our world.

References

Antick, P. (2002), 'Bloody Jumpers: Benetton and the Mechanics of Cultural Exclusion', *Fashion Theory,* 6: 83–110.

Arnheim, R. (1977), *The Dynamics of Architectural Form*, Berkeley: University of California Press.

Bargh, J. A. (2002), 'Losing Consciousness: Automatic Influences on Consumer Judgment, Behavior, and Motivation', *Journal of Consumer Research,* 29 (2): 280–5.

Barthes, R. (1981), *Camera Lucida: Reflections on Photography*, trans. R. Howard, New York: Noonday.

Bauman, Z. (1998), *Globalization: The Human Consequences*, Cambridge: Polity.

Belk, R. W. (1998), 'Multimedia Approaches to Qualitative Data and Representations', in B. B. Stern (ed), *Representing Consumers: Voices, Views, and Visions*, London: Routledge, 308–38.

Borgerson, J. L. and Schroeder, J. E. (2003), 'The Lure of Paradise: Marketing the Retro-escape of Hawaii', in S. Brown and J. F. Sherry, Jr. (eds), *Time, Space and the Market: Retroscapes Rising*, New York: M. E. Sharpe, 219–37.

Cadava, E. (1999), *Words of Light: Theses on the Photography of History*, Princeton, NJ: Princeton University Press.

Coleman, A. D. (1998), *Depth of Field: Essays on Photography, Mass Media, and Lens Culture*, Albuquerque: University of New Mexico Press.

Crawshaw, C. and Urry, J. (1997), 'Tourism and the Photographic Eye', in C. Rojek and J. Urry (eds), *Touring Cultures: Transformations of Travel and Theory*, London: Routledge, 176–95.

Czarniawska, B. (2000), 'The European Capital of the 2000s: On Image Construction and Modeling', *Corporate Reputation Review*, 3 (3): 202–17.

Firat, A. F., Dholakia, N. and Venkatesh, A. (1995), 'Marketing in a Postmodern World', *European Journal of Marketing*, 29: 40–56.

Hall, J. (1979), *Dictionary of Subjects & Symbols in Art, Revised Edition*, Boulder, CO: Westview.

Hirschman, E. and Thompson, C. J. (1997), 'Why Media Matter: Advertising and Consumers in Contemporary Communication', *Journal of Advertising*, 26, 1: 43–60.

Holt, D. B. (2002), 'Why Do Brands Cause Trouble? A Dialectical Theory of Consumer Culture and Branding', *Journal of Consumer Research*, 29 (June): 70–90.

Kaplan, S. and Kaplan, R. (1982), *Cognition and Environment*, New York: Praeger.

Kress, G. and van Leeuwen, T. (1996), *Reading Images: The Grammar of Visual Design*, London: Routledge.

Leiss, W., Kline, S. and Jhally, S. (1990), *Social Communication in Advertising*, 2nd edn. Scarborough, ON: Nelson Canada.

McKenna, R. (1991), 'Marketing is Everything', *Harvard Business Review*, January-February, (reprint) 1–10.

McQuarrie, E. F. and Mick, D. G. (1999), 'Visual Rhetoric in Advertising: Text-interpretative, Experimental, and Reader-response Analyses', *Journal of Consumer Research*, 26, 1: 37–54.

Mick, D. G. and Buhl, C. (1992), 'A Meaning Based Model of Advertising Experiences', *Journal of Consumer Research*, 19 (December): 317–38.

Moxey, K. (1994), *The Practice of Theory: Poststructuralism, Cultural Politics, and Art History*, Ithaca, NY: Cornell University Press.

Mullins, E. (1985), *The Painted Witch: How Western Artists have Viewed the Sexuality of Women*, New York: Carroll & Graf.

Murray, S. (2000), 'Dull Tomes Replaced by Designer Message', *Financial Times*, June 30, 5.

O'Donohoe, S. (2001), 'Living with Ambivalence: Attitudes to Advertising in Postmodern Times', *Marketing Theory,* 1 (1): 91–108.

Peñaloza, L. (1999), 'Just Doing It: A Visual Ethnographic Study of Spectacular Consumption Behavior at Nike Town', *Consumption, Markets and Culture* 2 (4): 337–400.

Reynolds, T. J. and Gutman, J. (1984), 'Advertising is Image Management', *Journal of Advertising Research*, 24: 27–37.

Ritson, M. and Elliott, R. (1999), 'The Social Uses of Advertising: An Ethnographic Study of Adolescent Advertising Audiences', *Journal of Consumer Research*, 26, 3: 260–77.

Schroeder, J. E. (1997), 'Andy Warhol: Consumer Researcher', in D. MacInnis and M. Brucks (eds) *Advances in Consumer Research*, Vol. 24, Provo: Association for Consumer Research, 476–82.

— (1998), 'Consuming Representation: A Visual Approach to Consumer Research', in B. B. Stern (ed) *Representing Consumers: Voices, Views, and Visions*, London and New York: Routledge, 193–230.

— (2000), 'Édouard Manet, Calvin Klein and the Strategic use of Scandal', in S. Brown and A. Patterson (eds), *Imagining Marketing: Art, Aesthetics, and the Avant-Garde,* London: Routledge, 36–51.

— (2002), *Visual Consumption*, London: Routledge.

— (2003), 'Building Brands: Architectural Expression in the Electronic Age', in R. Batra and L. Scott (eds), *Persuasive Imagery: A Consumer Response Perspective,* Mahwah, NJ: Lawrence Erlbaum Associates, 349–82.

— and Borgerson, J. L. (1998), 'Marketing Images of Gender: A Visual Analysis', *Consumption Markets & Culture*, 2: 161–201.

— (2002), 'Innovations in Information Technology: Insights into Consumer Culture from Italian Renaissance Art', *Consumption Markets, and Culture*, 5: 153–69.

— (2003), 'Dark Desires: Fetishism, Ontology and Representation in Contemporary Advertising', in T. Reichert and J. Lambiase (eds), *Sex in Advertising: Perspectives on the Erotic Appeal,* Mahwah, NJ: Lawrence Erlbaum Associates, 65–87.

Scott, L. A. (1994), 'Images of Advertising: The Need for a Theory of Visual Rhetoric', *Journal of Consumer Research,* 21, September: 252–73.

Shapiro, C. and Varian, H. R. (1999), *Information Rules: A Strategic Guide to the Network Economy,* Boston: Harvard Business School Press.

Sirgy, M. J. and Su, C. (2000), 'The Ethics of Consumer Sovereignty in an Age of High Tech', *Journal of Business Ethics,* 28: 1–14.

Stern, B. B. and Schroeder, J. E. (1994), 'Interpretative Methodology from Art and Literary Criticism: A Humanistic Approach to Advertising Imagery', *European Journal of Marketing*, 28, 3: 114–32.

Strom, S. (2000), 'In Japan, an Established Company is Transformed', *New York Times*, December 20, 19, 22

Surowiecki, J. (1999), 'A Cowboy is Gone from the Highway, but He Rides on in the Art World', *The New Yorker*, 10 May, 37–8.

Wagstaff, J. (2001), 'Web Navigation Proves Difficult to Get Right', *Wall Street Journal Europe*, 8 March, 25.

Venkatesh, A. (2003), 'The Catalog and the Web Page: An Existential Tension?', in S. Brown and J. F. Sherry, Jr. (eds), *Time, Space and the Market: Retroscapes Rising*, New York: M.E. Sharpe, 271–92.

Zaltman, G. (1997), 'Rethinking Market Research: Putting People Back In', *Journal of Marketing Research*, 34: 424–37.

— and Coulter, R. A. (1995), 'Seeing the Voice of the Customer: Metaphor-based Advertising Research', *Journal of Advertising Research*, 35, July/August: 35–51.